"*Born to Buy* is so grounded in appalling data about both kids and advertising companies, it has the effect of making even the most TV-and-advertising-wary parents among us realize that we haven't been half vigilant enough."

—Amy Bloom, *O, The Oprah Magazine*

"*Born to Buy* is an eye-opener. It illuminates marketers' unrelenting exploitation of our youth; the well-being of children has been made secondary to maximizing corporate profit. This book is certain to shake us out of our complacency. I highly recommend it."

—Alvin F. Poussaint, MD, professor of psychiatry,
Harvard Medical School and
Judge Baker Children's Center, Boston

"This brilliant, informative, and deeply important book tells us what the advertisers don't: the more advertising children see and hear, the more likely they are to be depressed and anxious and to suffer family conflict. The American dream isn't something we buy, Schor wisely tells us; it's something we make and can, if broken, repair. A book that will start a revolution . . ."

—Arlie Russell Hochschild,
author of *The Commercialization of Intimate Life: Notes from Home and Work* and *The Time Bind: When Work Becomes Home and Home Becomes Work*

Also by Juliet B. Schor

The Overworked American

The Overspent American

Born to Buy

Juliet B. Schor

SCRIBNER
New York London Toronto Sydney

SCRIBNER
1230 Avenue of the Americas
New York, NY 10020

First Scribner trade paperback edition 2005

For information about special discounts for bulk purchases, please contact Simon & Schuster Special Sales:
1-800-456-6798 or business@simonandschuster.com.

DESIGNED BY ERICH HOBBING

Text set in Bembo

Manufactured in the United States of America

1 3 5 7 9 10 8 6 4 2

The Library of Congress has cataloged the Scribner edition as follows:

Schor, Juliet.
Born to buy: the commercialized child and the new consumer culture/Juliet B. Schor.
p. cm.
Includes bibliographical references and index.
1. Child consumers—United States. 2. Young consumers—United States. 3. Advertising and children—United States. 4. Materialism—Social aspects—United States. 5. Child development—United States. 6. Children—United States—Social conditions. 7. Child welfare—United States. I. Title: Marketing and the transformation of childhood and culture. II. Title.
HF5415.33.U6S355 2004
305.23'0973—dc22
2004045411

ISBN-13: 978-0-684-87055-7
ISBN-10: 0-684-87055-X
ISBN-13: 978-0-684-87056-4 (Pbk)
ISBN-10: 0-684-87056-8 (Pbk)

For Krishna and Sulakshana,
my wonderful children

Contents

Tables and Figures

TABLES

FIGURES

Author's Note

This book relies on two types of primary research. The first is a qualitative investigation of advertising and marketing to children, conducted through interviews and participant observation in the advertising industry. The second is survey research and data analysis. I want to say a word about each.

My industry research began in the summer of 2001, when I participated in the Visiting Professor Exchange program run by the Advertising Education Foundation. The AEF arranged for me to visit a number of advertising agencies, including a longer stay at one of them. During this time, I heard about twenty presentations on a variety of topics. My industry host also put together approximately fifteen private meetings with key individuals in the field of children's marketing. During those meetings, I conducted informal interviews and discussions and took notes. I also spent time with a group of professionals who were working on children's products, observing what goes on in an agency. In the eighteen months following my fellowship, I broadened my contacts and conducted approximately twenty-five more interviews, which ranged in length from an hour to five or six hours. I also had the opportunity to shadow researchers at a small firm, observing meetings and focus groups. I went to two industry conferences and talked to as many people as I could. I read trade books, newsletters, magazines, and other publications. Although the bulk of my work was within the industry, over the years I have been doing this research, I have also gotten to know many of the nation's leading critics of marketing to children, attending meetings and conferences and exchanging information with them.

My aim in this research was to identify and understand how children are being marketed to and how that has changed over time. I took a broad-brush approach, looking across product groups, including toys and food. I looked at television advertising to discern thematic approaches in the messages. I collected information on a wide variety of marketing, promotion, and sponsorship activities. And I studied the expansion and transformation of research on children.

As a complement to my investigation of marketing practices, I conducted a survey of 300 fifth- and sixth-grade children, which is described in detail in Chapter 8. The major contribution of the survey is the development of a new scale to measure children's level of involvement in consumer culture, which I call the "consumer involvement scale." I used this scale in a statistical model that tested the impact of consumer culture on a variety of psychological measures, including depression, anxiety, and self-esteem, and on the quality of parental relationships. I also conducted approximately twenty-five interviews with parents at one survey site that explored their children's relationship to consumer culture.

Advertising is a field in which confidentiality is extremely important. In comparison to other types of workplaces, such as factories and offices, academic research inside advertising agencies has been relatively sparse. Clients are often careful about secrecy, and agencies are wary about giving information to outsiders. Furthermore, most research and findings about children are proprietary, in order to protect the economic return that the data yield. During the period of my research, there was a lot of controversy about marketing to children, as various groups were actively protesting and organizing against the people I was attempting to study. Industry participants had good reason to be cautious about outside researchers. I expected that I would have a hard time getting people to meet with me because of the critical nature of my earlier work on consumer society. Instead, most of the people I approached were willing to talk.

It is hard to know what accounted for my success in gaining access. My initial entrée, through the AEF, occurred in part because of my affiliation with Harvard University. Once I began to meet people, they were willing to refer me to others. I benefited from a generally positive, and at times enthusiastic, attitude toward academic researchers. There are now a fair number of former academics in the field, and some of them were especially gracious and open. Another factor was that some of the people I interviewed seemed interested in the public exposure my book might provide. Others were hopeful I could help them in return in my capacity as an academic expert who studied consumer trends. While I did offer my views in our conversations and expressed a general willingness to be helpful, no one ever followed up with specific requests.

I also encountered some fairly closed companies. My calls to Saatchi and Saatchi were never returned. Channel One was unwilling to talk. At MTV Networks, I found a more polite, but nevertheless standoffish, attitude. Both Channel One and MTV explicitly cited their desire to avoid criticism. I was unable to arrange firsthand experiences of certain research practices that I was interested in. I did not sense overt resistance, but after repeated attempts, nothing materialized. I rarely asked to see confidential material, knowing that I would probably be unable to write about it. Occasionally, I was given access to confidential materials or meetings, but usually without my asking.

To protect their privacy, I have not revealed the names of the agencies I spent time at. I have also used pseudonyms for a number of industry people I interviewed and indicated this in the text. I have also used pseudonyms for all the parents and children from the survey. For the most part, however, and unless explicitly noted, the names, titles, and affiliations appearing in the book are real.

The majority of direct quotations in the text came from interviews I conducted. All the parent interviews were taped and transcribed. Some industry interviews were taped, and those I draw most heavily on were also transcribed. With the remainder, I took detailed notes, and the quotes come from those. In most cases, I have not provided endnotes for these quotes. Wherever I quote from other sources, such as conference presentations, printed materials, or journalistic accounts, I have put a reference to the source in the endnotes. The endnotes also contain some discussion of the scholarly literature, elaboration of points, and additional sources. To make for an easier reading experience, I have taken numbered cues out of the text. All endnotes are cued by page and surrounding text in the endnote section.

Things change fast in the world of marketing and advertising. People move around and change titles frequently, accounts move from agency to agency, and campaigns come and go. Expenditure estimates are also rising rapidly. During the time I was finishing the book, there were almost daily developments related to food marketing. I have made every attempt to keep my information current, but my revisions ended in 2003.

Acknowledgments

My work on this book has spanned a number of years. Along the way, I have incurred many debts and relied on the assistance of a large number of people. I am grateful to all those who gave me introductions or otherwise facilitated my access to the world of advertising and marketing. These include Susan Fournier, John Deighton, and Douglas Holt of Harvard Business School; Tim Brunelle of Arnold Worldwide; and Paula Alex and Sharon Hudson from the Advertising Education Foundation. I also thank people in the industry who agreed to be interviewed, especially Donna Sabino, Paul Kurnit, Roberta Nusim, Thomas Kouns, Langbourne Rust, Laura Groppe, and the people I refer to by the pseudonyms Amanda Carlson, Mary Prescott, Mark Lapham, Alex Houston, and Lisa Morgan. Special thanks are due to Wynne Tyree. Spending time with me took all these people away from paying clients, and I appreciate their generosity.

For assistance with the school survey in Doxley, a suburban Boston town that I refer to by this pseudonym, I am thankful to Henry Bolter, who made the initial contact with the Doxley schools; principals Walter McGrail, Lisette Kaplowitz, and Joann Little; and the fifth- and sixth-grade teachers who participated in the survey. For research in the Boston schools, I am grateful to Ethan D'Ablemont Burnes and Lisa Dodson, both of whom used their contacts to help get me access; to all the Boston teachers; and to administrators Yolanda Burnett and Laurie Carr for their cooperation. These teachers and administrators were willing to give up valuable class time. Two people were especially important, and I am particularly appreciative of their efforts. Jonathan Landmann of Doxley and Manuel Fernandez of Boston both immediately saw the value in the research and took a personal interest in making sure it happened.

Many people sent me materials, papers, or data. I thank Marvin Goldberg, James McNeal, James Sargent, Amy Aidman, Gary Ruskin, Marnie Glickman, Diane Levin, Donna Sabino, Nancy Johnston, Wynne Tyree, Gary Colen, Genevieve Pan, Charles Elberson, Laura Groppe, Langbourne Rust, Gerald Zaltman, Douglas Holt, Viviana Zelizer, Eric

Brown, Tracy Fisher, Thomas Robinson, and Daniel Cook. I thank Suzy Conway for her generous search of the medical literature.

I had administrative support from two institutions. From Harvard, I am grateful to Christiana Morgan and the community surrounding Women's Studies. From Boston College, I thank Jess Geier, Jessica Bickley, Toni Vicari, and Paul Emery.

During the course of this project, I worked with a number of research assistants. At Harvard, Elisheva Lambert and Leah Plunkett began the search for material on this topic, and Shauna Shames continued it. Alissa Sakai did a case study on Pokémon for me. At Boston College, Kristna Evans gave bibliographic assistance; Leah Schmalzbauer helped with the survey and arranging interviews; Jenna Nobles did the initial analyses of the data; Michael Yaksich did media analysis and formatted tables; and Chiwen Bao graciously helped with many different tasks. I am grateful to them all for their excellent work. I particularly thank Leon Litchfield and the Boston College Center for Work and Family for overseeing the data entry and coding, and Beverly Miller for her excellent copyediting.

I thank Ranjini Reddy for her work on an initial collaboration to investigate these issues in a large-scale data set, and Tim Kasser for his good advice. Both Ranjini and Tim helped in the development of the consumer involvement scale. Lisa Feldman Barrett also gave helpful input. Thanks to Eric Brown, Betsy Taylor, and the board and staff of the Center for a New American Dream. My work with the center is an ongoing source of intellectual and political stimulation. I also thank Boston College, Dean Joseph Quinn, Stephen Pfohl, and my colleagues in the Sociology Department. I appreciate the teaching leave they offered when I arrived, and consider myself very lucky to have such a supportive and welcoming place to do my work.

I owe special debts to a number of people. Jean Rhodes was an invaluable source of advice and expertise as I entered the field of psychological research for the first time. She gave generously of her time, and I reaped the benefits. Douglas Holt has been a valued collaborator and friend. Doug is one of the most insightful interpreters of consumer culture I have encountered, and I have learned an enormous amount from him. Bob Kunovich and John Shandra worked with me on the structural equation estimates and collaborated on the analysis of the survey. I could not have done this work without them. Gary Ruskin was immensely helpful in many ways. I am also deeply grateful to my host during my Advertising Education Fellowship who opened so many doors for me, with so much grace. I cannot reveal her identity without revealing the agency she works at, so she will have to remain anonymous. Finally, I thank Charles Terry, whose ready support in the form of a generous grant from the Philanthropic Collaborative enabled me to do this work.

I am indebted to the Doxley parents who were willing to be interviewed for this project. They welcomed me into their homes, shared personal information, and gave freely of their time. I am also grateful to all the parents who trusted me to survey their children, and most of all to the children themselves, without whose input this book would not exist. Their enthusiasm and seriousness of purpose was inspiring.

Thanks also are due to my agent, Gerry McCauley, in part because he brought me to Alexis Gargagliano and Nan Graham. They have helped me immeasurably as I struggled to turn a skeleton of a manuscript into a book. Their sensibilities, intelligence, and skill resonate throughout the manuscript. My husband, Prasannan Parthasarathi, is my intellectual compass and soul mate. He has my daily thanks and love.

CHAPTER ONE

Introduction

The United States is the most consumer-oriented society in the world. People work longer hours than in any other industrialized country. Savings rates are lower. Consumer credit has exploded, and roughly a million and a half households declare bankruptcy every year. There are more than 46,000 shopping centers in the country, a nearly two-thirds increase since 1986. Despite fewer people per household, the size of houses continues to expand rapidly, with new construction featuring walk-in closets and three- and four-car garages to store record quantities of stuff. According to my estimates, the average adult acquires forty-eight new pieces of apparel a year. (She has also been discarding clothes at record rates, in comparison to historical precedents.) Americans own more television sets than inhabitants of any other country—nearly one set per person. Observers blame TV for plummeting levels of civic engagement, the dearth of community, and the decline of everyday socializing. Heavy viewing has also resulted in historically unprecedented exposure to commercials. And ads have proliferated far beyond the television screen to virtually every social institution and type of public space, from museums and zoos, to college campuses and elementary school classrooms, restaurant bathrooms and menus, at the airport, even in the sky.

The architects of this culture—the companies that make, market, and advertise consumer products—have now set their sights on children. Although children have long participated in the consumer marketplace, until recently they were bit players, purchasers of cheap goods. They attracted little of the industry's talent and resources and were approached primarily through their mothers. That has changed. Kids and teens are now the epicenter of American consumer culture. They command the attention, creativity, and dollars of advertisers. Their tastes drive market trends. Their opinions shape brand strategies. Yet few adults recognize the magnitude of this shift and its consequences for the futures of our children and of our culture.

* * *

I have been studying consumer issues for twenty years. An economist by training and inclination, I became interested in commercialization through studying the culture of work. My first book, *The Overworked American,* reported my findings of an unrecognized and unexpected rise in working hours. The average employee now spends 200 more hours per year on the job, or five extra weeks of work, than he or she did thirty years ago. Fifty years ago, American work hours were substantially lower than those in Western Europe; they now exceed them by more than 300 a year (or about eight weeks). Even Japan, the world's workaholic when I began my research in the early 1980s, now has shorter annual hours of work than the United States.

My earlier book's analysis of why hours were increasing pointed to workplace factors such as employers' cost structures and the persistence of corporate cultures of face time and long hours. I found that employers were unwilling to allow workers to trade income for time, and that for the past half-century, most people got higher incomes but also had to work longer hours. What I did not understand was why so few employees had chosen to resist these schedules. Polling data showed that most people were satisfied with their balance of work time and pay, despite rising hours. Although eventually dissatisfaction grew, the extent of acquiescence to long schedules remained puzzling.

So I began to investigate consumer behavior, where I found an answer. Americans had gotten caught in what I called the cycle of work-and-spend, in which the compensation for longer hours was a rising material standard of living. People were accumulating stuff at an unprecedented rate. Demanding jobs and escalating debt in turn resulted in high levels of stress and enormous pressure on family life. Some tried to buy their way out of the time squeeze by contracting out more household services, jetting off for stress-busting vacations, or finding a massage therapist, strategies that themselves require greater and greater household income. Through the boom years of the nineties, as new wealth led to a dramatic upscaling of consumer norms, the pressures intensified. Luxury replaced comfort as the national aspiration, despite its affordability for only a fraction of the population. In my second book, *The Overspent American,* I catalogued these changes and identified the social trends driving them. Americans had come under strong imperatives to keep up with the escalating costs of basics, like health care and education, as well as luxuries, such as branded goods, bigger vehicles, and outlays for leisure and recreation. A trip to Disneyworld became an expensive, but urgent, social norm. Households spent more, saved less, and took on more debt. Meanwhile, commercialization proceeded apace as branding became ever more sophisticated, ads proliferated, and shopping turned into a 24/7 affair. The country was preoccupied with getting and spending.

As I was writing *The Overspent American* in the mid-1990s, I was aware of the pressures parents felt to provide for their children, with requisites ranging from extracurricular activities, to quality education, to fancy athletic footwear. I knew how anxious people were feeling about their kids' futures in a highly competitive global economy. I wrote a bit about these issues. But I conceptualized the consumer market in terms of its orientation to adults, as I watched SUVs replace cars, McMansions replace homes, and designer labels proliferate for everything from sunglasses to jockey shorts. I also studied downshifters—the millions of Americans who were rejecting the work-and-spend lifestyle, opting instead to work less, spend less, and live more simply. As it turned out, they provided a powerful clue to the growing importance of children in consumer culture.

One part of my research for the spending book was interviews with people toward the far end of the downshifting spectrum—those who were intentionally rejecting the consumer lifestyle rather than merely working less. I discovered that downshifters who were raising children were almost impossible to find. At the time, I reasoned that children are expensive or that most parents would not want to impose a regime of reduced consumption on their kids.

Eventually I realized that this dearth of downshifting among parents revealed a significant trend in consumer culture. Children have become conduits from the consumer marketplace into the household, the link between advertisers and the family purse. Young people are repositories of consumer knowledge and awareness. They are the first adopters and avid users of many of the new technologies. They are the household members with the most passionate consumer desires, and are most closely tethered to products, brands, and the latest trends. Children's social worlds are increasingly constructed around consuming, as brands and products have come to determine who is "in" or "out," who is hot or not, who deserves to have friends, or social status. In such a world, how many parents opt to downshift or simplify? It's a radical step many children don't welcome.

By the end of the 1990s, I began to take notice of the central role of children in consumer culture, not only as a social scientist, but also as a parent. Our first child, Krishna, had been born in 1991, so I was already encountering commercialized childhood personally. The standard rituals of preparing for a baby centered on consumer choices. Which brand of stroller and car seat? What licensed characters for decorating the baby's room? Is a video camera really necessary? Although we were committed to moderation in our material lives, it was hard as middle-class Americans to avoid many of the features of the work-and-spend lifestyle. I'll never forget our first weekend trip after Krishna was born. As we gathered our gear to pack up the car, my husband, who is from India, stared in disbelief. "There's more stuff in this pile than the average Indian family owns in a lifetime," he observed. What's more, by today's standards, that pile would be considered meager. In the past decade, product innovation and the expansion of "must-have" goods in the infant and toddler category has been nothing short of extraordinary. But as I learned, an excess of baby gear is the least intrusive of the challenges of commercialized childhood. Controlling consumption becomes far more difficult as children reach the preschool years and turn into consumers in their own right.

Our daughter, Sulakshana, was born in 1995. She afforded us firsthand experience of how deeply and pervasively commercialized childhood is gendered. With boys, parents worry about violent products and obsessions with video games. With girls, it's sexualized products and distorted body image. As our children grew, I watched the experience of childhood changing. Kids were coming under increasing pressures to succeed, as homework assignments became longer and performance expectations rose. Overscheduling became a norm in middle-class communities. Many children were growing materialistic, even spoiled. Television, video game, and computer time appeared to be rising, and in many communities, including ours, the streets were empty after school. One Saturday morning after a rare snowstorm, I was struck by the pristine snow and the pervasive quiet: all the kids were inside. I felt sad about their lack of autonomy and lost connection to the outdoors. I became determined to reclaim some of that for my kids and to protect them from the commercial influences I was uneasy about.

As I struggled with these issues as a parent, I also became intellectually captivated by them. I began to think that the most important change in consumer culture was not what the analysts were focusing on—Internet shopping, branding, consumer credit, or customization of products. It was that the imperative to target kids was remaking the marketplace. By 2003, Martin Lindstrom, one of the world's leading branding gurus, opined that 80 percent of all global brands now required a tween strategy. (Tweens are a marketing category roughly comprising children from first grade to age twelve.) Lindstrom is referring not only to acknowledged tween targeted products such as food, music, fashion, and culture, but also expensive items traditionally thought of as adult oriented, such as consumer electronics, hotels, and cars. For example, his findings suggest that 40 percent of urban tweens worldwide are strongly attached to particular car brands and that 30 percent of their parents ask them for advice on car purchases. Marketing is also fundamentally altering the experience of childhood. Corporations have infiltrated the core activities and institutions of childhood, with virtually no resistance from government or parents. Advertising is widespread in schools. Electronic media are replacing conventional play. We have become a nation that places a lower priority on teaching its children how to thrive socially, intellectually, even spiritually, than it does on training them to consume. The long-term consequences of this development are ominous.

The Commercialization of Childhood

Plenty of evidence now confirms how far-reaching this process of commercialization has become. Contemporary American tweens and teens have emerged as the most brand-oriented, consumer-involved, and materialistic generations in history. And they top the list globally. A survey of youth from seventy cities in more than fifteen countries finds that 75 percent of U.S. tweens want to be rich, a higher percentage than anywhere else in the world except India, where the results were identical. Sixty-one percent want to be famous. More children here than anywhere else believe that their clothes and brands describe who they are and define their social status. American kids display more brand affinity than their counterparts anywhere else in the world; indeed, experts describe them as increasingly "bonded to brands."

At the same time, evidence of distress among children has been mounting. Rates of obesity are at epidemic levels. Diagnoses of attention deficit disorder and attention deficit hyperactivity disorder have risen dramatically, and record numbers of kids are taking drugs to help them achieve self-control and focus. Anecdotal reports of electronic addictions—to video games, Internet surfing, and online gaming—have begun to surface. Teasing and bullying is rampant in schools, and includes a new protagonist, the "alpha girl," a mean-spirited social enforcer. A comprehensive study of anxiety finds a dramatic increase in recent decades. Today's average (i.e., normal) young person between the ages of nine and seventeen scores as high on anxiety scales as children who were admitted to clinics for psychiatric disorders in 1957. Increasing numbers of parents are sending their children off to expensive "behavior-modification" camps in the hope that these harsh and often abusive environments will cure them of their problems.

Researchers and advocates have focused primarily on social trends to explain the problems that beset children—working mothers, poverty, divorce. But these explanations are insufficient. After years of study, there is decisive evidence that children suffer no ill effects from maternal employment. And while poverty has strong negative effects on kids, middle-class and suburban youth have also been afflicted. Similarly, plenty of children from intact families are in trouble. Conservatives have blamed liberal values and the decline of patriarchal authority. But the research shows that children with authoritarian parents tend to have more, not fewer, behavioral problems.

The ills young people are suffering span a wide range, from the physical to the psychological to the social. I began to wonder if there weren't connections among them. Consumption excess is widespread, whether it's unhealthy food, electronic media, or drugs and alcohol. Psychological distress, especially feelings of alienation and meaninglessness, is a common message in popular music. Drug and alcohol consumption often exacerbates psychological problems. Social pathologies are promoted by the materialistic and exclusionary messages of ads and marketing. Indeed, Martin Lindstrom reports that "fear and pressure are the two most common elements characterizing the daily lives of tweens" and that the exploitation of anxiety in ads has steadily increased in the past few years.

As I began to investigate the impact of consumer culture on children, I found that the existing studies focused on the adverse effects of a particular consumer experience or product on a child. There were studies on the relation between junk food and obesity, between television violence and aggression in children. But no study had assessed the impact of the new consumer environment as a whole. I suspected that the growing commercialization of childhood was at least partly responsible for the decline in children's well-being.

A Historical Perspective on Children and Consumer Culture

But I didn't want to jump to unwarranted conclusions. Children have a long history as consumers. Some children's products, such as literature and clothing, have been around for centuries. Historians report that as early as

1870, toys began to serve as status symbols. Throughout the twentieth century, kids have liked to shop, and they have been avid consumers of popular culture offerings, such as comics, movies, radio serials, and books. What scholars have dubbed "moral panics," that is, exaggerated adult fears about children's fads, are longstanding. In recent years, moral panics have been triggered by comic books, trading cards, electronic games, even stuffed animals such as Beanie Babies. Children also have a rich history as economic actors—not merely as workers, but also as traders, wrapped up in acquiring, exchanging, and collecting. As long as we have had consumer capitalism, children have had a relationship to it.

The historical record also suggests how important it is to avoid overly romantic notions of childhood. Princeton sociologist Viviana Zelizer has convincingly argued that in the early part of the twentieth century, adult attitudes about children changed dramatically. Once considered almost expendable, children were increasingly thought of as sacred, priceless, and irreplaceable. This was also the time when ideas of innocence and purity came to dominate adult views of children. That legacy remains with us: childhood is designated the period of "innocence and wonder." But as cultural theorists have cogently argued, the concept of childhood innocence is less a description of reality than a way for adults to project their own fantasies onto children. Henry Giroux has argued that these fantasies "allow adults to believe that children do not suffer from adult greed, recklessness, and perversions of will and spirit." Flesh-and-blood children are not merely innocents, but complex beings, with conflicting desires and impulses. As we consider how childhood is changing, it's important to avoid our own nostalgia, wishful thinking, or culturally specific experiences.

Nevertheless, the sheer extent of children's immersion in consumer culture today is unprecedented. In the past, consuming was modest in comparison to other activities, such as work, play, school, and religious involvement. Now, marketed leisure has replaced unstructured socializing, and most of what kids do revolves around commodities. Children's purchasing power and influence have exploded as they spend their days shopping and watching more television.

A second difference is that today's commercialization is coinciding with major changes in the nature of childhood itself. In comparison with baby boomers, today's youth have earlier exposure to and more involvement with adult worlds. Children from single-parent families, a growing portion of the population, shoulder significant family responsibilities. Social analysts, media critic Neil Postman, and others have argued that these developments constitute a "disappearance of childhood." Evidence of the blurred boundaries between children and adults includes the decline in children's games, such as marbles, stickball, or hand-clapping, the disappearance of special clothing styles for children, early sexual activity, drug and alcohol use, and the widespread eroticization of children through beauty pageants, ads, and fashion. Advocates of the disappearance of childhood thesis have their critics, and there is some evidence that a counterreaction has set in, with the growth of homework, school uniforms, and increased supervision of kids. But there's little question that emotionally, children are growing up faster and that they are more integrated into adult spaces and activities and wield far more power in family decision making.

Marketing and advertising have been influential in transforming children into autonomous and empowered consumers. They have done this by overturning the original 1920s formula for selling children's products, which was an alliance with mothers. Advertisers had to convince moms that the product was beneficial for the child. Wheatena's proteins built bodies. Milk contained Vitamin D. This approach, which the industry termed the "gatekeeper model," was practiced through the postwar era as well. Today, marketers create direct connections to kids, in isolation from parents and at times against them. The new norm is that kids and marketers join forces to convince adults to spend money.

In some sense, this shift is not surprising. Important changes in consumer society have historically involved new forms of triangulation. One such shift occurred a century ago as women and merchants formed an alliance to overcome opposition to the emerging consumer economy from frugal, conservative husbands. In both England and the United States, the success of retail establishments, including department stores, was partly predicated on merchants' willingness to let women purchase goods on credit, which they could arrange without their husbands' consent. The merchants pursued these policies of easy credit even in cases when the husbands' approval was in doubt or had been explicitly denied. (Sometimes men would take out ads in newspapers repudiating responsibility for any future debts their wives might incur.) The merchants' motivation, of course, was that buying on credit expanded sales far beyond what they would have been had wives been required to obtain their husbands' permission—and dollars—in advance. Husbands for the most part owned the marital property but in return were required to support their wives at a "customary" level that was set by social class and past practice. As one might imagine, the customary number or quality of dresses and household items turned out to be a matter of disagreement. Many of the overdue credit cases ended up in court, because husbands refused to pay what they considered outrageous bills incurred by their wives at dressmakers' and milliners' establishments or department stores. The courts usually sided with the husbands, and the bills often went unpaid. Nevertheless, the alliance made it possible for women, despite their lack of control over family purse strings, to emerge as the nation's dominant consumers. Opposition to the emerging consumer economy came from men, who worried that its hedonistic aspects threatened self-control, sobriety, chastity, and, perhaps most important, male authority.

I note this history in some detail because it shows how a new alliance can remake a culture. Today, the partnership is between children and marketers, who are sometimes implicitly, sometimes explicitly, allied against parents. The gatekeeper model has become an archaic remnant of another era, operating only in the market for very young children. Advertisers have direct access to kids because they watch television without their parents. Marketers have also pried open other parent-free environments, most notably schools and the Internet, where they speak directly to their target market. Indeed, marketers are connecting with children in an increasingly close embrace that parents find difficult to penetrate and is even affecting how kids and parents get along.

These developments have not been beneficial for children. My research shows that those who are more involved in consumer culture fare far worse in psychological and social terms. What's more, my findings reverse the conventional wisdom that dysfunctional kids are drawn to consumer culture; in fact, the reverse is true. Involvement in consumer culture causes dysfunction in the forms of depression, anxiety, low self-esteem, and psychosomatic complaints.

Many adults respond to the critique of media and consumerism by shrugging it off, on the grounds that this culture is inescapable. Some are fatalistic; others contend that the critics exaggerate or are missing the true causes of kids' distress. Many reason that they themselves grew up on television with no untoward effects. But this stance is increasingly untenable. Day by day, marketers are growing bolder. Year by year, the scientific evidence about harmful effects is mounting. I offer this book both as a record and in hopes of breaking through what seems to me to be a case of collective denial about the nature and consequences of children's consumer culture.

CHAPTER TWO

The Changing World of Children's Consumption

> A nation of kids and they Drive purchases; Kids influence 62% of family SUV and minivan purchases! Nickelodeon owns 50% of the K2–11 GRP's [Gross Rating Points] in Kids' Commercial TV.
>
> —From a Nickelodeon ad, with a smiling kid in an SUV

The typical American child is now immersed in the consumer marketplace to a degree that dwarfs all historical experience. At age one, she's watching *Teletubbies* and eating the food of its "promo partners" Burger King and McDonald's. Kids can recognize logos by eighteen months, and before reaching their second birthday, they're asking for products by brand name. By three or three and a half, experts say, children start to believe that brands communicate their personal qualities, for example, that they're cool, or strong, or smart. Even before starting school, the likelihood of having a television in their bedroom is 25 percent, and their viewing time is just over two hours a day. Upon arrival at the schoolhouse steps, the typical first grader can evoke 200 brands. And he or she has already accumulated an unprecedented number of possessions, beginning with an average of seventy new toys a year.

By age six and seven, girls are asking for the latest fashions, using nail polish, and singing pop music tunes. The day after the dELIA*s clothing catalogue arrives in the mail, marketers report that "everyone brings their catalog to school" to talk about the products in it. (When I wrote those words dELIA*s was hot; when they appear in print, who knows? Trends move at the speed of light in this world.) Eight-year-old boys are enjoying Budweiser commercials (the consistent favorite ad for this age group), World Wrestling Entertainment, and graphically violent video games.

Schools routinely ban the toy fads that sweep the market, from Power Rangers to Pokémon, on the grounds that they lead to fights, antisocial behavior, and disruption. The average eight to thirteen year old is watching over three and a half hours of television a day. American children view an estimated 40,000 commercials annually. They also make approximately 3,000 requests for products and services each year.

As kids age, they turn to teen culture, which is saturated with violence, alcohol, drugs, and guns. Teen media depict a manipulated and gratuitous sexuality, based on unrealistic body images, constraining gender stereotypes, and, all too frequently, the degradation of women. The dominant teen culture is also rife with materialism and preaches that if you're not rich, you're a loser. Adolescents are subjected to unremitting pressure to conform to the market's definition of cool. MTV has been the global leader in promoting these values, and its worldview has become pervasive among youth. And now, teen culture has migrated down to younger children. Eight and nine year olds watch MTV and BET (Black Entertainment Television), reality shows, and other prime-time fare ostensibly aimed at teens and adults. Marketers are deliberately investing children's culture with the themes and sensibilities that have worked with teens. As Betsy Frank, head of research for MTV Networks, explained, "If something works for MTV, it will also work for Nickelodeon." It's a widespread process, known as tweening.

The Marketing Juggernaut

This commercialization of childhood is being driven by a number of factors, including broad social trends. But underlying them all is a marketing juggernaut characterized by growing reach, effectiveness, and audacity. One clue to the marketing mentality is industry language. It's a war out there. Those at whom ads are directed are "targets." When money is committed to an ad campaign it is referred to as "going against the target." Printed materials are called "collateral." Impromptu interviews with consumers are "intercepts." The industry is heavily into the metaphor of biological warfare, as in the terms "viral marketing" and "sending out a virus." Other conventions include "converting [a kid] into a user" (a phrase from drug culture), delivering the "eyeballs," and becoming "top of mind." There's not much doubt about who's winning this war either. When Nickelodeon tells its advertisers that it "owns kids aged 2–12," the boast is closer to the mark than most of us realize.

The companies' successes are partly attributable to their enormous outlays of money. James McNeal, the nation's most influential estimator of the size of the children's market, has calculated that by 2004, total advertising and marketing expenditures directed at children reached $15 billion, a stunning rise from the mere $100 million in television advertising spent in 1983.

Researchers have chopped up the 52 million plus children in the age-twelve-and-under demographic into discrete age, gender, ethnic, and product segments, each with tailored messages. Nearly every segment warrants a yearly conference. For those who want to capture Hispanic youth, there's the Annual Hispanic KidPower meeting, which promises to unlock the special secrets of the most rapidly growing market segment in the country. The Annual KidPower Food and Beverage conference teaches participants how to sell more junk food to kids. There are conferences devoted to teens, to tweens, to Latin America, Asia, and Europe. African American children sometimes get special attention, as do themes such as girl power or technology. Hundreds of representatives of the client companies come to hear the latest findings about what kids are up to from researchers, psychologists, and ad agency reps. At one conference, I was treated to the pitch of the Gepetto Group, which created a simulated safari video, *The Nature of Kids.* The animals, of course, are children, defined as "nature's most elusive creature." The narrator has a British colonial accent, to conjure up images of safari suit and pith helmet. The kids slink through the jungle on all fours, guzzling soda and eating toaster pop-ups, speaking their own commercially inspired lingo. They're a species apart. But have no fear. Gepetto, the intrepid hunter, can help. It has snared and dissected these strange creatures we call our children and is ready to sell that information to anyone with cash to spend. Its representative promises to teach the client "how to get a grip on cool all the time" or do an assessment of kids' innermost dreams, aspirations, and fears.

Other companies have less elaborate come-ons but offer similar messages. Their workshop titles include "Emotional Branding: Maximizing the Appeal of Your Brand to Hispanic Youth," "Purchasing Power: Capturing Your Share of the Tween Wallet," and "Seeing the World Through Kids' Eyes: An Intimate Peek into the Minds and Hearts of Kids." Companies promise to "create an experience so engaging that the consumer won't have another option but to pay attention to it."

The growth of specialized kid expertise is made possible by a deluge of industry-generated research. Companies have created scores of surveys, polls, and other research instruments. They've gone anthropological, using ethnographic methods that scrutinize the most intimate details of children's lives. Marketers are videotaping children in their private spaces, providing in-depth analysis of the rituals of daily life. They are taking to the streets, to stores, and even into schools to observe and record. Researchers are paying adults whom kids trust, such as coaches, clergy, and youth workers, to elicit information from them. Online, they're offering money, products, and prizes directly to kids in return for saleable consumer information.

Once the research has been done, message crafting begins. Ads depict kid-friendly worlds free of annoying parents and teachers. They rely on "attitude" and use increasing daring in terms of shock value or sexuality. There's a growing sense of license. Marketing is also being delivered in new ways, as stealth, guerrilla, and peer-to-peer techniques have taken hold. Companies enlist children to market to each other at school, in chat rooms, on playgrounds, even inside their homes. Marketing to children is occurring almost everywhere—at market festivals, concerts, and public schools, which have been a major staging ground for advertisers in the past decade. Trusted social institutions, such as the Girl Scouts and Boys and Girls Clubs, are teaming up with marketers. When the *Los Angeles Times* decided to create a children's version of its well-known book fair, it turned, tellingly, to a marketing group. All the while, the industry claims that it is empowering kids and promoting their self-esteem.

A recent poll by the Center for a New American Dream reveals that children are well aware, and even critical, of these efforts. Among those aged nine to fourteen, 63 percent expressed concern that there is too much advertising that tries to get kids to buy things, 74 percent say "it's too bad you have to buy certain things to be cool," and 81 percent believe that "lots of kids place way too much importance on buying things." Fifty-seven percent agree that they sometimes feel they spend too much time trying to "get their parents to buy you things rather than doing fun things with them." And the same fraction worry that "advertising that tries to get kids to buy things causes trouble between kids and parents."

The Explosion of Youth Spending

Companies are advertising because kids are buying. Every half-second, somewhere in the world another Barbie is sold. More than 120 million kids worldwide have watched Children's Television Workshop. McDonald's, despite its current woes, still manages to attract 8 percent of the

American population every day, and a fifth of its business is in Happy Meals. Whether it's music, food, movies, video games, apparel, footwear, toys, television, sports, school supplies, retailing, e-tailing, health and beauty products, consumer electronics, entertainment, or travel, there is now a thriving children's market segment.

Children's purchasing power has risen rapidly. McNeal reports that children aged four to twelve made $6.1 billion in purchases in 1989, $23.4 billion in 1997, and $30.0 billion in 2002, an increase of 400 percent. The number one spending category, at a third of the total, is for sweets, snacks, and beverages. Toys are number two and apparel is growing fast. Older kids, aged twelve to nineteen, spend even more: they accounted for $170 billion of personal spending in 2002, or a weekly average of $101 per person. This teen market is important because the children's market tracks it, and because trends and styles now migrate quickly from adolescents to kids. Teens have become a leading indicator for tween and child behavior.

Children are becoming shoppers at an earlier age. Six to twelve year olds are estimated to visit stores two to three times per week and to put six items into the shopping cart each time they go. Eighty percent of them shop regularly with their parents, a change necessitated by the decline of stay-at-home mothers. But kids are also going solo. McNeal estimates that one in four make trips to stores alone before they enter elementary school and that the median age for independent trips is eight. Youthful shoppers are now often buying for family needs, particularly in single-parent households. The proliferation of children in stores is also leading to changes in retail environments. In 1996, the world's first mall catering exclusively to children opened in Alpharetta, Georgia. It has been enormously successful, and its "kids' village" concept has been copied around the country. Expect one on your local interstate before too long.

"Kid-fluence"

The more children shop, the more voice they have in parental purchases. In the industry, this is called the influence market, and it is enormous. McNeal estimates that children aged four to twelve directly influenced $330 billion of adult purchasing in 2004 and "evoked" another $340 billion. And he believes that influence spending is growing at 20 percent per year. Global estimates for tween influence topped $1 trillion in 2002. That persuasive power is why Nickelodeon, the number one television channel for kids, has had Ford Motor Company, Target, Embassy Suites, and the Bahamas Ministry of Tourism as its advertisers. (This explains why your child has been asking for an SUV, a vacation in the Bahamas, and a Robert Graves teapot.)

Children's influence is being driven by a number of factors, including changes in parenting style. Older generations were more authoritarian, believing that they knew what was best for their kids. The famous "children should be seen and not heard" adage also meant that parents made most buying decisions. Baby boom and later generations of parents have been far more willing to give voice and choice, to see consumer decisions as "learning opportunities." (Cheerios or Fruit Loops? Cherry Popsicle or grape?) As one marketer explained to me, "When I was a kid I got to pick the color of the car. Kids nowadays get to pick the car." While that may be an exaggeration, there is little doubt that parental attitudes have changed markedly. One industry estimate finds that 67 percent of car purchases by parents are influenced by children. Marketers have put tremendous effort into discovering just how far kid influence has permeated into household purchasing dynamics and for what types of products. And what they have found is that for a growing array of expenditures, children, not parents, are making choices.

What's more, kids' opinions are solicited from the earliest ages. According to a consumer panel run by New York agency Griffin Bacal, 100 percent of the parents of children aged two to five agreed that their children have a major influence on their food and snack purchases. For video and book choices, the rate of major influence was 80 percent, and for restaurants, clothes, and health and beauty products, it stood at 50 percent. The Roper Youth Report has found that among six and seven year olds, 30 percent choose their own grocery store food items, 15 percent choose their toys and games, and 33 percent make fast food and candy decisions. As kids age, their influence grows.

Food is an area where influence marketing and the decline of parental control has been most pronounced. Consider the case of Fruit Roll-ups, a phenomenally successful snack food represented by Saatchi and Saatchi's Kid Connection. When the product was introduced, the ads had both kid and mom appeal. For moms, they called attention to the fruit aspect of the snack. But over time, the agency realized that this "dual messaging" was unnecessary. As a former Saatchi employee explained to me: "For years we used to say 10 percent fruit juice. And finally we're just like, okay, forget it. Who are we kidding? . . . That was also a conscious effort to move toward direct kid marketing and not even worrying about Mom. Just take her out of the equation because the nag factor is so strong on something like that, that you can just take advantage of that."

Parental time pressure and longer working hours have also driven this trend. Time-starved households have become easy prey for marketers, whose research shows that parents who spend less time with their children will spend more money on them. "Guilt money," as they call it, came up in almost all my discussions about why kids have so much influence now. Research done by one of my students is consistent with this view. She found that parents who spent more hours working bought more discretionary items such as toys, videos, and books for their children. This effect is in addition to the fact that the additional income from working more also leads to more spending. By contrast, parents who spent more time with their children bought fewer of these items. The amount of extra spending was larger for mothers than fathers. And it was greater for toys than for other items. In higher-income families, spending was even more sensitive to time spent with children. These results do not show that parental guilt is motivating purchases, but marketers' belief in the power of guilt, and their ability to exploit it, remains strong.

Time pressure operates in other ways as well. Parents have less time to cajole kids to eat products they don't like or to return rejected purchases to stores. This is part of why 89 percent of parents of tweens report that they ask their children's opinions about products they are about to buy for them. Kids are also technologically savvy and eagerly seek out consumer information. Many parents now believe that their children know more about products and brands than they do, and they rely on that knowledge.

"Bonded to Brands"

These days, when kids ask, they ask for particular brands. A 2001 Nickelodeon study found that the average ten year old has memorized 300 to 400 brands. Among eight to fourteen year olds, 92 percent of requests are brand specific, and 89 percent of kids agree that "when I find a brand I like, I tend to stick with it." A 2000 Griffin Bacal study found that nearly two-thirds of mothers thought their children were brand aware by age three, and one-third said it happened at age two. Kids have clear brand preferences, they know which brands are cool, they covet them, and they pay attention to the ads for them. Today's tweens are the most brand-conscious generation in history.

The increased salience of brands is a predictable outcome of kids' greater exposure to ads. Companies spend billions to create positive brand associations for their products, attempting to connect them with culturally valued images, feelings, and sensibilities. This is especially true in the youth marketplace, where so many of the products are hardly differentiable without the labels. There's a copycat sameness to sodas, fast food, candy, athletic shoes, jeans, and even music and films. And in light of that, companies have to work overtime to establish brand identity and loyalty. They turn brands into "signs," pure symbolic entities, detached from specific products and functional characteristics. This has been a winning strategy, and youth have eagerly embraced an ethic of labels and logos. But brand value is a hard quality to sustain, especially in today's supercompetitive environment. The intensification of what scholars Robert Goldman and Stephen Papson have dubbed "sign wars," that is, corporate competition centered on images, has led to an ever-accelerating spiral of changing symbolism and brand vulnerability. And that vulnerability fuels marketing innovation and sometimes desperation.

In what industry insiders call the "kidspace," much of the action has been in what is called brand extension. Products are inserted into a vast matrix of other products. There's the Pokémon TV program, the collectible cards, the handheld electronic game, Pokémon toys at the fast food outlet, Pokémon versions of classic board games, Pokémon clothing, school supplies, plastic cups, backpacks, Pokémon everything and anything. Indeed, the process of extensive branding has become a profoundly normalized part of children's lives. It's now a lack of branding that's out of the ordinary. One of my friends explained to me that her son, a five year old with sophisticated musical tastes, was baffled by the fact that there was no "Talking Heads" stuff—no show, no toys, no logo, no nothing. What was going on, he wondered, with this band he liked so much?

Increasingly the brands kids want aren't just any brands. They crave designer duds and luxury items. By the mid-1990s, parents and buyers reported a sea change as girls aged six to ten became more fashion and label conscious. They wanted trendy styles like platform shoes and black clothing. They started asking for Hilfiger and Donna Karan labels. The designers claim that "kids are driving the trend," but they have been advertising heavily to them. Meanwhile, children's lines have sprung up at fashion houses such as Armani and Calvin Klein. Burberry opened Burberry Kids, and Abercrombie & Fitch, the current bad boy of youth apparel, became tweens' favorite brand. Upscaling has gone beyond designer clothes. By the end of the 1990s, Marianne Szymanski, founder of the Toy

Research Institute, reported that "kids are starting to want more expensive toys like computer software, cell phones, VCRs, e-mail, stereos, bedroom microwaves (for making popcorn while they watch movies in their own 'bedroom theater'). And guess what? Parents are buying all these items." Kids are also amassing far more toys than ever before. The number of toys sold annually rose 20 percent between 1995 and 2000. The United States, despite having only 4.5 percent of the world's population, now consumes 45 percent of global toy production.

Consumer experiences are also going luxe, and they're often more adult-like. The London salon MiniKin Kinder offers eight year olds its "Princess Treat," with haircut, manicure, and minifacial. Even cosmetic surgery has begun to reach down into childhood, according to journalist Alissa Quart, who reports that the year between elementary and middle schools is becoming a popular time for aesthetic enhancements for eyes, lips, chins, and ears. For those seeking the ultimate experience, FAO Schwartz offered birthday sleepover parties at a price of $17,500, and they were booked solid. Restaurateurs report that "crayons just won't do it anymore." Now they're providing menus attached to Magna Doodle sets, watercolor paint boxes, and Chinese carryout boxes with chopsticks, fortune cookies, and toys. In perhaps the most dramatic example of restaurant upscaling to come along yet, in 2002 McDonald's gave away Madame Alexander dolls, full-sized versions of which go for $50, with its Happy Meals.

Real-Life Monopoly

The commercialization of childhood is certainly being driven by the fact that kids have more money and more say, the explanation most marketers articulate. But there's another side to what scholars Shirley and Joe Kincheloe have insightfully called the "Corporate Construction of Childhood." It's the growing scope, market power, and political influence wielded by the small number of megacorporations that sell most of what kids buy. Far from being a consumers' mecca ruled by diverse and rich choices, children's consumer culture is marked by bigness and sameness. Four companies now dominate the children's media and entertainment market almost entirely. There's Disney, with its global reach, anodyne cultural products, and long history of racial and sexual stereotyping. Number two is Viacom, king of cool, whose MTV Networks is the parent company's most profitable division, whose annual revenue in 2001 exceeded $3 billion. We have MTV to thank for shows such as *Beavis and Butthead,* which has been accused of inspiring copycat antics that led to real-life death and destruction. (Viacom also published this book.) Rupert Murdoch's News Corp is the parent to Fox, which has brought us such contributions to youth culture as *Fear Factor.* And finally, there's AOL Time Warner, owners of WB, Cartoon Network, *Sports Illustrated for Kids,* and DC Comics. In 2002, the company announced it would begin showing paid sponsorship on its CNN-branded school news broadcast, but backed down after criticism. In the midst of these behemoths, PBS is overmatched, and anyway, it has joined up with Nickelodeon (Viacom) to infiltrate the "educational" market.

In the toy category, it's Mattel and Hasbro, which together have gobbled up virtually all the other toy companies. Playskool, Fisher-Price, Parker Brothers, Milton Bradley, Tonka Trucks, Tyco, Hot Wheels, American Girl, Cabbage Patch Dolls, Tinker Toys, Avalon Hill, Wizards of the Coast, and Mr. Potato Head are all owned by the big two. In early 2002, eight of the top-selling ten toys belonged to these two companies. Video games are dominated by a small number of producers—Nintendo, Sony, and Microsoft among them. The big-two model prevails in other markets as well. In candy it's M&M and Hershey. In soft drinks it's Coke and Pepsi. In fast food McDonald's and Burger King. Philip Morris (the tobacco giant, renamed Altria) owns Kraft with its Lunchables product, kids' second favorite lunch choice after pizza, as well as Nabisco and Post cereals. Frito-Lay is part of PepsiCo, as are Tropicana, Gatorade, and Quaker Oats. PepsiCo tries to retain a wholesome oatmeal image with the venerable Quaker on the box, but it's the same company that sells Cap'n Crunch's Choco Donuts cereal. Throughout the world of children's products, the markets are dominated by a few powerful companies.

This matters for a number of reasons. One is that with monopoly comes uniformity. Economic theory predicts that when two opponents face off, the winning strategy for both entails their becoming almost identical. This model explains why gas stations congregate at intersections, why Democrats and Republicans cleave to the political center, and why Coke and Pepsi are hard to tell apart with a blindfold. What it means for consumers is that true variety and diversity of products is hard to find. If you want greasy pizza, sugared drinks, plastic toys, and violent programming for your kids, no problem. It's the other stuff that's missing.

Monopoly also means bigger profits and market power for producers and less value and influence for consumers. That's standard economic reasoning. Finally, many of these companies have spent the past two decades stockpiling money and political influence. At the end of the 1970s, the

Federal Trade Commission was investigating practices in children's advertising and didn't like what it saw. It advocated a ban on advertising sugared products to kids, as well as an end to commercials aimed at children under age eight. Today, such a stance seems almost inconceivable, given the tremendous growth in political influence enjoyed by media corporations and food processors. Philip Morris gave more than $9 million in soft money to the two political parties between 1995 and 2002 ($7.8 million of it went to Republicans). AOL Time Warner gave more than $4 million (nearly equally divided). Disney contributed $3.6 million. Coca-Cola gave $2.3 million (mostly to the Republicans). The U.S. Sugar Corporation is also among the top "Double Givers." Two decades of corporate monies have eroded the regulatory, legislative, and judicial environment, making it far harder to protect children.

Playing Less and Shopping More

Memories shape adult views of childhood. Many in my generation—the baby boomers—have vivid recollections of endless hours of unsupervised, spontaneous play. We remember outdoor activities such as pick-up games on an empty sandlot. Many of us had a "gang" (in the wholesome sense) of neighborhood kids, often of mixed age and sex, who met up after school. When I was a kid, we would get obsessed with particular games, often ones we invented ourselves. There was plenty of traditional indoor play as well, such as house, war, and board games. We made concoctions, played dress-up, built forts, and fought with our siblings. Sometimes we even watched television.

We were lucky. Earlier generations of children spent much of their time working, on farms, in factories, and in domestic service. Paid child labor wasn't eliminated in this country until the 1920s. Baby boomers also escaped the sobering effects of depression and war. And we were a group of girls who were unusually liberated, both because we were allowed out on our own and because we were increasingly excused from household work. Children born in the late 1940s and afterward had more carefree, play-oriented upbringings with less family responsibility than the generations that preceded them. It was a childhood experience that took many decades to achieve, and unfortunately, the era was short-lived. In recent years, children's unsupervised time has declined. They spend more hours in worklike activities. More of daily life is structured by commercial and consumer activities than was true for previous generations.

Table 1

Weekly Time Children Spend in Various Activities, 1981–1997 (in hours and minutes)

	Ages 3–5		Ages 6–8		Ages 9–12		All Ages	
	1981	1997	1981	1997	1981	1997	1981	1997
Household work	2:09	2:20	2:49	2:07	5:18	3:42	3:46	2:49
Shopping	2:35	3:44	0:59	2:38	1:57	2:24	1:52	2:53
Personal care	6:18	8:32	6:13	7:53	6:21	7:53	6:18	8:05
Eating	9:43	9:24	9:08	8:05	8:13	7:23	8:52	8:13
Sleeping	77:19	76:11	70:04	70:49	65:36	67:24	70:01	71:07
School	14:30	12:05	27:52	32:46	29:02	34:03	24:45	26:48
Studying	0:25	0:36	0:52	2:08	3:22	3:41	1:53	2:16
Visiting	2:58	3:04	3:40	2:48	3:48	2:40	3:32	2:50
Sports	1:31	4:08	6:01	5:13	4:51	6:33	4:15	5:25
Outdoors	0:13	0:37	0:28	0:30	0:46	0:36	0:32	0:35
Art activities	0:28	1:12	0:21	0:45	0:22	0:54	0:23	0:57
Playing	25:50	17:21	14:58	11:10	7:24	8:54	14:30	12:12
Television	15:14	13:52	15:55	12:54	20:01	13:36	17:35	13:29
Reading	0:29	1:24	0:59	1:09	1:03	1:14	0:53	1:16
Household conversations	0:37	0:48	1:07	0:30	0:53	0:27	0:53	0:35
Other passive leisure	2:59	2:35	1:58	1:33	3:24	2:19	2:53	2:11
Day care	0:10	7:30	0:12	1:33	0:18	0:24	0:14	2:57

Source: Hofferth and Sandberg (2001b, Table 2).

Large-scale studies of children's time use are rare. In 1997, the Panel Survey of Income Dynamics conducted a major survey on children and their environments, and gathered data on how they spend their time. The "Child Development Supplement" was a nationally representative sample with more than 3,500 children from approximately 2,400 households. Time use was measured through a daily activity diary. The data show that time spent in leisure and unstructured play is limited. After subtracting eating, sleeping, personal care, schooling, studying, day care, shopping, and household work, only 25 percent of children's time remains discretionary. For six to twelve year olds, the fraction is a percentage point lower. (See Table 1.)

How do children spend that time? While three to five year olds still play a considerable amount, what study authors Sandra Hofferth and John Sandberg define as play comprises only about ten hours per week for the six-to-twelve age group, lower than school hours (thirty-three), and fewer than the thirteen hours spent watching television as a primary activity. Nine to twelve year olds play fewer than nine hours a week. There are other play-oriented activities during discretionary time, such as art and hobbies, measured at one hour, and "outdoors," at thirty-five minutes.

There is a widespread belief that in comparison with the past, today's children are harried, sped up, herded into productive activities, and less able to be kids. Book titles such as *The Hurried Child* and *The Over-Scheduled Child* reveal these social anxieties. Investigation of time-use patterns two decades ago suggests these worries may not be misplaced. In comparison to 1981, today's children spend more hours in school, and they spend more time on homework. They spend a lot less time visiting others and having household conversations. And their passive leisure time has fallen. They also have somewhat less free time. These trends may help to explain why there are now stress management workshops for kindergartners and why marketing studies report that one of the major problems articulated by kids today is that they want less pressure, less overload, and more time to relax.

Contemporary children also do far more shopping. In 1997, the average child aged six to twelve spent more than two and a half hours a week shopping, a full hour more than in 1981. Children are frequent visitors to the grocery store and the pharmacy. They run errands to the dry cleaners and accompany parents to the mall. They spent as much time shopping as visiting, twice as much time shopping as reading or going to church, and five times as much as playing outdoors. They spent half as much time shopping as playing sports. More children go shopping each week (52 per-

Table 2
Average Daily Time Exposed to Each Medium
(in hours and minutes)

	Ages 2–7	Ages 8–13
Total media exposure	4:17	8:08
Television	1:59	3:37
Taped TV shows	0:03	0:20
Videotapes (commercial)	0:26	0:29
Movies	0:02	0:26
Video games	0:08	0:32
Print media	0:45	0:50
Radio	0:24	0:35
CDs and tapes	0:21	0:47
Computer	0:07	0:32

Source: Kaiser Family Foundation (1999, Table 8-A).

Table 3
Amount of Daily Media Exposure and Media Use
(in hours and minutes)

	Total exposure	Person hours
All ages	6:32	5:29
Ages 2–7	4:17	3:34
Ages 8–13	8:08	6:47

Note: Total exposure is the sum of the amount of time children spend with each type of media, which includes double-counting. Person hours adjusts exposure time to avoid double-counting and represents total daily time spent with media.

Source: Kaiser Family Foundation (1999, Table 7).

cent) than read (42 percent), go to church (26 percent), participate in youth groups (25 percent), play outdoors (17 percent), or spend time in household conversation (32 percent).

Postmodern Childhood: The Electronic Generation

The change that has attracted most attention is kids' heavy involvement with electronic media, prompting some to posit a new, postmodern childhood, driven by television, Internet, video games, movies, and videos. To see the magnitude of these changes, we need to move beyond the diary data, which focus mainly on television, to more detailed surveys of media use.

One such study is the Kaiser Family Foundation's 1999 *Kids & Media @ the Millennium,* a high-quality, large-scale survey that combined a time diary with questions about yesterday's media viewing. It found that daily television viewing for two to eighteen year olds was two hours and forty-six minutes, plus an additional twenty-eight minutes watching videotapes. Viewing is most intense at ages eight to thirteen, when television takes up three hours and thirty-seven minutes a day, plus an additional twenty-nine minutes with videotapes. That's nearly thirty hours per week. The averages conceal wide variations, because there is a substantial group of very heavy watchers: 27.5 percent of kids aged eight to thirteen report more than five hours a day of TV viewing.

These estimates accord with most surveys of media use, including Nielsen's, but are much higher than traditional time diaries, which yield average viewing times of only thirteen to fourteen hours per week. One reason for the difference is that the diaries focus on primary activities, and television is often watched while doing other things. For example, in the Kaiser study, 42 percent of respondents reported that in their house, the television was on "most of the time." In 60 percent of households the television is on during meals.

When we combine all types of media—video games, computers, music, radio, and print—media time almost doubles. The average American child is estimated to spend five hours and twenty-nine minutes a day with media, for a weekly total of more than thirty-eight hours. About forty-five minutes a day is spent with print media. Forty-six percent of eight to thirteen year olds report total media exposure (which double counts media being used simultaneously) of more than seven hours per day. (See Tables 2 and 3.)

Television viewing varies significantly by race, income, and parental education, with the racial variations being most pronounced. For example, among eight to eighteen year olds, white children watch an average of two hours and forty-seven minutes a day, Hispanic children watch three hours and fifty minutes, and black children watch four hours and forty-one minutes of television a day. All three groups also watch an additional thirty minutes of video. In households with lower incomes, there is more television watching, especially among younger children. And in households where parents have lower educational levels, viewing times are higher, especially among younger children.

How Children Are Faring

The conservative take on the trends I've described is that we've produced a generation of couch potato kids, scarfing down chips and soda, driving their parents crazy about those hundred-dollar sneakers. They're spoiled, unable to delay gratification, and headed for trouble. An alternate view stresses the enormous accomplishments of young people today, their volunteer spirit, resiliency, and tolerance. Setting aside these value judgments, what do we know about how children are doing? The past fifteen to twenty years have witnessed big changes in what kids have been eating, drinking, watching, and doing. How are they faring?

Let's start with child nutrition. Historically, poverty has been the major culprit in malnutrition and poor diet. And despite the nation's wealth, we have significant levels of poverty-induced hunger and malnutrition. In 1999, 16.9 percent of children were subject to what is called "food insecurity" and did not have adequate food to live active, healthy lives. Millions of American children still go hungry. But now there's a new problem with food. Diets have gotten far out of line with recommended nutritional standards. Most kids are eating the wrong foods, and too many of them. A 1997 study found that 50 percent of children's calories are from added fat and sugar, and the diets of 45 percent of children failed to meet any of the standards of the USDA's food pyramid. Children eat excessive quantities of advertised food products and not enough fruits, vegetables, and fiber. Among children aged six to twelve, only 12 percent have a healthy diet, and 13 percent eat a poor diet. The rest are in the "needs improvement" category.

As has been widely reported, rates of youth obesity are skyrocketing. Using the eighty-fifth percentile Body Mass Index as a cutoff, about 25 percent of American youth are now overweight or obese. By the stiffer ninety-fifth percentile criterion, 15 percent of children are obese. Since 1980, obesity rates for children have doubled, and those for teens have tripled. Weight-related diseases, such as type II diabetes and hypertension, are rising rapidly. Alongside the rise in obesity is excessive concern with thinness and body image and a host of eating disorders. Record numbers of girls are on diets, and they are beginning to diet at an increasingly young age.

Other forms of consumption are similarly troubling. Kids are smoking, drinking alcohol, and taking illegal drugs at alarming rates. As early as the eighth grade, more than 7 percent of kids are regular smokers, and that number nearly triples by twelfth grade. Despite the tobacco settlement, more than 2,000 children and teens still start smoking every day, a third of whom will die of smoking-related causes. In the eighth grade, 14 percent of kids report that they have taken five alcoholic drinks in a row within the past two weeks. By the twelfth grade, twice as many answer affirmatively. Half of all high schoolers report that they currently drink alcohol. And 12 percent of eighth graders report that they have used illegal drugs within the past thirty days. Among twelfth graders, that percentage rises to 25 percent.

Children and youth are increasingly suffering from emotional and mental health problems. A study published in the *Pediatrics Journal* found that rates of emotional and behavioral problems among children aged four to fifteen soared between 1979 and 1996. Rates of anxiety and depression went from negligible to 3.6 percent; attention deficit hyperactivity disorder rose from 1.4 percent to 9.2 percent. Estimates of major depression are as high as 8 percent for adolescents. In recent decades, suicide rates have climbed, and suicide is now the fourth leading cause of death among ten to fourteen year olds. Suicide rates are highest among racial minorities. In 2001, the annual survey of incoming college freshmen by the University of California at Los Angeles found that self-reports of physical and emotional health reached their worst level in the sixteen years the questions had been asked.

The large-scale MECA study (Methods for the Epidemiology of Child and Adolescent Mental Disorders) yields similar findings. It found that 13 percent of kids aged nine to seventeen suffer from anxiety, 6.2 percent have mood disorders, 10.3 percent have disruptive disorders, and 2 percent suffer from substance abuse. Taken together, about 21 percent of this age group had a "diagnosable mental or addictive disorder with at least minimum impairment." Eleven percent had a significant functional impairment, and 5 percent were reported to have an extreme functional impairment. (See Table 4.)

Conclusions from the 1997 Child Development Supplement, which included children aged three to twelve, are also cause for concern. Although parents reported that their children were generally happy and healthy, one in five said that they were fearful or anxious, unhappy, sad, depressed, or withdrawn. Two in five reported that their children were impulsive, disobedient, or moody. All told, nearly 50 percent had at least one of these problems. This survey also asked about the quality of relationships between children and parents. It found that only 59 percent of parents reported that their relationships with their school-aged children are "extremely or very close," and only 57 percent reported engaging in very warm behaviors with their child several times a week. (Warm behaviors are defined as hugging, joking, playing, and telling them they love them.)

Taken together, these findings are not comforting. They show that American children are worse off today than they were ten or twenty years ago. This conclusion is especially notable when we consider that during the past fifteen years, child poverty fell substantially, from a high of 22 percent in the late 1980s to its current rate of 16 percent. The decline in child poverty should have led to improvements in measures of distress, because child poverty is correlated with adverse physical and psychological health outcomes. The deterioration of the well-being indicators suggests that some powerful negative factors are undermining children's well-being.

Table 4
Youth Mental and Addictive Disorders
Children and Adolescents Age 9–17

	Pecentage of Youth, Ages 9–17
Anxiety disorders	13.0
Mood disorders	6.2
Disruptive disorders	10.3
Substance use disorders	2.0
Any disorder	20.9

Source: Data cited in U.S. Office of the Surgeon General (1999, Table 3-1).

One of them may be the upsurge in materialist values. Children's top aspiration now is to be rich, a more appealing prospect to them than being a great athlete, or a celebrity, or being really smart, the goals of earlier eras. Forty-four percent of kids in fourth through eighth grades now report that they daydream "a lot" about being rich. And nearly two-thirds of parents report that "my child defines his or her self-worth in terms of the things they own and wear more than I did when I was that age."

Psychologists have found that espousing these kinds of materialist values undermines well-being, leading people to be more depressed, anxious, less vital, and in worse physical health. Among youth, those who are more materialistic are more likely to engage in risky behaviors. In the light of these findings, the survey data are worrisome. One of the few large national surveys of children's materialism found that more than a third of all children aged nine to fourteen would rather spend time buying things than doing almost anything else, more than a third "really like kids that have very special games or clothes," more than half agree that "when you grow up, the more money you have, the happier you are," and 62 percent say that "the only kind of job I want when I grow up is one that gets me a lot of money." To understand how and why American children got this way, it's time to take a stroll down Madison Avenue.

CHAPTER THREE

From Tony the Tiger to *Slime Time Live*

The Content of Commercial Messages

It's a great gig.

—Lisa Morgan (pseudonym),
New York account executive,
talking about marketing to children

Proponents of the "there's nothing new under the sun" view of history remind us that children have been marketed to for decades, even centuries. When special children's products, such as literature and clothing, appeared in the eighteenth century, kids had to be sold on them. In the late nineteenth century, Chicago department store Marshall Field's produced a thirty-six-page catalogue devoted exclusively to toys. Not long afterward, department stores converted their seasonal toy departments to year-round displays and staged fashion shows for children's apparel. Children's radio shows in the 1930s contained advertising directed to kids. But as I have already noted, in the first half of the twentieth century, products were mainly sold through mothers.

One reason was that opportunities to target children directly were limited until the introduction of television programs specifically for children. In 1954, ABC aired its highly successful *Mickey Mouse Club* in the after-school period, and Mattel advertised on the show. By the late 1950s, the popularity of Barbie solidified a long and profitable relationship between television and toy commercials. Saturday morning programming also began at this time, and Kellogg's created its classic characters Tony the Tiger, Rice Krispies' Snap, Crackle, and Pop, and the Trix rabbit to sell cereals. In these early days, toys and breakfast cereals were already the two major categories of products being advertised. Interestingly, brand awareness and influence purchasing, two central themes of contemporary marketing wisdom, were already present in the 1950s. But in comparison to today, the advertising of the past was far less ambitious. The kids' market was an industry backwater, ruled by standard formulas. Boys' ads had announcers speaking at high decibels, car crashes, and animation. Girls got bouncy, sweet, pink-washed commercials. Ads tended to focus on the attributes of the product, in contrast to the more symbolic appeals of today. Those who have seen the children's advertising of this period will remember it as a low-budget, low-creativity affair.

Early television advertising also had an almost Wild West, anything-goes quality. Selling techniques were largely unregulated. Ads showed children getting superhuman strength by eating cereals and employed special effects that enhanced toys. Ads did not have to distinguish between fantasy and reality, as they do today. Host selling within shows was widespread. Early ads were often crude and relied on pressure tactics and sometimes deceptive formulations.

For these reasons, television commercials directed at children eventually became highly regulated, through a voluntary guideline system put forward by the Children's Advertising Review Unit (CARU) of the Better Business Bureau, and more specific but similar guidelines at the networks. These guidelines include a variety of prohibitions, such as bans on host selling, celebrity endorsers, and the use of superhuman effects. All child-directed ads are also required to refrain from suggesting that a child needs the product to be accepted by peers or that ownership of the product confers superiority. Exhortative language to "buy" the product or "ask a parent for it," which is termed hard sell, is also prohibited. However, these guidelines apply only to ads for which the primary target is children. Ads for beer, autos, and any other products where 51 percent of the viewing audience is adults are covered by the far less restrictive adult guidelines. Widespread child viewing of adult shows has undermined the relevance of the children's guidelines. (By the late 1990s, more than half of the top twenty most popular programs among two to twelve year olds were adult programs.)

Toy advertisements, which are second to food in terms of size of expenditures, are the most highly regulated category. Guidelines stipulate that a portion of a toy commercial must show the product in a realistic setting, which has resulted in the so-called island shots at the end of all toy ads, with toys shown in a neutral backdrop. The ad must not imply that the toy can do things it cannot, such as move alone when it requires human assistance, and if batteries or other accessories are necessary, that fact must be stated. Toy ads must also distinguish clearly between realistic play and play in fantasy environments, and fantasy cannot comprise more than a third of the length of a spot. A typical toy commercial now begins with a realistic play sequence, a fantasy sequence in the jungle, outer space, prehistory, or a magical kingdom, and then a return to realism. Ads also have to be careful about showing unsafe activities that real kids might mimic. This is in contrast to the leeway given to programs, despite their having been implicated in a number of dangerous copycat incidents. Legal findings concerning false or deceptive ads have also been a major influence in regulating toy advertising. In the 1970s, the Federal Trade Commission issued consent orders against some of the major toy companies, such as Mattel and Kenner, which remained in force for decades. The orders involved ads that depicted toys doing things they couldn't, and one of their effects has been to create caution in these companies' subsequent advertising.

Advertising for food is less strictly regulated than for toys, because the industry view is that kids need to be encouraged to eat. The major guideline is the so-called balanced breakfast shot, in which cereals and other breakfast foods must be shown in the context of a balanced breakfast. Other regulations include the stipulation that claims linking food and energy must be reasonably accurate, and a prohibition on advertising special enriched foods as substitutes for meals, such as Slim-Fast or Carnation Instant Breakfast.

The 1980s brought major changes in children's advertising. Companies began to see more potential in selling to kids. Credit for this realization is typically given to James McNeal, whose estimates of children's purchasing power were widely circulated in the industry. McNeal reports that in the 1960s, when he pitched his expertise to firms, his message fell on deaf ears: "They practically laughed me out of the place. 'Kids as a market? You gotta be kidding.' " By the late 1980s, when his first book appeared, companies were taking children far more seriously. McNeal's estimates helped to expand the types of products that were marketed to kids, as well as increase the volume of dollars companies were willing to commit in categories such as food and leisure. Kraft started targeting kids for cheese, pasta, Jell-O, and puddings, in addition to longstanding child foods such as snacks and cereals. As Paul Kurnit, one of the deans of kid marketing, explained to me, "There was the recognition that you could drive macaroni and other foods to kids themselves, you know, 'Mom, please get me Kraft macaroni and cheese.' "

A second development was that the expansion of children's media offered new opportunities for advertisers. In the 1980s, cable television stations specifically designed for children were introduced. And although some of them, such as Nickelodeon, did not initially accept ads, those policies eventually changed. Cable became an inexpensive and effective venue for advertisers. The emergence of Fox as a fourth network also helped propel the kids' market. Fox skewed toward youth, using edgy new formats with "cool" and African American, urban themes that appealed to children who hadn't yet reached adolescence.

Finally, the 1980s witnessed the dramatic upsurge in kids' influence power. There were fewer of what marketers called the "authoritarian mom"—the woman who, in the words of Paul Kurnit, said, "No way, no how is there going to be a pre-sweetened cereal in our house no matter how hard Johnnie tries to convince her." Instead, 1980s mothers were far more likely to be permissive or ambivalent moms, willing to buy the products on offer. "Another piece of it is that today's mom grew up with all this stuff, so she tends to be much more of a culture creature herself, and if her parent wasn't authoritarian, why should she be?"

By the 1990s, the stage was set for a thorough revolution in youth marketing. Kids had unprecedented spending power. They had unprecedented influence over their parents' spending power. They were watching unprecedented levels of television. And they were on their own far more than the previous generation had been. Now the trick was to get them to buy the products on offer.

The companies responded by upping their ad budgets substantially. Once that happened, the agencies needed to bring in more expertise. In the past, kid marketers had mostly relied on personal intuition and the experiences they themselves had as parents. With so many more dollars at stake, that strategy was risky, so companies hired psychologists, child development specialists, anthropologists, and sociologists to help craft more compelling messages. They developed far more capacity for testing and research and they began delivering those messages in new ways. In the remainder of this chapter and the next three, I describe these developments in some detail, looking at the content of marketing messages, the expanding venues through which they are delivered, and the infrastructure of research that supports these activities.

The Child Psyche According to Marketers

Virtually all the marketers I interviewed and the printed sources I used relied on a common psychological model of the child. It's an old-fashioned view that sees children steadily developing or emerging into adulthood. Developmentalism conceptualizes change in a linear fashion, with a biologically predetermined set of cognitive and emotional stages. Children are thought to go through these stages at more or less the same rate. The stages are seen as universal, applying to children regardless of race, ethnicity, social class, or sexual orientation. The father of developmentalism and perhaps its most influential thinker of all is Jean Piaget, whose model of cognitive advance is still widely taught.

Developmental psychology and children's marketing have a long history of close alignment. Marketers took the psychology and reconceptualized the process of growing up as a process of learning to consume. University of Illinois sociologist Daniel Cook, who has studied the expert discourse on marketing to children throughout the twentieth century, argues that the common thread has been the view that children are small but emergent consumers. In the 1930s, the characterization of children was as growth machines who needed to be educated. In the 1950s, kids were seen as novelty seekers. In the 1970s and 1980s, the field took up the idea that kids are molded by their parents in a consumer socialization process. By the 1990s, child consumers were described as autonomous and savvy. What all these conceptualizations shared was their belief in an immanent process of unfolding product needs. Furthermore, Cook argues, developmental thinking in the early part of the century gave marketers a "template of sorts upon which to organize the child's experience, abilities and 'needs' and a justification to target young children in a modified form of 'education.' " Then, as today, companies were using teaching materials to promote their products. Lifebuoy produced a chart about washing up. Shredded Wheat had a color-coded account of the product's journey from field to factory. Magazines such as *Parents* and *Child Life* merged commercial messages with academic research, and child development and child marketing evolved together.

While the developmental paradigm has attained an almost sacred, commonsense status in our culture, most of its adherents fail to recognize how culturally and historically skewed much of its lore really is. As an example, consider that the toddler stage, now a mainstay of parenting books and developmental thinking, was popularized by department stores in the 1930s, as they segregated children's apparel into separate sections, and even separate floors. Cook has shown that the term *toddler* gained currency as a size and style range for clothing (e.g., 2T, 3T), which spurred its conceptualization as a stage of childhood. Writers in apparel industry publications began to describe toddlers as the "third stepping-stone" in building an infants' department. Developmental language was linked to clothing: "The child at this age is leaving babyhood and each day becoming more of a personality. His clothes, too, must begin to have personality." Notably, this was also the point at which clothing was differentiated by gender. Cook has argued that the concept of the teen developed in tandem with the introduction of new teen sizes in the mid-1930s. Popular awareness of a sub- or preteen phase, the precursor to today's tweens, was also partly attributable to clothing advertising.

The construction of the toddler stage is just one example of what academics term the naturalization of childhood. Naturalization denotes a situation in which socially constructed phenomena come to be seen as inherent in the individual, that is, an inalterable part of human nature. Kids' consumer desires are now considered natural, despite the fact that children in different cultures and different historical periods in our own culture vary widely in how much they covet stuff or care about consumer trends. Not one of the industry professionals I interviewed revealed any consciousness of this tendency within their field.

In contemporary marketing, the naturalization of consumer desires has been codified into a set of timeless emotional needs all children are believed to possess. Standard practice consists of matching those universal needs to particular products and advertising messages, in which the role of the ad or product is to satisfy the need. Kids need to be scared to help them overcome their fears, so make a scary movie. Kids need to belong, so suggest that if they buy brand X, they'll have friends.

These needs are defined similarly throughout the field. The first "need" is for gender differentiation. Virtually every marketing professional I encountered contends that boys and girls like different products and need segregated marketing. With the exception of food, almost all products, messages, and campaigns are subjected to gender analysis that asks, Is it for boys, or is it for girls? (Some products do emerge as unisex.) Despite efforts to raise awareness about the role of toys in the reproduction of unhealthy gender stereotypes, the major toy chains still segregate by gender. The so-called timeless emotional needs also skew in one direction or another, and boys get a wider range of messages. The conventional wisdom is that boys want power. Boys also want action, and they want to succeed. By contrast, girls are thought to want glamour. And although girl power (the idea that girls are powerful and active) has now entered the pantheon of innermost needs, girls are still thought of in stereotypical ways and remain tethered to traditional ideals of glamour and femininity, even when they're powerful.

In ads, these ideas play out in standard formulas. The old themes of car crashes for boys and pink-washing for girls have by no means disappeared, but they are less common, and the gender rules have become more subtle. For example, boy characters and masculine messages must dominate in ads for any products that are aimed at boys or both sexes. If four children are used to advertise a unisex or boy product, the rule is that at least three will be boys. Three girls are used only for girl products. The rationale for these conventions is that boys are more skittish about gender identities and highly sensitive to anything that smacks of the feminine. As a consequence, boys are still preferred when casting ads. Other gender differences are that girls remain more likely to be portrayed in indoor domestic spaces, and boys are shown out of doors. While passivity is no longer required for girls, behavioral differences remain, such as the fact that boys are frequently shown engaging in antisocial behavior, while girls act only in socially sanctioned ways.

Despite the growth of girl heroines, gender imbalance remains in certain programming mediums. A 1997 Kaiser Family Foundation study found that 63 percent of movie characters are male, as are 78 percent of those in music videos. (The breakdown on television is now closer to parity, with 55 percent male characters.) But there are some signs that the consensus is cracking. The phenomenon of gender blending has been getting attention recently, with examples such as boys wearing nail polish or girls liking "gross." However, for a field that portrays itself as on the cutting edge, the extent to which gender stereotypes still predominate is striking.

After dividing the sexes, marketers go to work trying to match products with basic human needs. About half of the so-called needs look harmless enough. They're the ones mainly targeted to the youngest kids and include mastery and the need to succeed, sensory stimulation, and love.

Success and mastery are thought to be common kid fantasies and show up repeatedly in advertising. They are addressed through showing challenging toys and games, where kids are portrayed achieving and winning. Success and mastery are also used as themes in cases where the product is unrelated to the need. In one Eggo commercial, an old codger in a farmhouse eats an Eggo with mud on it, mistakes it for a chocolate chip waffle, and calls the company to complain about the taste. The young whippersnapper who answers the call parlays the idea into career success, in the process becoming a child CEO, complete with corner office, suit and tie, and a servile staff. Getting rich, becoming the boss, and beating out the competition are messages that emanate from the so-called need to succeed. One feature of this theme is that it skews heavily toward boys, on the grounds that girls don't really care about being successful. When mastery, accomplishment, and achievement are portrayed in commercial messages, boys are usually the target.

A second need is sensory stimulation. This approach is thought to be a sure winner with kids, again, skewing male. When two tween boys bite into an Oreo cookie, all of New York City is engulfed in a tsunami of creme. Some ads create a blitz of sensations, using noise, flashing lights, and images in rapid succession. Many ads are designed to capture attention through high levels of stimulation. The need for sensory stimulation is often translated into what Lisa Morgan, an executive from a major agency, described as the "need to create sensory overload" for kids. "The product," she explains, "is a trigger for over-satisfying kids' senses."

Marketers also concur that kids want love, especially those in what they call the zero-to-three age target. Common strategies for conveying love are the use of stuffed animals, sweet-looking dolls, and objects with rounded surfaces. Child development experts, brain scientists, and psychologists have helped marketers translate the desire for love into concrete objects, shapes, music, and themes for ads. This category skews girl. It is now rather rare in marketing to school-aged children, who are thought to prefer edgier themes.

Fear also shows up on virtually all marketers' lists, on the grounds that children need to face and overcome their fears, and ads provide opportunities for doing so. Regulation prevents kid-directed commercials from being too frightening, but combining excitement with some element of fear is common in fantasy scenes. The fear level is far greater in films and programs. However, scaring children is a controversial practice. Some advertisers and Hollywood executives advocate it. But many psychologists and educators are critical. Joanne Cantor, a long-time researcher and author of *Mommy, I'm Scared,* believes that television programs and movies are the main preventable cause of nightmares and anxieties in children and that media-induced fright can have substantial negative effects on children's emotional well-being.

These themes are the least controversial of the approaches advertisers take with children. Whether they are as benign as they appear is a question

I will come back to. There's also a second set of more innovative approaches that define the direction of the field. The industry describes them as the marketing of cool, attitude, nag factor, age compression, dual messaging, and trans-toying. With these strategies, corporations have ventured into some highly questionable territory.

The Marketing of Cool

Cool has been around for decades. Back in the fifties, there were cool cats and hipsters. In the sixties, hippies and the Beatles were cool. But in those days, cool was only one of many acceptable personal styles. Now it's revered as a universal quality—something every product tries to be and every kid needs to have. Marketers have defined cool as the key to social success, as what matters for determining who belongs, who's popular, and who gets accepted by peers. While there is no doubt that the desire for social acceptance is a central theme of growing up, marketers have elevated it to the sine qua non of children's psyches. The promotion of cool is a good example of how the practices of marketing to teens, for whom social acceptance is even more important, have filtered down to the children's sphere. In a recent survey of 4,002 kids in grades 4 through 8, 66 percent reported that cool defines them. Part of why is that cool has become *the* dominant theme of children's marketing.

Part of the genius of cool is its versatility. Cool isn't only about not being a dork. Cool takes on many incarnations. It can incorporate dork and jock, if necessary. It can be driven by neon or primary colors; it's retro or futuristic, techno or natural. Today, Target is cool. Yesterday it was the Gap. Good-bye Barney. Hello Kitty. By the time you read these words, today's cool will not be. But although cool is hard to pin down, in practice it centers on some recurring themes, and these themes are relentlessly pushed by marketers in the conception and design of products, packaging, marketing, and advertising. At every step, these principles apply.

One theme is that cool is socially exclusive, that is, expensive. In an earlier era, cheap stuff dominated kids' consumer worlds, mainly because they didn't have much money. They bought penny candy, plastic toys, and cheap thrills. In those days, the functional aspects of products were paramount, such as the fact that the toy is fun to play with or the candy tastes good. Social symbolism and status weren't wholly absent, but they were far less important. Now that kids have access to so much more money, status and its underlying values of inequality and exclusion have settled at the heart of the kid consumer culture. Branding expert Martin Lindstrom reports that for tweens, the brand took over from function as the main attraction of products in the 1990s. From video games, to apparel, to that ubiquitous symbol of status, the athletic shoe, kids' products have upscaled, in the process becoming both more unaffordable and more desirable. Gene Del Vecchio, former Ogilvy and Mather executive and author of *Creating Ever-Cool: A Marketer's Guide to a Kid's Heart,* is more candid than most others about the exclusionary nature of cool: "Part of cool is having something that others do not. That makes a kid feel special. It is also the spark that drives kids to find the next cool item." When Reebok introduced its computerized Traxtar shoe, it was banking on a message of "superiority" ("I have Traxtar and you don't"), according to the people who designed the program. The shoe became the top seller in its category, a notable accomplishment given its significantly higher price. Marketers convey the view that wealth and aspiration to wealth are cool. Material excess, having lots of money, career achievement, and a lifestyle to go with it are all highly valued in the marketing world's definition of what's hot and what's not. Living modestly means living like a loser.

Cool is also associated with being older than one's age. Marketers and advertisers take this common desire of kids and play into it in a variety of ways. They put a few older kids in ads that are targeted to younger kids. They have young kids in ads morph into older kids or into adults. They use adult celebrity endorsers for products or brands that kids buy. They depict fantasy worlds in which a young kid sees himself or herself grown up. Cool is also associated with an antiadult sensibility, as ads portray kids with attitude, outwitting their teachers and tricking their parents. Finally, cool is about the taboo, the dangerous, the forbidden other. Among advertisers, *edgy* has been and remains the adjective of the moment—not "over the edge," because that is too dangerous, but "at the edge," "pushing the edge."

Edgy style has associations with rap and hip-hop, with "street" and African American culture. In the 1990s, ads aimed at white, middle-class Americans began to be filmed in inner-city neighborhoods with young black men as the stars. The ads made subtle connections to violence, drugs, criminality, and sexuality—the distorted and stereotypical images of young black men that have pervaded the mainstream media. As Harvard University's Douglas Holt wrote in 1999 in a paper we coauthored, "Street has proven to be a potent commodity because its aesthetic offers an authentic threatening edginess that is very attractive both to white suburban kids who perpetually recreate radical youth culture in relation to their parents' conservative views about the ghetto, and to urban cultural elites for whom it becomes a form of cosmopolitan radical chic. . . . We now have the commodification of a virulent, dangerous 'other' lifestyle . . . Gangsta."

The story of how street came to be at the core of consumer marketing began more than thirty years ago. Chroniclers of the marketing of "ghetto" point to the practices of athletic shoe companies, starting with Converse in the late 1960s and, more recently, Nike and its competitors. The shoe manufacturers intentionally associated their product with African American athletes, giving free shoes to coaches in the inner cities, targeting inner-city consumers in their research, attaching their brand to street athletics and sociability. They also developed a practice dubbed "bro-ing" by industry insiders, that is, going to the streets to ask the brothers which designs deserve the moniker of cool. Apparel companies, beginning with Tommy Hilfiger, became active in this world, giving rap stars and other prominent tastemakers free samples of their latest styles. While the connection to inner-city life may sound like a contradiction with the idea that cool is exclusive and upscale, it is partially resolved by the fact that many of the inner-city ambassadors of products are wealthy, conspicuous consumers such as rap stars and athletes driving fancy cars and living luxurious lifestyles.

Eventually soft drink companies, candy manufacturers, culture producers, and many others that sell products to teens and kids would be on the street, trying desperately to get some of that ineluctable cool to rub off on their brand. As advertiser Paul Kurnit explains, "What's going on in white America today is [that] the inner city is very much a Gold Standard. We've got lots of white kids who are walking around emulating black lifestyle." Of course, mere association with ghetto style is not a guarantee of success. Some campaigns have been flat-footed with their mimicry. Others lack basic credibility, such as preppy tennis shoe K-Swiss, which tried to position itself as a street brand. The brands that have been skilled at this approach are those with images that are more plausibly and authentically connected to it.

Although many aspects of African American culture have had a long historical association with cool, such as jazz and sartorial styles, as well as a legacy of contributions to popular culture, what's happening now is unique. Never before have inner-city styles and cultural practices been such a dominant influence on, even a primary definer of, popular culture. The process is also no longer one of mainstreaming, in which a cultural innovation from the margins is incorporated into the larger culture. Rather, in the words of Douglas Holt again, "It is now the local, authentic qualities of Street culture that sell. Instead of black cultural products denuded of their social context, it is now primarily the context itself—the neighborhood, the pain of being poor, the alienation experienced by black kids. These are the commodifiable assets." The other new development is the role of large corporations in the movement of styles and cultural forms from the ghetto to the suburb. The process no longer develops through an organic movement as it once did. Instead, cool hunters manage the process of cultural transmission. Another novel aspect is the evolution of a back-and-forth dynamic between the companies and the grass roots, with cool-hunting and street marketing creating what media critics have called a feedback loop.

The feedback loop is a sharp departure from decades past, when consumers blindly followed where advertisers led. In Holt's words, marketers once possessed a monopoly on "cultural authority," in which they set the tone and agenda, and consumers eagerly looked to them to learn what to wear, eat, drive, and value. That cultural authority has virtually disappeared. Its demise can be traced to the backlash against advertising that originally emerged in the 1950s with the popularity of books such as John Kenneth Galbraith's *The Affluent Society* and Vance Packard's *The Hidden Persuaders*. By the 1960s, some of the most successful marketers were those who took their cues from consumers. Since then, advertisers have increasingly attempted to figure out what people already value and let those findings direct ads. With youth, the process has gone a step further, because they know the advertisers are relying on them, and consciously play to their influence. That's the feedback idea, which has been identified by observers such as Douglas Kellner, Holt, and Douglas Rushkoff. As Rushkoff explains, in a plea to the industry: "It's turned into a giant feedback loop: you watch kids to find out what trend is 'in,' but the kids are watching you watching them in order to figure out how to act. They are exhibitionists, aware of corporate America's fascination with their every move, and delighting in your obsession with their tastes." Although there's a democratic veneer to the feedback loop, that perspective obscures the fact that giant businesses orchestrate, control, and profit from the process. Furthermore, kids are increasingly pulling outrageous and even dangerous stunts to get themselves noticed by the great big marketing machine.

Originally, the marketing of edgy was a teen and young adult development. Now it too has trickled down to the children's market, though with some adjustments. Kid advertisers had to become far more discriminating, screening out what had become an anything-goes ethic. By way of illustration, consider the heroin-chic fashion photography of the mid-1990s. At that time cool hunters routinely included drugs, including hard ones, on their lists of what's hot and what's not. As one now-famous accounting from a cool-hunter publication that appeared in the *New Yorker* had it: "In San Francisco it's Nike, heroin, and reggae; in Chicago, Jungle music, Tag watches, and drugs." Similarly, in kids' ads, violent images are more restricted, although this is less the case in movie ads, video games, and on the Web. The situation is similar with sexuality, exploitative racial imagery, and certain antisocial themes, all of which are prominent in cultural forms for teens and young adults. While going edgy can almost guarantee cool, it can also jeopardize a brand that depends on maintaining its wholesome image. Advertisers calibrate the degree of edginess and strive to go as far as, but not beyond what, a brand's image can tolerate.

Kids Rule: Nickelodeon and the Antiadult Bias

What else is cool? Based on what's selling in consumer culture, one would have to say that kids are cool and adults are not. Fair enough. Our country has a venerable history of generational conflict and youth rebellion. But marketers have perverted those worthy sentiments to create a sophisticated and powerful "antiadultism" within the commercial world.

This trend also has a history. Advertising agencies have been co-opting youth rebellion for years, beginning with Bill Bernbach's embrace of the counterculture in Volkswagen ads in the 1960s, a development insightfully chronicled in Thomas Frank's *The Conquest of Cool.* More recently, the entity most responsible for the commercial exploitation of youth rebellion has been Viacom. The trend began with MTV and its teen audience, as the enormously popular network capitalized on teen desires to separate from and rebel against their parents. MTV allowed teens to immerse themselves in an increasingly separate culture, with its own fashions, language, and attitudes. Over time, some of that sensibility has trickled down to Nickelodeon's younger target.

Nickelodeon was founded in 1979 as a cable network, but it has since become a transcendent brand identity, selling a wide array of products and a relationship with kids. Nickelodeon would eventually dominate children's media. Nickelodeon's audience outpaces all other kid-oriented networks by a wide margin. At 80 percent, its household penetration tops the children's cable networks. As I write these words, it is enjoying its best ratings year ever, surging far above the competition. The Nickelodeon Web site is the number one children's online destination. Its magazines boast 1.1 million subscribers and 6.3 million readers. Nickelodeon is shown in 158 countries. Incredibly enough, given its limited demographic target, Nickelodeon has become one of the nation's most profitable networks. In the process, it has remade children's programming and advertising.

Early on, Nickelodeon earned a reputation for offering quality shows. Its graphics were visually arresting, and the content was fresh. In comparison to the tired world of program-length commercials, that is, shows whose primary purpose is to sell products, Nickelodeon's offerings stood out. The network has also benefited from its recognition that children are a diverse group in terms of race and ethnicity, family type, and age. On the revenue side, Nickelodeon has made hay with the insight that children are a major influence market for parental purchases. A senior executive explained their stance: "The whole premise of our company was founded on serving kids, and what we've found is that when you do good things for kids, it happens to be good for business."

The secret of Nickelodeon's success is its core philosophy: *kids rule.* In everything that they do, Nickelodeon tries to take the child's perspective. The network has positioned itself as kids' best friend, on their side in an often-hostile environment. Donna Sabino, director for research and development at Nickelodeon's Magazine Group, explained the thinking to me: "It's hard to be a kid in an adult world. The adult world doesn't respect kids. Everywhere else adults rule; at Nick kids rule." The Nickelodeon worldview is that childhood has gotten tough. "Kids are experiencing increased pressure for achievement and activity. They don't have enough time for homework, they're overscheduled." Nickelodeon gives them what they need: "funny, happy, empowering." There are thirteen criteria a program must have to pass muster at the network, including good quality, a kid-centered message, humor, and edgy visual design. In theory, these are good criteria. But in practice, when kid-centric and edgy come together, what often results is attitude—an antiauthoritarian us-versus-them sensibility that pervades the brand.

Nickelodeon's 2001 back-to-school campaign featured a teacher who looked like a battle-ax, advice on how "to make the substitute teacher screech," and opportunities to "slime the teacher." (Sliming derives from the popular *Slime Time Live* show and involves throwing slimy green goop on a person.) The campaign included a contest sponsored by a tobacco company, for which the prize was a slime shower for their principal and the chance to have Nickelodeon "take over" their school. In the kid-centric hip world, adults are the bothersome, the nerdy, the embarrassing, and the repressive—that is, perfect and deserving targets for sliming. The network also pushes the boundaries of acceptability in terms of vulgarity and manners. *Butt-Ugly Martians* premiered in the fall of 2001, targeted at four to eight year olds. On *The Amanda Show,* which one parent I interviewed complained about, the girls have "attitude." When her fourth grader started going around the house imitating one character with a sassy, "My name is Joyce. You got a problem with that?" the mother replied in the affirmative: "I do have a problem with that, so stop it, please." *Nickelodeon Magazine* delivered its Jumbo Prank Kit to almost 2 million kids, complete with annoying songs to sing in the backseat of the family car.

Nickelodeon knows not to go too far with its portrayal of adults and other authority figures. The brand needs approval from parents. In the words of Don Steinberg, writing in the *Philadelphia Inquirer,* the company knows what it's about "confidently enough to go, on occasion, right up to the edge of parental acceptance without ever crossing that line."

Nickelodeon is not unique in its positioning. The world of children's marketing is filled with variants of the us-versus-them message. A prominent example is the soft drink Sprite, one of the most successful youth culture brands. One witty Sprite ad depicted an adolescent boy and his parents on a road trip. The parents are in the front seat singing "Polly wolly doodle all the day," the epitome of unnerving uncool. He's in the back, banging his head on the car window in frustration, the ignominy of being stuck with these two losers too much to bear. "Need a CD player?" the ad asks.

A Fruit-to-Go online promotion tells kids that "when it comes to fashion class, your principal is a flunkie." A spot for Sour Brite Crawlers has a group of tween boys in an elevator going into gross detail about how they eat this gummy worm candy, eventually sickening the adults and forcing them to flee. The creators of the spot consider it "a great example . . . where tweens demonstrate their superiority of the situation with control over the adults."

Adults also enforce a repressive and joyless world, in contrast to what kids and products do when they're left in peace. Consider a well-known Starburst classroom commercial. As the nerdy teacher writes on the board, kids open the candy, and the scene erupts into a riotous party. When the teacher faces the class again, all is quiet, controlled, and dull. The dynamic repeats itself, as the commercial makes the point that the kid world, courtesy of the candy, is a blast. The adult world, by contrast, is drab, regimented, BORRRR-inggg.

A study of 200 video game ads produced between 1989 and 1999 revealed a similar approach. Researchers Stephen Kline and Greig de Peuter report themes of boy empowerment through "oedipal rebellion" and rejection of home environments depicted as boring suburban spaces. "Nintendo ads," they write, "often construct the gamer as under siege by the adultified world while promising the young male gamers 'empowerment' and 'control' in an unlimited virtual world." This attitude pervades the company's marketing strategy as well. As one Nintendo marketer explained, "We don't market to parents. . . . We market to our target group, which is teens and tweens. . . . The parental seal of approval, while it is something that we like, it is not something that we actively encourage in our marketing because that might say to the kids that we're boring."

A related theme in some kid advertising is to promote behavior that is annoying, antisocial, or mischievous. There's usually a playful quality to these spots, as in the various ads involving stealing candy at the movies. Julie Halpin of the Gepetto Group explains the strategy they used for Kids Foot Locker: "We wanted to be able to show them the empowerment they could have with the shoes. . . . What's really fun about a new pair of sneakers is a lot of the things that kids do that are really mischievous: squeaking on the floor, giving each other flat tires, writing little messages underneath. . . . Sales during the advertising period were about 34 percent higher than they were the previous year."

Industry insiders and outsiders confirm the antiadultism in much of today's youth advertising. As one marketer explained to me: "Advertisers have kicked the parents out. They make fun of the parents. . . . We inserted the product in the secret kid world. . . . [It's] secret, dangerous, kid only." Media critic Mark Crispin Miller makes a similar point: "It's part of the official advertising world view that your parents are creeps, teachers are nerds and idiots, authority figures are laughable, nobody can really understand kids except the corporate sponsor. That huge authority has, interestingly enough, emerged as the sort of tacit superhero of consumer culture. That's the coolest entity of all."

Similar trends can be found in programming. Journalist Bernice Kanner notes that "television dads—and to a lesser extent moms—once portrayed as loving and wise are now depicted as neglectful, incompetent, abusive or invisible. Parenthood, once presented as the source of supreme satisfaction on TV, is now largely ignored or debased." It's "parents as nincompoops." After 9/11, Holly Gross, then of Saatchi and Saatchi Kid Connection, counseled companies that although "families *are* reconnecting and kids and parents *do* wish for more time together . . . that doesn't mean the tender moments must be shared in *your* marketing communication . . . some parents are just *sooooo* embarrassing." She advises going "parent-free" to market to tweens.

Marketers defend themselves against charges of antiadultism by arguing that they are promoting kid empowerment. Social conservatives, however, see treachery in the ridicule of adults. Wherever one comes down on this debate, it's important to recognize the nature of the corporate message: kids and products are aligned together in a really great, fun place, while parents, teachers, and other adults inhabit an oppressive, drab, and joyless world. The lesson to kids is that it's the product, not your parent, who's really on your side.

Age Compression

One of the hottest trends in youth marketing is age compression—the practice of taking products and marketing messages originally designed for older kids and targeting them to younger ones. Age compression includes offering teen products and genres, pitching gratuitous violence to the twelve-and-under crowd, cultivating brand preferences for items that were previously unbranded among younger kids, and developing creative alcohol and tobacco advertising that is not officially targeted to them but is widely seen and greatly loved by children. "By eight or nine they want 'N Sync," explained one tweening expert to me, in the days before that band was eclipsed by Justin Timberlake, Pink, and others.

Age compression is a sprawling trend. It can be seen in the import of television programming specifically designed for one year olds, which occurred, ironically, with Public Broadcasting's *Teletubbies.* It includes the marketing of designer clothes to kindergarteners and first graders. It's the deliberate targeting of R-rated movies to kids as young as age nine, a practice the major movie studios were called on the carpet for by the Clinton administration in 2000. It's being driven by the recognition that many children nationwide are watching MTV and other teen and adult programming. One of my favorite MTV anecdotes comes from a third-grade teacher in Weston, Massachusetts, who reported that she started her social studies unit on Mexico by asking the class what they knew about the country. Six or seven raised their hands and answered, "That's the place where MTV's Spring Break takes place!" For those who haven't seen it, the program glorifies heavy partying, what it calls "bootylicious girls," erotic dancing, wet T-shirt contests, and binge drinking.

A common argument within the marketing world is that age compression is being caused by social trends that make contemporary children far more sophisticated than their predecessors. These include the increased responsibilities of kids in single-parent or divorced families, higher levels of exposure to adult media, children's facility with new technology, early puberty, and the fact that kids know more earlier. In the 1980s, Hasbro sold its GI Joe action figure to boys aged eleven to fourteen. Now, Joe is rejected by eight year olds as too babyish. Twenty years ago, *Seventeen* magazine targeted sixteen year olds; now it aims at eleven and twelves. In a telling gesture, the toy industry has officially lowered its upper age target from fourteen to ten.

Marketers have even coined an acronym to describe these developments. It's KAGOY, which stands for Kids Are Getting Older Younger. The social trends become part of the license for treating kids as if they were adults. Indeed, some advertisers are even arguing that current approaches are too protective of children. In a presentation at the 2001 annual Marketing to Kids Conference, executive Abigail Hirschhorn of DDB New York argued that it's time to stop talking down to kids and start "talking up" to them and that too much advertising denies kids what they really crave—the adult world. She argued for more "glamour, fashion, style, irony, and popular music."

Nowhere is age compression more evident than among the eight- to twelve-year-old target. Originally a strategy for selling to ten to thirteen year olds, children as young as six are being targeted for tweening. And what is that exactly? Tweens are "in-between" teens and children, and tweening consists mainly of bringing teen products and entertainment to ever-younger audiences. If you're wondering why your daughter came home from kindergarten one day singing the words to a Britney Spears or Jennifer Lopez song, the answer is that she got tweened. Tween marketing has become a major focus of the industry, with its own conferences, research tools, databases, books, and specialty firms. Part of why tweening is so lucrative is that it involves bringing new, more expensive products to this younger group. It's working because tweens have growing purchasing power and influence with parents. The more the tween consumer world comes to resemble the teen world, with its comprehensive branding strategies and intense levels of consumer immersion, the more money there is to be made.

In some cases, it's the advertisers pushing the trend with their clients. But clients are also initiating the process. Mark Lapham (pseudonym), president of a company that has focused almost exclusively on the teen market, says, "We're being asked all the time about it" by makers of school supplies, apparel manufacturers, cosmetics companies. Lapham explains how his clients are thinking: "Hey, we can actually sell a cosmetic, not just bubble gum lip gloss . . . we can sell foundation possibly . . . nail polish."

Abigail Hirschhorn's plea for industry change is well behind the times. Children are being exposed to plenty of glamour, fashion, style, irony, and popular music, that is, sex. Even the family-friendly Disney Channel is full of sexually suggestive outfits and dancing. One radio Disney employee explained to me that the company keeps a careful watch on lyrics but is hands-off with the other stuff. A stroll down the 6X–12 aisles of girls' clothing will produce plenty of skimpy and revealing styles. People in advertising are well aware of these developments. Emma Gilding of Ogilvy and Mather recounted an experience she had during an in-home videotaping. The little girl was doing a Britney Spears imitation, with flirting and sexual grinding. Asked by Gilding what she wanted to be when she grew up, the three year old answered: "A sexy shirt girl." As researcher Mary Prescott (pseudonym) explained to me in the summer of 2001, "We're coming out of a trend now. Girl power turned into sex power. A very sexy, dirty, dark thing. Parents were starting to panic." While Prescott felt that a reversal toward "puritanism" had already begun, other observers aren't so sure. Not long after Prescott's prediction, Abercrombie and Fitch came under fire for selling thong underwear with sexually suggestive phrases to seven to fourteen year olds. And child development expert Diane Levin alerted parents to the introduction of World Wrestling Entertainment action figures recommended for age four and above, which include a male character with lipstick on his crotch, another male figure holding the severed head of a woman, and a female character with enormous breasts and a minimal simulated black leather outfit and whip. Four year olds are also targeted with toys tied to movies that carry PG-13 ratings.

Some industry insiders have begun to caution that tweening has gone too far. At the 2002 KidPower conference, Paul Kurnit spoke out publicly about companies "selling 'tude' to pre-teens and ushering in adolescence a bit sooner than otherwise." Privately, even more critical views were expressed to me. Mark Lapham revealed that he finds this "kind of an amazing thing . . . this is where personally my guilt comes out, like gosh, it's not really appropriate sometimes." But, he continues, "that's where society's going, what do you do?" Prescott, who is more deeply immersed in the world of tweening, confessed that "I am doing the most horrible thing in the world. We are targeting kids too young with too many inappropriate things. . . . It's not worth the almighty buck."

Dual Messaging: When Kids and Parents Like Different Things

Nickelodeon's "kids rule" principle is successful because it reflects a reality about children's lives. Adults do have power over children. And children do attempt, through their consumption, to create autonomous, self-defined spaces. As British anthropologist Allison James has argued, "Children, by the very nature of their position as a group outside adult society, have sought out an alternative system of meanings through which they can establish their own integrity. Adult order is manipulated so that what adults esteem is made to appear ridiculous; what adults despise is invested with prestige." James argues that this alternative system is most pronounced in food. Children take the symbolic order of adults and turn it on their head, going wild for food that adults deem inedible or gross. Kids like brightly colored candy that transforms their tongues or other body parts. They like food that tingles, pops, or fizzes. They delight in blue, a color that is particularly taboo for adult food. And they enjoy eating character likenesses, even human ones. In her research on candy, James explored what is at stake in these differentiations. In Britain, cheap children's sweets are called kets, but in adult parlance, kets refer to useless items, or rubbish. "It is thus of great significance that something which is despised and regarded as diseased and inedible by the adult world should be given great prestige as a particularly desirable form of food by the child." The people who sell to children have figured all this out. Johann Wachs, an experienced food marketer now at Ogilvy and Mather, noted that "if it grosses out Mom, if it empowers me the kid by setting me apart from my parents, then it's good."

In the case of colored candies, the divergence between adult and children's tastes is largely symbolic. Adults are perfectly willing to eat artificial colors; it's just that we prefer muted tones, such as brown, or pastels. But differences in what kids and parents like stretch far beyond candy, into realms where the distinctions are substantive. These include not only the food and drinks that are staples of a child's diet, but also toys, apparel, accessories, consumer electronics—indeed, most product categories. Here the differences center on product qualities such as nutrition and durability, whether a toy is educational, the social class associations of the product, or whether it represents good value for its price. In these cases, there is frequently a gulf or even outright opposition between what children and their parents prefer.

Contemporary advertising has made great strides in overcoming this opposition, using sophisticated and Janus-faced techniques to close the sale. Mary Prescott explains that children's marketing relies on a push-pull approach. "Hit the kids because of the nagging and address the mothers." In practice, this often means dual campaigns, that is, different ads for kids and mothers. A famous example of how successful this approach can be is the rejuvenation of Kool-Aid.

Robert Skollar, executive creative director and managing partner at Grey Advertising, worked seven years on the Kool-Aid account. At the time of the campaign, Kool-Aid sales were stagnant, and it was no longer a favorite beverage of kids, losing out to soda. As Skollar explained, "Our job was to make it as exciting as possible." They did that by promoting the idea that Kool-Aid was cool and magical. A second set of ads was created for mothers. There the strategy was to give mothers license to give kids what they wanted, so they promoted the idea that Kool-Aid was good for kids, because it has vitamin C in it and because mothers can control the amount of sugar they put in. To give the spots strong appeal to mothers, the company hired directors and producers from the then-popular TV show *thirty-something*. When it ran, the campaign led Kool-Aid to become the third largest soft drink in the country and the beverage of choice for kids aged six to twelve.

Cereal marketing follows this dual campaign strategy, but only if the product can plausibly be sold to mothers. In practice, this means that it isn't among the obviously most sugary, gimmicky, or worst nutritionally. "We never talk to moms about [brand name omitted]," cereal marketer Lisa Morgan explained to me. Selling to mothers requires a nutritional claim or some other perceived benefit. Morgan reveals the strategic thinking: "With other sugary types of cereal we only talk to kids because that's a battle Mom is willing to lose." Cereal has what the industry calls a wholesome halo, which advertisers have figured out how to exploit: "Moms perceive it as wholesome whether it is or not," Morgan explained. Another example of this strategic thinking is Alpha-Bits. The regular version is targeted to moms, because the letters are seen as educational and beneficial for kids and it has less sugar than Alpha-Bits with marshmallows, which is targeted only to kids.

McDonald's pioneered another example of dual marketing that has been spectacularly successful—the Happy Meal. Colleen Fahey, the creative director of the team that invented the Happy Meal, explained that McDonald's was trying to get more business during the evening hours, but children resisted because they found the experience of fast food dining "boring." The marketing team's insight was to get the kids engaged through pictures, puzzles, games, and other things to play with during their stay. Eventually they began using toys, and, as they say, the rest is history. By giving a toy with the meal, McDonald's appealed directly to kids, for whom the offer was hard to pass up. According to Jerrie van Gelder of Arnold Worldwide, who has worked on the McDonald's account for many years, "We target kids directly with the toys . . . mother is the veto vote."

The practice of enticing children with toys has its critics. One problem is that the toys attract kids to fast food outlets, and fast food isn't good for them. A second is that food without toys may become less appealing. When I raised objections, van Gelder responded that McDonald's considers the Happy Meal part of a balanced diet. But the company encourages collecting these toys and offers them only during limited periods of time. In 1997, McDonald's sold about 100 million Teenie Beanie Baby Happy Meals within the space of about ten days in what has been described as one of the most successful marketing promotions in history.

Part of why the dual messaging campaigns in food have been so successful is that parents have gotten far more permissive about food. That's partly because they face ongoing conflicts for far more expensive products. Shoe companies have figured out how to make extra money by including flashing lights, computers, and air pumps. Apparel manufacturers promote the brand label as essential to social survival. The makers of consumer electronics have been extremely successful marketing all the latest gizmos and gadgets to kids, whether it's gaming toys, cell phones, personal digital assistants, or computers with fancy graphics cards, speakers, and the like. When parents are asked to fork over money for features that only their kids care about, dual messaging is not far behind.

As Mark Lapham explained, "There's still a lot of manipulation of parental pocketbooks." For example, one of the products he promotes is a backpack with a built-in CD case and earphone. Those are features kids love, but it's more expensive than a regular pack and parents care only about having a bag that carries books. He overcomes that gap with divergent messages. He explains that he's "aggressive" about the CD case and earphone when communicating to kids in his print and online advertising, "telling kids where to buy it and how to buy it and why they should buy it." But at the point of sale where parents will be present, "you might not be promoting the fact that it's good for music compatibility and that you can listen to music while people think you're doing your homework. . . . If the parent thinks it's a fashion product or a social product, they're not going to pay for it. If the parent thinks it's a school product, of course they're going to pay for it."

Pester Power

When all else fails, there's always nagging, or what the British side of the industry calls Pester Power. Thanks to Cheryl Idell's widely influential "nag factor study," and numerous derivative reports, this time-honored technique of kids has become heavy artillery in the industry arsenal. A number of research outfits now devote enormous time and energy to figure out how to get kids to get their parents to buy stuff. Child Research Services runs consumer panels called CAPS (child and parents studies), which study child-parent interactions. The Cincinnati-based Wondergroup, a prominent nag factor proponent, counsels clients that even preverbal babies can be effective naggers. How can companies get kids to make more purchase requests? How can they facilitate requests that will be effective? Once a benign nuisance, nag factor is now a topic of intense scrutiny.

Idell's study, which is from 1997–1998, created a stir because nagging had become extraordinarily effective. She found that 70 percent of parents are receptive to their children's product requests. A third of them are what she called indulgers, that is, impulse buyers who don't mind their children's requests for nonessentials. Fifteen percent are "kid pals." Childlike themselves, they allow children significant impact on brand selection. Another 20 percent are "conflicteds," who dislike kid advertising and don't like their children's requests for nonessentials, but find them hard to resist. That leaves only 13 percent unaffected by nagging, a "bare necessities" group Idell describes as conservatives whose purchases are well considered. Overall, Idell found that sales volume for items purchased for kids declined by one-third if kids did not ask for them, with larger declines for certain types of products, such as toys and entertainment. Marketers currently advise their clients that for certain age groups, such as tweens and teens, if they cannot get the kids to request it, it will not be purchased. Dave Siegel of Wondergroup warns that "Mom-centricity is a heinous disease" for marketers. Laurie Siegel of JustKid Inc. reports that "I can't think of one successful food product that has been targeted to moms." Who is the advocate for the product in the home? The party line is that it should be the kid.

A 2002 poll by the Center for a New American Dream that I collaborated on suggests that kids have embraced pester power in a big way. Eighty-three percent of youth in the twelve-to-thirteen age range report that they've asked their parents to pay for or let them buy something they'd seen advertised. Forty percent report they've done it for an item they thought their parents disapproved of or didn't want them to have. After their parents have denied the request, 71 percent of them keep asking. The average number of asks is eight, but over a quarter of kids ask more than ten times. Eleven percent repeat their request more than fifty times. Half of the twelve to thirteen year olds report that they are usually successful in getting their parents to let them have something they want that they saw advertised even if their parents won't want them to have it.

From the parent point of view, buying what children ask for makes good sense. There's little point in wasting money and time on things they don't like or will not use. Furthermore, many parents believe their kids know more about brands than they do in a variety of product categories. But marketers exploit this good-sense attitude of parents. For example, they promote the idea of kids "training" their parents, even without the parents' realizing it. Reports from focus groups suggest that mothers attempt to limit the number of product requests per shopping trip. Meanwhile, kids report that they have already trained their mothers to buy items previously requested, enabling them to use their requests for new items. Kid researcher Wynne Tyree agrees that training has become common. "The whole idea of moms calling the shots and kids having to beg or 'pester' their moms for what they want is a defunct paradigm. Particularly as kids get older, moms consult with their children and/or they allow them total control of the purchase. Over time, this often isn't based on a child's direct request. Moms learn what their kids will and will not eat, and they don't buy the things they won't eat. It saves them money to not have products in the refrigerator or pantry that go uneaten. And it saves them the time they might have to 'battle' with their kids to eat things they don't want."

Nag factor has now been widely exposed in the media, engendering a backlash. Even prominent proponents of this approach are starting to hedge their bets. Wondergroup is currently pushing the idea of a "four-eyed, four-legged consumer," in which mom and kid coexist harmoniously. ACCUPoll, a research outfit, is backing off its previous advice to clients to "forget moms." In 2003, the International Quality and Productivity Center, which organizes the Kid, Tween, Teen, and Food and Beverage Power conferences, added Mom Power to its annual offerings. In yet another example of marketing overkill, some marketers are beginning to wonder if they haven't killed the goose that lays their golden eggs.

Trans-Toying

Another strategy for reaching kids is to take everyday items and turn them into playthings, or what the industry calls "trans-toys." Although toy revenues are relatively stagnant—hard to believe, I know, given all the stuff kids have these days—trans-toying is hot. According to Rachel Geller, a longtime leader in the field of children's marketing, "Almost every single product can be a toy."

Some examples of trans-toying have been around for a while and have already faded into the landscape of daily life. These include toothbrushes with licensed characters and shampoo topped with rubber character heads. But the phenomenon is accelerating. 3M has turned the Band-Aid into a wearable toy, a tattoo for those few kids still too young to get a real one. School supplies are now branded. Clothes are turning into toys, with Scratch 'n' Sniff jeans and socks. Vitamins come in the form of gumballs. It's one of those "What will they think of next?" categories.

Trans-toying is most noticeable in the supermarket aisle, where packaged goods companies have gotten ingenious in their attempts to turn what we eat into things kids can play with. Frito-Lay has come up with colored Cheetos, now available in a mystery color version. You have to eat them to see what color your mouth and tongue become. Lucky Charms changes what it does with every box. Quaker Oatmeal contains dinosaur eggs and other hidden treasures. And Ore-Ida has come out with Funky Fries, which are blue, or sugar coated, or cocoa flavored. Food is changing color and texture, showing up in fancy packages, paired with contests, toys, and free stuff.

While cocoa french fries and green ketchup are not cause for alarm, the cumulative impact of trans-toying may be troublesome. Child development experts worry that this trend leaves little space for imagination, as every item in the environment becomes a toy. If all children's experiences are geared toward excitement, surprise, and thrills, they may not discover that happiness and well-being are mainly gained through an appreciation of the quotidian. They may never learn to appreciate the taste of good, wholesome food if they are taught that eating is equivalent to playing. Harvard psychologist Susan Linn, one of the nation's leading critics of marketing to children, thinks there's a moral vacuity in the whole approach. "Marketers would have us believe that the purpose of food is to play with it. Isn't that an obscene value, when there are people in the world who are starving?"

Assessing the Messages: How Do They Affect Children?

Advertisers select their thematic messages on the basis of what they think will trigger children's innermost psychological needs and states. How these messages affect those psychological states is another question. At first glance, some of the messages I've described, such as the themes of sensory stimulation, success, and love, appear to be benign. However, further reflection prompts questions. If an ad suggests that eating an Eggo leads to success, does it create an unrealistic view by downplaying the hard work necessary for actual achievement? Does sensory overload create an insatiable desire for constant stimulation? Does the unreal world of advertising become too real?

Research from the cultivation theory school pioneered by former University of Pennsylvania professor George Gerbner suggests that these questions are serious. Cultivation theory finds that heavy television watchers have their views of the real world shaped by what they see on the screen. For example, they overestimate the extent of crime in the real world because crime is so common in television shows. They are far more fearful of strangers because there's so much stranger crime on television. Other research has found that people who watch more television have pronounced biases in their perceptions of how wealthy Americans are, because television disproportionately shows wealthy and upper-middle-class lifestyles. Heavy viewers think that affluence is the norm, vastly exaggerating the proportion of the population with swimming pools, maids, and other luxuries. In statistical analysis I conducted, I discovered that heavier television viewing leads to higher spending and lower saving, presumably through the enhancement of consumer desires. I haven't found related studies for children that deal with the impacts of advertising themes, so we don't know how these dynamics are operating. One reason for the dearth of studies is that children's research has tended to focus on more pressing issues, such as the effects of media violence, body images, and advertisements for alcohol, tobacco, and junk foods.

Marketers don't tend to think about these issues either. Lisa Morgan admits she's never considered the consequences of what she dubs "over-the-top experiences"; however, she acknowledges that over-stimulation through excessive media use worries her. "How many kids these days just actually play with toys? . . . How do we entertain these kids," she wonders, "because nothing satisfies them?" It's possible that reality gets boring for kids who are constantly exposed to the hyperstimulated world of children's commercial culture. Marketers claim that the portrayal of loving relationships between kids and products is positive for kids. But in real life, products do not love back. Does the selling of love in ads help children to construct truly loving relationships in real life? Or do the ads implicitly promise something they cannot deliver on, creating disappointment and frustration in the long run?

The second set of themes (cool, age compression, antiadultism, dual messaging) is more problematic. Encouraging age-inappropriate behavior and desires can create confusion and erode genuine self-esteem. If antiadult messages drive a wedge between children and their parents or teachers, they undermine relationships that are vital to children's well-being. Telling kids that cool is everything can lead to the exploitation of psychological vulnerabilities. Nancy Shalek, president of the Shalek Agency, displayed a disarming level of candor when she argued that "advertising at its best is making people feel that without their product, you're a loser. Kids are very sensitive to that. If you tell them to buy something, they are resistant. But if you tell them that they'll be a dork if they don't, you've got their attention. You open up emotional vulnerabilities and it's very easy to do with kids because they're the most emotionally vulnerable." While most kid marketers would distance themselves from such a statement, the actual impacts of the messages they are putting out may be closer to Shalek's characterization than they realize.

What Do Kids Understand About Ads?

Ad content is one issue. An undue level of persuasiveness from advertising is another. One of the clues to how much power corporations have gained is the way the debate about children's advertising has been transformed. Twenty years ago, advertising to young children was widely believed to be unfair because children were thought to be unable to view it critically or with a discriminating eye. Today, the industry argues that kids have become supersophisticated and incapable of being manipulated. At the moment, the two sides are talking past each other. Much of the literature on what children understand about ads and how they respond to them dates from the 1970s and 1980s. Neither the government nor private foundations have been funding much research to revisit these questions, so industry's claims remain unaddressed.

Beginning in the 1970s, researchers began to look at what children do and do not understand when they are exposed to ads. A range of methodologies has been used, and expert opposition to advertising emerged on the basis of an accumulating body of evidence. The research has addressed a series of questions. At what age can children discriminate between advertising and programs? When do they understand the purpose of advertising? And when are they able to understand the notion of persuasive intent, that is, the idea that commercials are attempting to persuade viewers to buy products? On the first question, the evidence is mixed. One 1979 study (by Palmer and McDowell) showed videotapes to kindergartners and first graders and stopped the tape periodically to ask the children what they had just seen. The children were correct in identifying ads only about half the time. Blosser and Roberts, in a 1985 study, found that only one in ten children below age five correctly identified ads, but by age five to six, the fraction rose to 62 percent. Identification reached 100 percent by age ten and above. Other studies have found recognition at earlier ages, and reviews of the literature typically conclude that by age five, most, but not all, children are able to discriminate. (One 1982 study found 20 percent misidentification by five year olds.) At this age, they are typically able to describe the difference in very limited terms, noting that ads are shorter or funnier. Advertising is mainly seen as entertainment or unbiased information. The research also shows that the usual practice for differentiating ads from programs, the insertion of a separator, is not effective as a signaling device for this age group. Similarly, disclaimers and explanations such as "assembly necessary" or "batteries required," designed to prevent unrealistic expectations, have also been found to be ineffective with young children.

A second question is whether children can articulate the purpose of ads once they can identify them. The first explanations kids give are along the lines of "ads show you a product" or "they are to sell a product." Deeper understanding of the persuasive intent of ads occurs by about age eight. One study in which children were asked, "What is a commercial?" and "What does a commercial try to get you to do?" found that 53 percent of first graders (ages six and seven), 87 percent of third graders (ages eight and nine), and 99 percent of fifth graders (ages ten and eleven) noted the persuasive dimension of ads. In a more recent (1992) study, only 32 percent of four to six year olds mentioned that ads try to sell products, instead noting that ads are there to entertain or give information. Other research finds that contrary to what some believe, watching more television does not lead to earlier or more complete ability to discern advertising intent.

By age eight, children also recognize that ads do not always tell the truth, and they have begun to figure out why. The research finds that as they age, children become less trusting of ads. In a 1994 study of middle school students, most agreed with statements such as, "Advertisers care more about getting you to buy things than what is good for you," and "TV commercials tell only the good things about a product; they don't tell you the bad things." Industry practitioners point to this mistrust as proof that children can't be influenced. But the available research finds that the presence of skepticism doesn't have much impact on kids' desire for the advertised product, even for nine and ten year olds. Despite expressing doubts about ads, kids remain vulnerable to their persuasive powers. Furthermore, although media literacy has been encouraged as a solution to some of the problems raised by children's inability to watch ads critically, studies of its impact find that it does not affect kids while they are actually watching ads. In one study of nine and ten year olds, exposure to a media literacy film did not subsequently affect their thoughts while they viewed advertisements, because they did not retrieve the consumer knowledge they learned from the film and were therefore not better able to resist persuasion. And in recent years, advertisers have learned a lot about kids' skepticism and tried to use it to their advantage. They try to ally themselves with the skepticism by lampooning advertising, admonishing kids not to trust celebrity endorsers, or imparting a gritty realism to spots. These tactics are often successful in breaking down kids' defenses and fooling them about what is and is not an ad. Over time, a back-and-forth dynamic has evolved as advertisers respond to kids' mistrust in order to circumvent it.

Finally, do ads lead to purchases? While it is important to avoid a view that gives too much influence to ads, the literature does show that they are effective in creating purchase requests. Early research found that television commercials inflate children's perceptions of products and that television viewing time is positively correlated with requests. Food advertising has been shown to affect preferences. But the most compelling evidence comes from a recent experiment done by Stanford Medical School's Thomas Robinson. Robinson conducted a six-month classroom intervention to reduce television viewing among third and fourth graders in San Jose, California. The children whose television viewing time declined made 70 percent fewer toy requests than those in the control group, whose media habits were unchanged.

A long-standing argument is that if advertising really were ineffective, companies wouldn't use it. This doesn't imply that all ads are effective. But it does counter the common industry rebuttal that if advertising is as influential as its critics contend, rates of product failure wouldn't be so high. The flaw in that argument is that advertising may be a necessary but not sufficient component of market success. A reasonably good product and reasonably good advertising are both necessary. The products that fail may lack one or the other. The agencies have amassed a lot of data to support their claims that what they do results in higher sales, and the results for particular campaigns are sometimes dramatic. The reasonable conclusion is that companies aren't spending billions ineffectively or irrationally. And while advertising is hardly the whole story behind children's consumer expenditures, it's a vital part.

CHAPTER FOUR

The Virus Unleashed

Ads Infiltrate Everyday Life

> There are places people go to escape their worries. Where their defenses are down. Happiness abounds. And their minds are as malleable as putty. Sounds to us like the perfect opportunity to stick your product in their faces.
>
> —Eventive Marketing sales brochure

Once upon a time, the children's market was a spontaneous, intuition-driven business. Toys were dreamed up by eccentric inventors or savvy entrepreneurs. Wacky creatives wielded enormous influence at advertising agencies. Marketing a product heavily meant spending a lot on television ads. Now the process of designing, marketing, and advertising a product for the kid marketplace is meticulously planned and expensive. Indeed, the case I am about to relate involved a plan of such complexity that the man in charge of it, Alex Houston (pseudonym), a marketing executive at Hasbro Games, explained that "for me it was as much as if I took a graduate course, if not getting a doctorate in it. What we went through over probably two years . . . from the technicalities and manufacturing the product to the marketing effort . . ." At this point in the interview, Alex began to ramble, overwhelmed, perhaps, by the magnitude of the effort.

Today, new products often have their genesis in kid brainstorming sessions. The adults then get to work on the design and execution of the idea. They go back to the kids for focus group testing the product and perhaps the name. Next comes the job of positioning. What exactly is the unique selling proposition for this product? To which of the many age-based segments will it be targeted? Once that's established, the marketing team puts together a detailed plan. Increasingly, companies begin with a viral, that is, a person-to-person grassroots effort, or even a stealth campaign. Ideally it will be accompanied by a public relations push to get stories about the product into the news media. There will be a tie-in to a major retailer with local newspaper advertising. Depending on the product, there may be an in-school or fast food component, or a link to a packaged food item sold in grocery stores. Sometimes the company will pay to have the product placed in movies, television shows, video games, or on Web sites. There are also conventional spots on television, radio, and billboards, at movie theaters, and on the Internet.

POX: The Battle Unseen

The marketing effort that Alex Houston thought might have earned him a doctorate was for an electronic game called POX. The early stages of development involved extensive consultation with college students, video game enthusiasts, child development experts, editors of gaming magazines, even customers caught in the act of buying. The marketing plan called for coordinated local and national actions stretching over many months, and included a prestigious coming out at the International Toy Fair, a stealth campaign in a carefully chosen city, grassroots events at Toys 'R' Us outlets around the country, and a public relations effort capped by a cover story in the *New York Times Magazine.* If POX has escaped your attention, it's because the major rollout was scheduled to occur on September 23, 2001. Given that POX was billed as a game of "alien creation and universal destruction," the top brass at Toys 'R' Us and Hasbro got cold feet, and the big bang never happened. But much of the elaborate plan had already been executed, and the product looked to be a raging success. If it weren't for September 11, there's a chance we'd have been debating a POX ban in schools, whether the toy is destroying American youth, and if parental lawsuits against Hasbro have any merit. Those things happened with the last big toy fad, Pokémon. The general approach is one that may well be repeated many times over in coming years, so it's worth taking a careful look at it.

Like Gameboy but less expensive, POX is a handheld electronic toy. It can be played like an ordinary game, but it can also operate on radio frequencies. This technology, which was new for Hasbro, made it possible to incorporate features that are absent on most other handheld units and is part of the reason that the company was so heavily committed to the product. POX enables play against an opponent or even a group of opponents. Moreover, each unit can automatically engage another unit, or many other units, in a communal gaming experience. There's also a stealth component because the game can be activated from hidden places, such as inside a backpack or a school locker, without the owner of the other unit even knowing it is being attacked. The purpose of the game is to build a more powerful warrior creature than your opponents have and to use yours to defeat theirs. As with Pokémon, whose name is an abbreviation of pocket monsters, there is a large collection of parts, weapons, and qualities that is amassed to create these warriors. Success depends on strategy, the ability to remember arcane details, and a bit of luck. The POX name, which was tested in focus groups, is intended to conjure up visions of an invasion by invisible, contagious, and deadly extraterrestrials, ostensibly escapees from an alien laboratory. Its association with disease, contagion, and viruses was just what the kids loved.

Originally, the people at Hasbro expected that the gaming or collection aspect would be the draw, but in focus groups, they learned that secrecy was the most appealing feature to the eight-to-twelve-year-old boys to whom it was targeted. (Hasbro never bothered with girls; this toy was coded male from the very beginning. Other characteristics of the target were that they be "middle American," of all ethnic backgrounds, and have household incomes up to $60,000.) The secrecy insight was right in line with the direction kids' marketing was already moving—toward what marketers call viral and stealth techniques. And that's the route Hasbro decided to take, with a large but stealthy rollout in a single city, followed by nine more, and then to the national market. Houston described the strategy: "If you've got a germ or a cold, or a virus of some sort, you know it's at its strongest when it's got multiple hosts to go to. And that was really the genesis for our marketing launch."

Hasbro chose Chicago as the first city to be infected. Chicago is the largest and most important market for electronic game purchases in the country: it's a large population center with bad weather, which means kids spend a lot of time indoors. The spatial proximity of population to major retailers is also high, so that as the buzz spread, it would be easy for kids to get to stores to buy their units. By contrast, in some of the more spread-out western cities, the distances between the big retailers are large. And finally, although it's not New York or Los Angeles, Chicago is an important enough city that it could provide a national PR opportunity. That was crucial to the strategy, because spreading the virus from one locale to another was partly dependent on the free publicity Hasbro was expecting from the national media.

The plan called for identifying what are known as alpha kids, or as Matt

Schneider, president of Target Productions, the company that coordinated the operations for this campaign, called them, alpha pups. These are the coolest, most socially dominant, trendsettingest kids in the community. In this case, the kids were found through an elaborate, labor-intensive process of interviewing thousands of kids on playgrounds, in arcades, and at other kidspaces, and asking, "Who's the coolest kid you know?" until they got to the one who said, "Me!" The company also interviewed teachers and parents for leads on cool kids. By the end of April, they had identified 1,527 boys who fit the criterion of ultimate cool and were willing to participate in the program. The boys attended an "indoctrination" session where they watched a video about the invasion of POX, became official "secret agents," and accepted a secret mission and set of instructions on how to "infect" ten friends. Then they were given a backpack filled with tattoos, shirts, and hats, plus ten POX units, which they had to pass along to a list of friends, whose names would then be provided to the company. In return for their cooperation, each kid received $30. Each got a follow-up phone call a week later in which he was asked whether and to whom he had passed out his units. The callers were supposed to "reinvigorate the member to play and talk about POX, and to probe him for future POX ideas." The secret agent campaign was supplemented by television and radio spots, deejay endorsements, on-air giveaways, print ads, in-store giveaways, a Web site, and public relations efforts.

In contrast to many other viral programs, which rely on random infection patterns, this rollout was school-based. "SCHOOLS!" was Hasbro's PowerPointed answer to the question, "How do we reach target boys in a contained environment?" The screening process had identified two types of schools and recruited one to three boys from each. The A trendsetting schools had good population bases and proximity to major retailers; the B schools were smaller. There was also a subtext for attempting a school-based infection. Hasbro management, as well as their promotion and advertising agency partners, were aware that POX gaming might really take off in schools. This is partly because they thought it might be addictive, and kids would play during recess and lunch. They could also keep the game going during classes, with units hidden in desks or inside backpacks. Teachers wouldn't even know that play was occurring. Alex Houston insisted that "we certainly were never ever in the position of promoting game play during school. Never. But the fact of the matter is that kids will determine, and moms will determine, ultimately what gets in their backpacks." Even before the product was released, Alex had thought seriously about whether it was headed for a school ban. "Would that be a negative thing for POX? Probably not ultimately. . . . I even suggested at one point during our meetings [that] the ultimate philosophical emotional goal would be to get it banned from schools. And when I said that, my senior management wouldn't endorse that. But the idea was, if this is cool enough for kids to play it, that means they'll play it when they're not supposed to. If they're playing it when they're not supposed to, we get banned. That would, in my mind, indicate we have success; because they enjoy it, they can't stop."

As spring turned into summer and the buzz was ignited, executives at Hasbro were thrilled with the course of the infection. Kids loved the game. Sales were doing well in Chicago. The company believed it was reaching almost 17,000 boys directly, or one out of every six in their targeted geographical area. In fact, after much consideration, the company decided to skip step two, the rollout in nine more cities, and proceed directly to the national campaign. Toys 'R' Us wanted to put its considerable heft behind the product, with a 50-million-piece mailing and a commitment to host tournaments in stores around the country. When the company did a presentation to an industry conference on September 10, 2001, the message was totally upbeat.

They had also just scored the perfect 10 in the PR department. In early August, the *New York Times* published a cover story on POX in its Sunday magazine. As Houston explained to me, if they'd dreamed up such an outcome at a PR planning meeting, it would have been seen as pie in the sky. The genesis of the story was Toy Fair, February 2001, where Hasbro was debuting POX for toy buyers. POX was Hasbro's top new product, and the company had devised what Houston described as a highly "theatrical" (one might say gimmicky) exhibit. It had cordoned off an area of the showroom, which was accessible only at a certain time. Entrance required a VIP pass. The aim was to create "allure" and "mystique." The multimedia exhibit described the product proposition, the game experience, and the complex marketing plan Hasbro would be following. As it turned out, the gambit worked, and buyers were intrigued. So was a gaming enthusiast who wrote for the *Times* named John Tierney. Tierney indicated he'd be interested in doing a story on the launch.

When Toy Fair was over and the Hasbro management were back at headquarters debriefing, one of the topics that arose was the possible Tierney story. They were interested, but as Houston explained, "This is the *New York Times,* and we weren't sure what the real angle to the story would be. Would it be about a unique marketing approach, business angle . . . or would this be about exploiting kids? This wasn't what I'd call your conventional marketing effort with kids. And so there was a lot of risk, and there's certainly a lot of potential for embarrassment here at the very least." But the Hasbro public relations people were confident. They knew the writer and felt sure he'd have a "positive slant," so the company decided to cooperate fully, giving Tierney almost all its marketing documents, allowing him to sit in on the focus groups, and providing access to the kids in Chicago. They did, however, monitor the situation closely, keeping their senior management fully abreast at every step.

In the end, they had nothing to worry about, despite their lack of editorial control or even a chance to see the story before it went into print. In Houston's words, "It's as if, and I want to say this with all due respect . . . in many respects, it was almost as if it was written by someone from this organization. Because the facts were all there, but it was written in a truly . . . truly . . . truly complimentary fashion."

POX didn't become a runaway success story, perhaps because of superbly bad timing, perhaps because the product wasn't, in the end, as compelling as the company thought it would be. It's an instructive case nevertheless. The campaign to turn POX into the next big thing contained many of the elements of what has increasingly become standard practice in the kid marketplace. It used kids to test the product, vet the name, and weigh in on the unique selling proposition. It was school based. It involved an elaborate rollout through a viral campaign and the use of children's friendships as the vehicle for selling products. It made skillful use of the news media. The POX plan also mobilized a major retailer and a massive advertising blitz that reached directly into households. It may have started with buzz, but in the end, it was more like saturation bombing.

Buzz and the Transformation of Friendship

At the core of the POX launch was the idea that products need buzz, that is, getting consumers to be aware of, talking about, and buying a product. Once the province of boutique firms, buzz has been embraced by big agencies as well. Students of buzz rely on bibles such as Emanuel Rosen's *The Anatomy of Buzz* and Malcolm Gladwell's *The Tipping Point.* Andrew Banks (pseudonym), an affable recent college graduate working at the buzz unit of one of the large agencies, explained that successful marketing now absolutely requires a viral component. Consumers are harder to reach than ever before, busier than ever before, and suffering from information overload, with hundreds of television channels, including ad-free alternatives. Today's consumers are equipped with a cynical mental radar that the advertiser has to maneuver past. But how?

Banks's answer is the creation of a "360-degree world" in which the consumer is "constantly bombarded." The agency uses the somewhat more delicate term "infinite consumer touchpoint possibilities." But both terms amount to the same thing: the consumer is approached from all sides. Methods include television and radio; direct marketing; events and sponsorships; Web ads; product placement; using the editorial power of the press; billboards, posters, and graffiti; putting ads on buildings; point-of-purchase displays; and the use of packaging as a marketing tool. According to my guide to buzz, creating it requires five components: authenticity, or staying true to the brand; advocacy, in which the brand's sales force are the ordinary people who are enlisted in the viral messaging campaign; experiential messaging; fusion of strategies; and visibility and virality through a mix of overt and covert actions. Banks believes buzz practitioners are just getting started: "We'll have ten or fifteen more ways of encircling the consumer in ten years." Banks advocates a holistic approach: "Surrounding almost every move you make, that would be the ideal." Asked about consumers who didn't like being marketed to, Banks didn't hesitate: "Covert messaging. Use their best friend."

Buzz is part of why promotions seem to be almost everywhere these days—in subway stations, intersections, street festivals, water and amusement parks, and ski resorts. Buzz marketing is cheap, and is thought to deliver good bang for the buck. In teen apparel and footwear, it is now standard practice to seed a product with trendsetters. Rappers, artists, actors, athletes, and generally cool people get free New Balance shoes, Phat Farm and Sean John sweatshirts, and Levi's jeans. They wear them. Sometimes the products end up in their songs or their art. There are even ad agencies that specialize in getting celebrities to use clients' products at major award ceremonies and events. New CDs are frequent recipients of viral marketing plans. Indeed, conventional wisdom in the field now suggests that in genres such as hip-hop and rap, CDs cannot succeed without a viral campaign, which is why Sony's Epic Records dispatched a full-time street team to urban clubs to promote groups such as B2K and 3LW. Alcohol brands are promoted by hiring people to sit in bars and praise the drink. College kids are recruited to hold parties that feature products. In a widely reported story, two high school seniors from New Jersey sold themselves as more or less full-time pitchmen to a financial services company in return for college tuition. Viral campaigns are rampant on the

Internet and e-mail. Chat rooms are seeded with paid representatives to promote brands. E-mail lists are used to advertise products. While teens and young adults have been the target of many of the early viral campaigns, these techniques are filtering down to children.

The *New York Times Magazine* reported in late 2003 on a growing trend in street-level marketing: the use of kids, including very young ones, to market sports equipment and clothing. The magazine profiled Dylan Oliver, a four-year-old skateboarder who receives free products from skateboarding companies, and three-year-old L'il Mark, who has appeared shooting baskets in a Reebok commercial. Child endorsers have become common in the world of extreme sports, which are not restricted by NCAA or other rules, and contracts have become lucrative. These kids are unusual athletic prodigies. But ordinary kids can also get in on the act of buzz marketing.

One of the more intriguing companies in this business is the Girls Intelligence Agency. In 2002, its first year of operation, the company claimed to have a network of 40,000 girls, aged eight to eighteen, ready to swing into action on the drop of a dime to create buzz for whatever product the company sends their way. The GIA was founded by Laura Groppe, an Academy Award–winning film producer. Groppe is the founder of Girl Games, which promoted girls' video gaming. But girls' gaming hasn't taken off as she had hoped it would, so she jumped into the far more lucrative and rapidly growing business of peer-to-peer marketing.

Groppe began by using her existing contacts, staging events to draw in girls, and perhaps most interesting, working through organizations that "evangelize" for GIA. She was unwilling to name these organizations, explaining only that they are "regional and national organizations that are pro-girl." When I named the Girl Scouts and church groups, she didn't demur. Girls as young as age six are recruited to become GIA agents, and once they're accepted, they become part of an active online network. Profiles of agents are posted on GIA's Web site. Six-year-old "swimmergirl" lives in San Diego and loves swimming, cats, and chat rooms. Eleven-year-old "singsalot" loves fashion. The girls report going three to four times a week for style and fashion advice to Agent Kiki, a fictitious older-sister type whose answers are written by GIA staffers. Only GIA agents have access to Agent Kiki, who is described as "a big sis to all girls who need one!"

The GIA's trademark product is the Slumber Party in a Box, which takes place in what the company calls the "inner sanctum" or the "guarded fortress," that is, girls' bedrooms. There are marketing and "insight" (that is, research) parties, depending on the needs of the client. Parties have featured toys, films, television shows, health and beauty aids, and other products. The host girl (a GIA agent) invites up to eleven of her friends to the party. Their first instruction is to put on pajamas and "eat too much junk food." Then partygoers are given a product sample that they use during the evening. That's the only payment for the agent or her guests. The host is required to provide feedback to GIA after the event. The party becomes a natural, intimate focus group or sales session. Sometimes parties are videotaped with GIA staff in attendance, but most are run by the agents themselves. When they sign on, hosts are congratulated for winning the "distinguished honor" of becoming an "Official GIA Agent," described as a "VERY ELITE GROUP" with "EXCLUSIVE" access to products and events. Then they're asked to "be slick and find out some sly scoop on your friends," like what they're listening to, what the fashion must-haves for this year are, and what they buy for their bedrooms. The company's literature explains to agents that they've "gotta be sneaky" in promoting GIA.

GIA claims that each of their agents reaches an average of 512 other girls in virtually every area of daily life—in English class, at soccer practice, in carpool, even at equestrian club. With their growing network, the company estimates it can reach 20 million girls nationwide.

One of the most troubling aspects of viral marketing is that it asks kids to use their friends for the purpose of gaining information or selling products. GIA's network is called BFF, for Best Friends Forever, and its start-up relied on a friend-to-friend transmission mechanism. Many firms are involved in similar friend-based marketing such as the POX plan. Kids are hired to send out ads to their e-mail buddy lists. Others organize kids into "friendship pairs" and then listen to their discussions. Throughout the world of kids' marketing, using kids to pull in other kids is a rapidly expanding practice. A major reason is that word of mouth from friends is one of the remaining sources of credibility in a world that is oversaturated by commercial messages. These recommendations are assumed to be disinterested, unlike ads, which can carry the taint of deceptiveness or manipulation. However, if the trend toward more paid word-of-mouth advertising continues, it's likely that people will learn to be more skeptical of it, recognizing that the purveyor of the advice may be acting instrumentally. In the process, this valuable form of consumer information will be corrupted. An even more serious consequence is the corruption of friendship itself. Marketers are teaching kids to view their friends as a lucrative resource they can exploit to gain products or money. They even counsel kids to be "slick" with their friends.

But friendship is important precisely because it is insulated from commercial pressures. It is considered one of the last bastions of noninstrumentality, a bulwark against the market values and self-interested behavior that permeate our culture. It's part of what we cherish most about friendships. And that's precisely why the marketers are so keenly interested in them.

Under the Radar: 101 Ways to Disguise an Ad

As Andrew Banks explained, buzz works partly because consumers "are being marketed to without being aware that they're being marketed to." That's the best of all possible worlds, because it gets beyond the cynical radar that advertisers are so worried about. Toward that end, advertisers have developed 101 ways to disguise an ad.

The origin of what are termed "under-the-radar" practices is called product placement, in which companies pay to have their products included in media programming. Product placement began in earnest with Reese's Pieces, which were featured prominently in the film *ET: The Extra-Terrestrial* twenty years ago. Since then, the practice has been structurally incorporated into the making of movies, and huge sums of money are involved. *You've Got Mail* was a well-known example, and its deal with AOL may still be the most expensive product placement, at a reported $3 to $6 million. Paid placement has also developed on television. Remember the Junior Mint episode on *Seinfeld*? It was sponsored. Sarah Jessica Parker drank Fiji water for money. Burger King, Gatorade, Pokémon, Nintendo, Hello Kitty, Nick and Nora pajamas, and thousands of other products have paid sponsors. There are now more than a hundred specialized advertising agencies devoted to product placement, and they've even founded a trade association. In early 2003, the WB network announced it was going into within-program product placement as an alternative to standard thirty-second commercials. At the time I wrote this, WB had lined up Pepsi and was looking for a second major sponsor.

In programs for younger children, similar practices have a longer history. In the 1980s, deregulation led to program-length commercials for preexisting toys, such as He-Man and My Little Pony. Shows also spawn new products. *Arthur, Sesame Street, Pokémon,* and *Blue's Clues* all fit this mold. Virtually all the successful television shows and characters get extended to a wide variety of children's products through licensing agreements.

Placement has gone beyond the confines of Hollywood to encompass other media, such as books. In 1992, the *M&M Brand Counting Book* was published, and it has sold more than a million copies. Joining it on the shelves are *Kellogg's Fruit Loops Counting Fun Book,* Pepperidge Farm Goldfish books, and books with Cheerios, Reese's Pieces, Skittles, Hershey's chocolate, Sun-Maid raisins, and Oreo cookies. Placement has moved beyond food to other commercial characters, as in the example of Simon & Schuster, which teamed up with World Wrestling Entertainment to distribute a line of books.

A more recent development is called "real-life" product placement. The New York company Big Fat specializes in this type of activity, which puts a client's products into everyday life through paid users. Big Fat boasts thirty full-time very knowledgeable trendsetting staff in cities around the country. Their services include paying people to sit in bars and getting kids to go online and promote movies and other cultural products. Firms also recruit youth to call in to radio stations to ask for songs and stuff the ballot boxes for contests. Because so much market innovation is now coming from the grass roots, that is, from consumers themselves, companies feel the need to be there, manufacturing excitement for products from the bottom up.

Another strategy has been to place not just the product but an effective ad for it. I encountered one example of a company paying deejays to put their theme song into music mixes. At clubs and in malls around the country, the ad was heard by thousands (perhaps millions) of unsuspecting listeners. Mixing ads into other media is also getting a boost from the development of so-called virtual ads, which are digital insertions into programming, onto stadium walls "at sporting events, or into live filming." The virtualness is due to the fact that the ads aren't really there at the stadium, but they show up on the television set. This technology allows companies to change the billboards when a Times Square scene appears in a movie or to insert contemporary products into television reruns.

The deejay promotion was hard to identify because the jingle blended seamlessly into the music mix. Advertisers are keen on such camouflage, especially with skeptical youth audiences. This has led to the practice of creating spots that kids can't recognize as ads. Channel One, a daily in-school news and advertising program that millions of kids around the country see, has been a prime vehicle for such trickery. Some of its advertisers have produced spots that seem like public service announcements, because PSAs carry positive associations that companies cannot hope to evoke with ordinary ads. In his book on Channel One, teacher Roy Fox recounted his experience with a Pepsi ad filmed in documentary style that consisted of kids talking. Fox found that only 5 of his 150 kids understood that the ad was made by Pepsi. The students identified it as a documentary whose purpose was to help kids, and they came away feeling that Pepsi cares about kids. Procter & Gamble, through its Clearasil brand, has also made PSA-style spots for Channel One. Another deceptive practice I discovered is the stealth sponsorship in which a company that wants to keep a low profile gets a different company to be the public sponsor of an event. The true sponsor pays the money and retains the backstage influence. It also benefits because its free product samples can fold more seamlessly into the environment, because the brand isn't recognized as a paid advertiser. Meanwhile, the second company takes the credit.

Advertising is being disguised through the morphing of ads into content and through the incorporation of advertising material into editorial content in magazines and newspapers. This merger of ads and information has been most advanced on the Web, especially before the introduction of the Children's On-Line Privacy Protection Act (COPPA). The 1996 Center for Media Education report "Web of Deception" detailed a variety of troubling practices aimed at kids, such as Web sites based on interactive product-themed activities and character spokespeople, who are prohibited from host selling on television but unregulated on the Internet; the placement of ads that were not identifiable as such; and technologies that send children into advertisers' sites without their realizing it. Companies were also microtargeting children with ads in the form of personalized e-mail messages. Some of these practices have been stopped by COPPA, but media analyst Patricia Aufderheide has found that many Web sites are continuing practices that were identified in the "Web of Deception" report.

One of the hot online trends is a practice that has been dubbed "advergaming," in which a branded product is built directly into the game. Advergaming is expanding rapidly. One reason, industry professionals Jane Chen and Matthew Ringel argue, is that "savvy marketers can use Advergaming to encourage customers to provide rich and valuable information through both registration and game play." This means advergaming can realize a higher potential return on investment than other forms of advertising because it generates these ancillary revenue streams, in addition to having the gamer interact with the branded product in this sticky environment. The advergames are getting sophisticated. Nike's 3D Slam Dunk features NBA star Vince Carter and begins by having players choose shoe brands and colors to use during the game. Nickelodeon has an Advertoys program in which companies advertise a product, such as a sugared cereal, through games on the channel's Nick.com site. In November 2000, Gap Kids gave out a free CD-ROM with five interactive games starring characters wearing Gap clothing. In an added twist, kids had to return to the retail stores two times, to unlock games 4 and 5.

The Corruption of Public Information

Was the POX article in the *New York Times Magazine* news or an ad? The company enticed the writer into the topic at its Toy Fair exhibit. It screened his suitability in advance. It gave him materials it wanted him to see, provided access to the kids, and invited him to be present throughout the viral marketing campaign. In the end, Hasbro got a story that served its purposes far better than anything it could have written themselves. Not only was the story engaging and well written, but the writer's relative autonomy allowed for just enough of a critical edge to give his account maximum credibility. The story was masterful in its ability to raise and then dismiss criticism of what the company was doing. Even a determined opponent of this type of market manipulation would have been hard pressed to come away from Tierney's piece with much of an argument against Hasbro.

What happened in this case is exceptional only because a story about a children's product made its way into the nation's newspaper of record. As an example of how companies use the news media to promote children's products, it was routine. Public relations has become a standard feature of children's marketing campaigns, and advertising agencies offer PR divisions as part of their basic services. New products get press releases, with tie-ins to general trends or news, if possible. When a new academic study is published, PR firms rush to tie it to their clients' products, producing not only print releases but also video news releases. VNRs, as they are known, include the product in a subtle way and without identifying the sponsor. VNRs are provided free of charge to cash-strapped local stations, which air them as news rather than the advertising that they are.

Most commercial media have been happy to go along with this conflation of advertising and news. They've expanded their consumer coverage, with special sections of newspapers, a proliferation of tailored consumer magazines, and a steady stream of consumer news stories on television and the Internet. These stories become opportunities to solicit more paid advertising. Over the years that I've been studying children's consumer culture, the nation's top newspapers and online news organizations have been a major source of information about products and trends. They routinely report on which toys are popular, the clothing brands that kids like, the kinds of packaged foods they're bringing to school for lunch, and which video games are selling well. You may imagine the information comes from an enterprising reporter pounding the playground pavement, but the more likely scene is coffee with the agency's public relations representative.

Public relations has become attractive to advertisers because it bypasses consumers' cynicism about ads. News is considered more objective and more credible than pure commercial messages. But as the ties between the news and advertising divisions of media have gotten closer, consumers catch on and become skeptical about the news media as well. There was widespread reporting of a scandal at the *Los Angeles Times* when the paper heavily promoted, through its editorial side, a business venture it had a financial interest in. Viewers know that television networks and newspapers sometimes own the sports teams they cover. We notice that the same companies whose products are the subjects of stories are also advertisers. The corruption of news is an open secret. So advertisers are looking for new frontiers, untainted sources that can be mobilized to promote sales. In the children's market, the last frontier may well be academia.

The use of academic studies to promote sales has a long history in certain areas, such as drugs and health products. And academia has played a role in the kids' marketplace too, for example, when educators and psychologists endorse "worthy" toys and books. But a new development stirring has the potential to be far more insidious than these activities. During my research, I was briefed on an ambitious plan hatched by an executive from a client company. He'd gotten the idea for an ad and PR campaign focused on the claim that his product was good for health and well-being because it was an antidote to social isolation. He envisioned a message as dramatic as "This product cures cancer." He asked a couple of advertising agencies to pitch a plan for such a campaign. The account people went to work combing the academic literature for existing studies that bore on this question. They produced elaborate multistaged plans, the core of which involved hiring an academic researcher to set up clinical studies to discover the beneficial effects of using the product. Once the research was complete, they'd have the results publicized widely in the media and create a surge of interest in the product. The project went as far as choosing the agency, but was subsequently put on the back burner. Whether it will be implemented remains an open question.

I have no criticisms of this particular product. I'm perfectly willing to believe it does reduce social isolation, which makes people better off. But the virtues of this case shouldn't blind us to the pitfalls of such an approach. The next time, research could be manufactured to show that violent video games are good for kids or that a candy bar a day keeps the doctor away. If advertising agencies start dictating the agendas for academic research on children, we're into some potentially troubling territory. Just how troubling may be seen by recent revelations of the ways in which medical research has been corrupted by drug company funding. Results have been falsified. Failed experiments have been censored. Conflicts of interest have not been revealed. For the moment, these practices haven't gotten very far in the field of children's marketing, but if current trends continue, they probably will.

Enlisting Trusted Organizations

The infiltration of advertising into children's everyday lives has proceeded far faster and further than most adults are aware. One indication of that progress is the extent to which trusted, mainline organizations have become partners with companies and agencies in attempts to market to children. Beginning in 1995, the Girl Scouts began offering the "Fashion Adventure" experience with the Limited Too, the country's largest girl-oriented retail chain. Instead of camping out or learning about nature, the girls sign up for an overnight that begins at the mall. They're promised an experience emphasizing "smart shopping tips, personal money management and most of all, how to maximize your funds to have it all!" The girls try on clothes and return home with a discount coupon. Other organizations involved in partnerships with marketing firms include the National Boys and Girls Clubs, which has been collaborating to recruit children for the Strottman Group; the National Parent-Teacher Association, now aligned with Coca-Cola; and Unicef, which is collaborating with McDonald's. These are all in addition to the extensive commercial ties developed by public schools, the topic to which I now turn.

CHAPTER FIVE

Captive Audiences

The Commercialization of Public Schools

At one time, television ads represented two-thirds of total expenditures targeted to children. By the mid-1990s, television had been eclipsed by direct marketing, promotions, and sponsorships, which were estimated to account for 80 percent of all marketing dollars. With this shift, children's advertising has moved beyond the confines of the living room to virtually all public spaces and institutions, with houses of worship being the one major exception. The St. Louis Zoo houses the Monsanto Insectarium and the Anheuser-Busch Hippo Harbor. In Boston's Science Museum, the exhibitions are giant structures built from Lego and K'Nex toys. The children's hospital at UCLA was renamed Mattel's Children's Hosptial, and Hasbro's got an equivalent on the East Coast. Indeed, almost anywhere one finds children, there are attempts to market to them, whether it's at doctors' offices or nature centers. The jewel in the marketers' crown of commercial infiltration has been the nation's public schools.

Corporate influence in public schools is not wholly new. Packaged goods and agricultural companies have sponsored health and nutrition education for decades. But since 1990, commercial activities in schools have expanded substantially, with an explosive rise in nearly all types of school-based marketing since 1997. Schools were an especially appealing target to marketers. They had been relatively insulated from advertising, a rare clutter-free island in the larger sea of commercial messages. Teachers and administrators enjoy tremendous trust and authority, and products that appear under their imprimatur can benefit from their seal of approval. Finally, and most important, students are as close to a captive audience as advertisers are ever likely to get.

Force-Fed: Channel One and Mandatory Daily Viewing

The promise of a captive audience was the impetus for Channel One, a daily news and advertising broadcast that originated in 1989. In return for the use of video monitors and equipment, schools have agreed to deliver a certain number of "eyeballs" to watch the broadcast each day. The company quickly made deals with about 12,000, or a quarter, of the nation's nearly 50,000 middle and secondary schools. It reports that more than 8 million students in grades 6 through 12, including 40 percent of all U.S. teens, view the program on 90 percent of all school days. Channel One is reported to be second only to the Super Bowl in audience size. The daily broadcast purports to be ten minutes of news and current events, and this was the stated rationale for schools to sign up. But academic analyses of the program's content have found high levels of fluff, such as stories about celebrities, focus on the anchors' personalities, and lifestyle tidbits with relatively little serious news, although the program's defenders have tried to counter that view. But the most criticized aspect of the program is that it delivers its news along with two minutes of commercials.

From the beginning, Channel One has been controversial. Teachers, parents' groups, and conservative religious organizations have opposed the practice of forcing kids to watch ads. Virtually all other advertising requires at least passive consent from the viewer. One can zap a television spot, exit a Web site, or walk away from an offending billboard. These options do not exist with Channel One. Schools are contractually bound to provide students, sitting at their desks, with the volume turned on. (Volume controls on the sets are not adjustable.) This captive audience is one of the major selling points Channel One uses with its advertisers. Another criticism is that prominent among the advertised products are junk food, soft drinks, video games, Hollywood movies, television programming, and other products that do not enhance kids' well-being. Channel One has been used for military recruiting and messages that promote tobacco companies' brand names. Another point of contention is the cost. One study found that the six days of lost instructional time to Channel One cost the nation's taxpayers $1.8 billion. One of those six days was taken up by ads alone, at an annual price tag of $300 million.

Studies comparing Channel One to non–Channel One schools show that the program affects kids' attitudes. A study of two Michigan high schools found that Channel One students are more likely to agree that "a nice car is more important than school," that "designer labels make a difference," and that "wealthier people are happier than the poor." Channel One students have also been reported to feel that the products advertised are good for them, because they're being shown in the classroom. As one might expect, children in poorer districts are significantly more at risk of attending Channel One schools with their subsequent loss of class time and exposure to advertising messages. One study found that the risk was twice that for higher-income children. Chris Whittle, the company's founder, specially targeted poor Latino districts in California, giving money to school administrators, teachers, and parents, in hopes of gaining a foothold in the state.

Over time, opposition to Channel One has grown. Both of the national teachers' unions, the National Education Association and the American Federation of Teachers, oppose it, as do the National PTA and the National Association of State Boards of Education. The 15-million-member Southern Baptist Convention passed a resolution in 1999 that condemns Channel One because it advertises directly to schoolchildren. I've also encountered industry professionals who are critical of it. One executive I interviewed felt that it was "all packaged very prettily so it doesn't feel like advertising, which is even worse. . . . TVs in classrooms . . . I just don't think that's right." Besides, she continued, "there are other ways of getting to kids in schools," at which point she ticked off a long list of promotional possibilities, including free book covers and other product giveaways, direct ads, and sponsorships.

Channel One battles have raged at various state legislatures, including in New York State, which enacted a ban on the program. To defend itself, Channel One has done almost everything but change its ways. It has spent millions on lobbying efforts, sponsored "media-literacy" conferences, and hired academics to provide legitimacy. They've even offered kickbacks. Teachers from non–Channel One schools were recruited to try to convince their school administrators to sign up for the program. If they succeeded, they'd earn $500. This unethical, and in some states illegal, practice was stopped when activists exposed it. Meanwhile, part of how the company is able to survive is by hiding its product from the public eye and from parental scrutiny. Jim Metrock, an affable conservative from Birmingham, Alabama, reports that his daughter had been watching Channel One for years without his knowledge. When he found out, he started Obligation, an anti–Channel One group. As part of the research for this book, I attempted to view sample broadcasts. Channel One vice president Jim Brannan originally indicated a willingness to provide copies of the daily programs and have his staff meet with me, but he grew less generous when he heard I was writing a book. Eventually he told me he would give me information only if I promised to write about the company in a favorable light.

Opposition has prevented Channel One from growing for many years. But with some notable exceptions, it has mainly managed to hold on to its existing clients. A similar business model called Zapme! gave computers to schools in return for exposing kids to online ads for a certain amount of time each day, plus the right to collect information through the kids' computer use. Those data were then sold to marketing companies. In this case, activists raised enough awareness about the invasion of student privacy and the flaws in the basic agreement that the company was forced to suspend operations. Nevertheless, there are still firms doing school-based tracking of students' Internet use.

The Shop-Rite Gym, Exclusive Coke, and SweeTart Art: Sponsorships, Ads, Contests, and Revenue Deals

The school commercialization trend has proceeded quite far and encompasses a wide range of practices. In 2001, the Omaha, Nebraska, district hatched a plan to tear up its gymnasium floor and replace it with segments painted with corporate logos, each costing $10,000. A Pennsylvania school board announced plans to sell advertising time over the PA system. The Oscar Mayer corporation sponsors an annual elementary school contest for the best version of its familiar jingle, with the winning school receiving $10,000.

The practice that has drawn the most scrutiny is the sale of "pouring rights," in which school districts enter into exclusive contracts with soft drink companies. The first such contract was signed in 1997 in Madison, Wisconsin. Hundreds of other school districts followed suit, earning hundreds of thousands of dollars in the process, despite the association of sodas with tooth decay, obesity, and bone fractures. Vending machines began to proliferate through hallways. The Centers for Disease Control reports that soft and other sugar-added drinks are sold in 94 percent of the nation's high schools, 84 percent of middle and junior high schools, and 58 percent of elementary schools.

In some cases school officials encourage students to buy these drinks. Anticommercialization activists found and publicized a memo from a zealous Colorado administrator, who called himself "The Coke Dude," urging teachers to push Coke's products, to the point of allowing drinks inside the classroom, a typically taboo practice. Schools line up as either "Pepsi" or "Coke" and in some cases go to great lengths to prove their fealty to the corporate sponsor. In 1998, an independent-minded Georgia high school student named Mike Cameron was suspended by his principal for wearing a Pepsi shirt on "Coke Education Day." His plight attracted worldwide media attention and numerous questions about why the principal had chosen to have students devote a day to baking Coke cakes, devising marketing plans for Coke's discount cards, and using their bodies to spell out the four letters in Coke. Pressures on students to support their school's soda brand continue, as journalist Alissa Quart reported in the *New York Times,* discussing a Texas school where students are prevented from drinking any brand but the sponsoring one.

Schools are selling ad space on buses and stadium walls, and even inside school buildings and classrooms. In 2001, NetworkNext announced 500 contracts with schools to show ads in return for a mobile computer unit to use for PowerPoint and other presentations. When the teacher shows a slide, banner ads for Rock Star video games, Wal-Mart, Visa Buxx cards, and Coty products appear on the screen. This promotion also incorporates a survey feedback component in the contracts to let advertisers know how effective the technique proved to be. Product giveaways with corporate logos or ads are also common. Cover Concepts distributes millions of ad-festooned book covers a year. At the beginning of the 2003 academic year, 500,000 New York City kids received "free" annual planners with thirty pages of national advertising. In a telling example of how deeply corporate branding has infiltrated the education process, math textbook writers began to insert brand names, even without payment from the companies involved, on the grounds that kids would better relate to the word problems if they involved branded products. That practice is now illegal in California, following widespread publicity about word problems in a McGraw-Hill math textbook that included Nike, Gatorade, Topps trading cards, and Disneyland as examples. Advertising and sponsorship of athletic programs, teams, and activities are everywhere, with logos on uniforms and corporate branded scoreboards. In-school sports are reported to be one of the fastest-growing areas in all of American corporate marketing.

In what was publicized as the first deal of its kind, an elementary school in Brooklawn, New Jersey, sold naming rights for its gymnasium to the supermarket chain Shop-Rite, in return for what ended up being about $5,000 a year. Superintendent John Kellmayer noted, "We'll be the first school district to be branded with a corporate logo. You hope children can become sophisticated enough to deal with it." Naming rights discussions are cropping up at school board meetings around the country, as more and more schools mull selling off sponsorships of classrooms, libraries, and other marketable pieces of real estate.

Another major area of corporate infiltration is incentive programs, in which sponsors agree to give discounts or free products if students collect a requisite number of coupons or shop at certain stores. General Mills Box Tops for Education, supermarket loyalty programs, and Pizza Hut's Book-It program fall into this category. The Pizza Hut program, which gives free pizzas to kids who read a certain number of books, has involved tens of millions of students and has been expanded to preschools. Other fast food companies are also heavily involved in incentive and sponsorship programs. McDonald's McTeacher Nights send teachers (to work) and families (to spend) to the restaurants, with a portion of wages going to the schools. Ironically, former California governor Gray Davis, whose legislature led the way in efforts to decommercialize education, made McDonald's McTeacher Night official with a state proclamation. Corporate contests have also become common across the country. There's a Dunkin' Donuts competition for the best one-minute commercial to "sell" kids on the value of homework. The grand prize is $6,000, but many of the participants get coupons for free doughnuts at the stores. Nestlé's sponsors the SweeTart contest, in which more than 5,000 schools participate, submitting entries such as a Mona Lisa made of SweeTarts and a Sweetmobile car covered with the candy. Georgia Pacific, through its Angel Soft toilet paper brand, gives money to winners of a community service program. Corporations are also trying to enlist teachers to push their products or the company's point of view. A Crayola marketer I talked to explained they use teachers as "brand ambassadors." Logging giant Weyerhauser runs a six-week summer program on science and environment that pays teachers to attend. General Mills paid Minnesota teachers $250 each to paint ads for Reese's Puffs cereal on their cars and instructed them to place the cars next to where the school buses parked. Eventually opposition forced the company to end that program.

The main impetus for commercialization is the chronic underfunding of schools. As budgets tighten, officials become more receptive to selling access to their students. Debates about exclusive soda contracts, Channel One, corporate sponsorships, and naming rights have all focused on the challenges of funding, with proponents of the deals stressing the monies they anticipate. But there's another factor operating as well. Alex Molnar, author of *Giving Kids the Business: The Commercialization of America's Schools* and the nation's leading expert on school commercialization, has shown that current trends have roots in a larger push, which began during the Reagan administration, to increase corporate influence and activity in public schools. Corporate involvement has extended to training, curriculum development, the promotion of new technologies, and partnership models. Alongside these efforts is an ongoing attempt by conservatives and their business allies to privatize public education through voucher systems, for-profit schools, private testing services, anti-union activities, and charter schools. One part of the plan is to siphon public money out of the schools and into profit-making ventures, such as testing companies and education providers, to ease the path to privatization. The public debate about testing has focused on the failures of schools and the need to improve education, but behind the rhetoric, for-profit companies with ties to the Bush administration are reaping millions of public dollars. The ongoing criticism of public education has also opened the doors to for-profit education companies that have long wanted to capture streams of public revenue. A second component is to open up schools as places to advertise, market, and sell. The career of Christopher Whittle, founder of Channel One and current president of Edison, the nation's largest for-profit education provider, combines both objectives.

Corporations Write the Curriculum

Perhaps the most egregious of the in-school commercial activities is the corporate incursion into academic content. Roberta Nusim is a pioneer in the business of corporate-sponsored curricular materials. As an English teacher in New York's South Bronx in the 1970s, Nusim became dissatisfied with the materials she had to work with. Curriculums were textbook based, and textbooks were out of date. Nusim, who had attended the same school she was teaching in, recounts that she would find herself opening textbooks only to find her own name on the inside cover. These materials lagged one and even two decades behind, and weren't chronicling either the momentous social changes that were occurring in the sixties and seventies or the differences in the ways kids were growing up. Nusim felt that her students, the "*Sesame Street* generation," needed a more visually oriented presentation and faster-paced materials. She improvised for a while, bringing in cereal boxes to teach from and assigning television programs for her children to watch and discuss. But her improvisation prompted a thought. Why not go to corporations and ask them to sponsor innovative curricular materials? Nusim ruled out approaching her own school administration or district, because she felt those bureaucracies moved too slowly and didn't have money for new initiatives. With corporations, she anticipated success, because she could sell her venture as a clear case of self-interest. "Corporate America was waking up to kids' buying power," she explained. Companies were starting to take notice of James McNeal's estimates of child spending and recognizing that their influence was expanding beyond what cereal moms would buy.

Nusim's first project was in 1978 with Columbia Pictures, producer of the film *Kramer versus Kramer.* Together, they developed a curriculum on family living and communication, thinking that the growth of divorce was a good subject for in-school conversations. Children saw the film and then spent class time discussing the issues it raised. Teachers could not require that students go to the movie, but they could strongly encourage it. Soon enough, the phones were ringing off the hook with calls from companies, and Nusim's venture became a raging success.

Since then, Nusim has branched out to a wide range of issues. In the late 1970s, in the wake of the energy crisis, she began doing curricula for utility companies. In the 1980s, as the country was becoming more health conscious, she approached food companies with the idea of doing nutrition curricula, and over the years she has worked with all the major food corporations and soft drink manufacturers, including Pepsi, Coke, and the National Soft Drink Association. Nusim gets clients by keying in on social trends and current events, especially those she feels are underrepresented among existing school materials, and then approaching those companies whose products are relevant.

Nusim's company, Youth Marketing International, has produced 1,500 curricular programs. She now has many competitors, who annually produce thousands of these sponsored educational materials, or SEMs. They start targeting virtually after birth and stick with the kids through high school. Lifetime Learning Systems, which publishes *My Weekly Reader,* is now a national leader in corporate-sponsored materials. Scholastic alone boasts a staff of forty professionals dedicated to in-school marketing, and it promises its clients that it can "harness the incredible brand building power" not of educational materials but of educationally based "marketing programs." Scholastic trades on its long-term relationships with teachers but also gets them on board by offering rewards, such as free products. The company claims that 92 percent of U.S. teachers use its programs and that its reach extends to 53 million of the nation's 69 million students.

Scholastic has also turned its magazines into advertising vehicles by creating special issues that are sponsored by individual companies. Canon sponsored a special issue of *Art and Man Magazine* with three pages of company ads. Discover credit card is another Scholastic sponsor.

SEMs have made huge inroads into American classrooms in the past two decades, with little awareness by parents and the public. The cost of an SEM ranges from lows of about $25,000 to more than $1 million. These large sums of money have yielded an unprecedented ability to put out corporate messages. Revlon's curriculum taught kids about "good and bad hair days" and asked them to list their three must-have hair care products if they were stranded on a desert island. Campbell Soup Company's Science Curriculum included the "Prego Thickness Experiment" with a "slotted spoon test" to figure out whether Prego or Ragu spaghetti sauce was thicker. The Gushers Wonders of the World package included free samples and instructions to kids to bite down on the candy to create an in-mouth volcanic eruption. The Sunkist "Just One Orange" a day unit teaches children such educational facts as the theme of the first ad by the California Fruit Exchange, the number of growers that make up the Sunkist Growers corporation, and how to make a smoothie with a Sunkist orange. Other nutrition curricula are even more problematic in their selective use of information. For example, a Kellogg's breakfast curriculum presents fat content as the only thing to worry about when choosing breakfast food. There is no mention of the sugar and salt in Kellogg's cereals. A first-grade reading curriculum has the kids start out by recognizing logos from K-Mart, Pizza Hut, M&M's, Jell-O, and Target. Another first-grade program has children design a McDonald's restaurant, explains how it works, and gives them information on how to apply for a job at McDonald's. SEMs have also established a strong presence at earlier ages. In the summer of 2003, Nusim's company targeted a third of the nation's preschools with a Care Bears promotional package from American Greetings, and Scholastic placed a curriculum based on the cartoon dog Clifford in preschools all over Texas. For corporations, one of the appealing aspects of SEMs is that they can market covertly, and thereby more effectively. Evan Shapiro, senior vice president of marketing for Courtroom Television, brags about the Forensics in the Classroom Curriculum, a $60,000 investment that "reaches 400,000 students and 1.2 million consumers without EVER seeming like marketing" and has had "enormous impact for Court TV on brand awareness, ratings and revenues."

Another development in sponsored curricula is the use of school trips for marketing purposes. A ten-year-old Chicago-based company, the

Field Trip Factory, has organized more than 20,000 outings in forty-four states to important educational institutions such as Domino's Pizza, The Sports Authority, Petco, and Toys 'R' Us stores. The trips often include free samples, discount coupons, and exposure to advertising materials. More than 600,000 elementary school students, including kindergartners, have taken part in these exercises in early brand exposure and loyalty building.

In the mid-1990s, after sponsored materials began to flood into schools, Consumers Union undertook a study of their nature and quality, surveying seventy-seven corporate-sponsored kits and packets. It found that nearly 80 percent of the materials surveyed were guilty of blatant bias, commercial pitches, significant inaccuracies, or all of these. It judged more than half to be "commercial or highly commercial." These materials are intentionally biased in their choice of information, in order to make the corporate point of view seem reasonable, objective, and educational. One California administrator whose job involved screening materials explained how difficult her task was. She kept sending back the slanted submissions, but the corporations got the message and began to circumvent her, sending materials directly to schools. In the end, it didn't matter, because she was laid off, her position cut due to budget shortfalls, the very problem that opened the door to corporate-sponsored curricula to begin with.

Some of the worst examples of bias have been found among corporate environmental materials. In the early 1990s, energy, paper, and other primary materials companies became concerned about what they considered an excessively proenvironmental attitude among the nation's youth. They worried that existing environmental education curricula were exacerbating those sentiments. So the companies began what can only be described as an expensive propaganda effort to obscure the nature of the environmental problems facing the planet. For example, Consumers Union concluded that Exxon's elaborate Energy Cube curriculum "implies that fossil fuels pose few environmental problems and that alternative energy is costly and unattainable." It minimizes the problem of oil spills and strip mining. American Coal Foundation materials dismiss the greenhouse effect, saying the "earth could benefit rather than be harmed from increased carbon dioxide." A Chevron lesson plan took a similar tack and attempted to rebut the existence of global warming. One waste curriculum defined plastics' incineration as "recycling." Materials from the Pacific Logging Congress described clear-cutting as "environmentally responsible." Procter & Gamble stopped distributing its Decision Earth, which taught that clear-cut logging is good for the environment, after attorneys general in eleven states were asked to investigate its truthfulness. Overall, Consumers Union found a "distorted picture of the problems, choices and trade-offs inherent in the issues these materials cover."

These corporations were trying to put a good face on themselves, but sometimes it seems that they prefer to hide their involvement, to make propaganda look like truth. One example is a classroom video that promoted the idea that plastics were not a threat to the environment. All but one of the "experts" who appeared in the video were full-time employees of the plastics industry. At one viewing session, arranged by a newspaper investigating corporate-sponsored materials, students thought the film was produced by an environmental group. Stewart Allen, the journalist who organized the viewing, noted that the students missed "the minuscule Mobil copyright sign that appears at the end of the video, the only indication it was created by one of the country's largest manufacturers of plastics." A similar stealth sponsorship approach has been used by the governments of Saudi Arabia and Israel, each of which collaborated (separately, of course) with U.S. firms to produce classroom materials that portrayed their countries in a positive light.

Why do teachers use these materials? In the early days, Nusim got her products into schools through an intensive grassroots effort. She began by relying on her contacts in the field. She attended industry conferences, setting up a booth to showcase the materials she was offering, free of charge, to any teachers or administrators who wanted them. She was a frequent speaker at education meetings. All of this effort paid off. Nusim developed a core of teachers who use her materials on an ongoing basis. They then recruited other teachers through word of mouth and targeting of potential new recruits to corporate curricula. Eventually she developed access to every school in the United States and Canada, and the ability to cull specialized lists from her database (for example, chairs of middle school English departments). She attributes her success in large part to money. Current estimates are that the average teacher spends more than $521 of his or her own money each year to purchase classroom materials, and that number has been climbing steadily. The corporate materials are provided free of charge and designed for easy duplication. But schools are often getting what they pay for—shoddy and biased materials that serve commercial interests. Nusim emphasized that "educational value is first and foremost for me," but her company's survival depends on serving her clients' interests. Moreover, she concedes that others in the industry lack standards.

The growth of sponsored materials, advertising within schools, and schools' deliberate marketing of junk food can ultimately be traced to the very real problem of inadequate funding. But commercialization is a troubling response and raises important questions. Businesses are willing to spend millions of dollars on crummy classroom materials, but have proven unwilling to pay taxes to support high-quality, serious curricula for the nation's children. There's a national discourse paying homage to equality of opportunity, but schools in low-income districts have far fewer resources and are more likely to turn to insidious products like Channel One. As Molnar and others have detailed, right-wing efforts to increase corporate influence in schools have succeeded, to the detriment of children's education and well-being.

In the past few years, a backlash to school commercialization has gathered momentum. The soft drink companies are on the defensive, as some districts, including Madison, have rejected or failed to renew contracts, citing health impacts, parental opposition, and revenue streams that did not meet expectations. After a spate of bad publicity, Coca-Cola announced that the parent company, although not its bottling affiliates, would no longer promote (in contrast to enter into) exclusive contracts. In 2002, the Los Angeles Unified School District, where 40 percent of the children have been found to be obese, voted to enact a ban on soft drink sales to take effect in January 2004. The Oakland School District banned sales of sugared drinks and candy in schools in what is perhaps the nation's strictest regulation.

There has been opposition to other school-based commercial activities as well. After defeating Zapme! a coalition of organizations put together by the Nader-inspired group Commercial Alert was instrumental in Senate passage of the Dodd-Shelby privacy provision that requires schools to obtain parental permission before allowing marketers to elicit personal information from children. Seattle, where there is an active anticommercialization group, has enacted a new policy curtailing advertising on school property, and Channel One will be banned in 2004. Whether these victories signal a longer-term trend is unclear. Vigorous corporate lobbying by the soft drink industry, Channel One, and others defeated the Maryland legislature's attempt in 2001 to ban ads and exclusive soft drink contracts in public schools. As fast as activists can win victories, the marketers develop new schemes.

Under the Wholesome Halo

One of the keys to corporate successes in gaining access to kids has been that they glide in under the "wholesome halo." That glow is not merely reserved for cereals. Whole companies bask in it. And increasingly, those are some of the most aggressive commercializers around. Scholastic is a good example. It has a longstanding reputation as a quality educational enterprise and represents itself as the "most trusted name in publishing, education and entertainment." While it enjoys a reputation as a benign, educationally based company, Scholastic is a $2 billion giant that has been one of the leading and most aggressive forces for introducing corporate influence into schools through its sponsored curricula, licensed products at fairs, and sales of toys and other products on its book order forms. A telling example of Scholastic's transformation is the content of its well-known and loved book order forms. Once a cheap and convenient way of getting books to children, they have become a bonanza for media and toy companies. A recent order form includes four different Nickelodeon sections selling SpongeBob figurines, cards, and stickers; a *Rugrats* movie promotion; and offers of key chain giveaways with Nickelodeon characters. Disney has a number of sections, including a *Life with Lizzie* (McGuire) pack and poster next to an ad urging kids to "Watch it on Disney ABC Kids," and other products promoting Disney movies *The Hulk* and *Freaky Friday.* Other branded products represented were Hershey's, with its Hershey's Kisses math book, Hello Kitty toys and art supplies, as well as products featuring Scooby Doo, DragonBall Z, and Mary Kate and Ashley. There are guidebooks for PlayStation 2 and Lego's Bionicle action figures. There is also an array of unbranded toys.

PBS is another company that has been able to pursue commercial activities aggressively under its wholesome halo, such as its market research in schools and the introduction of *Teletubbies,* TV for one year olds, complete with fast food toy tie-ins. Lego's Bionicle action figure line benefited from the company's reputation as a maker of nonviolent toys, although its story line is violent and the figures come with extensive weaponry. Companies without the halo team up with those that have it to get access to kids and places they might not otherwise succeed with. Agencies enlist nonprofits to partner with for marketing efforts. For those who care to look, the wholesome halos are looking awfully tattered. But the companies are counting on the fact that few of us are looking.

CHAPTER SIX

Dissecting the Child Consumer

The New Intrusive Research

> At the end of the day, my job is to get people to buy things. . . . It's a horrible thing and I know it.
>
> —New York advertising executive Mary Prescott

Picture the following scene: Caitlin, a five-year-old girl, and Mary Prescott, a thirty-something woman with a video camera, are sitting on the floor in Caitlin's bedroom. Caitlin's mother is in the kitchen, because Mary has explained that for this project, she needs private time with Caitlin. They're talking about baths and what Caitlin does when she takes one. The client, a health and beauty aids company with a bubble bath product, wants to explore Caitlin's feelings about bath time and learn what she actually does while she's bathing. After some talk, Caitlin leads Prescott and her camera into the bathroom, where Mary spies a shelf full of empty shampoo and bubble bath bottles. She learns that Caitlin plays with them during her bath, which leads to the consumer insight that kids turn soap containers into toys. Prescott explains that had she done the research in a focus group facility or even in the kitchen, she wouldn't have happened upon the empty containers. And they were the key finding of the study.

Caitlin's mom was happy to oblige Prescott's request for an in-home taping, almost without thinking about it. The company doing the research is a reputable one, it's paying a fair amount of money, and Caitlin seems to feel comfortable with Mary. They had already met at a focus group facility, where Caitlin had been recruited to provide feedback on another product. By the end of their relationship, Mary would have been at the house a couple of times and had plenty of one-on-one private time with Caitlin. When the taping is over, Prescott lingers in the kitchen, eliciting some extra information from the mother, even though the one and a half hours they'd agreed on has passed. The interaction has become relaxed and casual, as Prescott needs it to be. After taping a number of Caitlins, Prescott will write a report about this research and show the highlights from the tapes to her client. On the basis of the findings, the bubble bath producer will redesign its package.

The Ethnographic Turn

Interactions like the one I have just described have become commonplace across American cities and suburbs, examples of the burgeoning field of naturalistic or ethnographic data-gathering with children. Marketers are now scrutinizing virtually every activity kids engage in. They watch them eating, playing, and grooming. Marketers want to know the contents of children's closets, how they interact in the classroom, and what really goes on at a tween slumber party. They are probing how kids talk about and even use drugs.

When I interviewed her, Mary Prescott was a vice president at a youth division of a major advertising agency. She began her career at a more traditional children's research firm, when the field was far more staid. Now she's one of its leading ethnographic researchers, well respected by her peers and at the cutting edge of consumer insights. Prescott attributes her success to the unique qualities of ethnographic research. Unlike more traditional methods, her observations are child directed and proceed at a slow pace. Part of the process is simple persistence. She often spends her time in previously unresearched spaces, such as homes, and their most private areas—bedrooms and bathrooms—where kids can be themselves. Prescott has learned that a one-shot approach doesn't work. She needs three visits before she is confident that she's getting the real deal. "Before that the children are performing. By the third time they're used to you." Multiple visits also allow a second component of this research, which is creating enough trust that the children are willing to open up. Prescott "establishes a friendship" and "builds a rapport." Her preference is to have a one-on-one session with the child, unlike in the past, when mothers were much more likely to be present when children were interviewed. Once they trust her, she can gain valuable information about them to pass on to her clients. This method avoids some of the pitfalls of focus groups, such as the fact that the dynamics of the group affect the answers and one influential person can skew responses or that people can be reluctant to be honest in front of others. It also bypasses the problem of kids who show off, or perform, during focus groups, thereby undermining true insights.

For these reasons, Prescott and scores of other researchers are now engaged in painstaking, face-to-face scrutiny of children's daily lives. They sit and film kids doing what they do and then try to use that information to figure out how to sell them more stuff. They watch them playing with their dolls and games, eating yogurt and cereal, and brushing their teeth. Contending that traditional interviews and surveys do not get at how consumers live or interact with products, practitioners of this daily life research aim to uncover insights that we consumers cannot articulate because we are unaware of them. They are also searching for consumer habits that kids are unwilling to talk about because they do not jibe with a child's self-image, such as the fact that tween girls still love to play with their Barbies and tween boys do the same with their action figures. Actually being in the places where consumers live lets researchers see many things that would never even surface in standard interviews. Emma Gilding, the researcher behind AT&T's mlife campaign, which focuses on the everyday realities of life and how cell phones have been woven into ordinary moments, explains that the method is about "trying to find moments of truth," especially during the times when language breaks down. Gilding, a senior partner at Ogilvy and Mather's Discovery Group and one of New York's hottest practitioners of this type of work, contends that what she's doing goes beyond standard practice: "It's not research, we live with them . . . not anthropology, we're in the frame." She's trying to get at deep intangibles that cannot be accessed by interviews or surveys.

If the product Prescott had been researching were a toy, or apparel, or food, she would have taped Caitlin using it. And although she didn't observe kids actually bathing in this project, I did find researchers who have done bath and shower observation. One woman I interviewed described how she'd have the child pull the curtain closed while she sat on the toilet, taking notes. She explained that after a few minutes, the kids forget she's in the room. That's when they perform the private behaviors it's her job to discover, such as grabbing the shampoo container and pretending it's a microphone, singing the latest Britney Spears tune, and exiting the tub with a towel wrapped around the neck, play-acting a superhero.

In market research, the ethnographic turn dates to the 1980s. One of the first companies to use these methods was Levi Strauss, the jeans company, which started sending researchers into homes to look into kids' closets as a way of finding out what they were into and what the newest trends might be. Ethnography got a big boost in 1998 with an influential Saatchi and

Saatchi study called "Digital Kids." Saatchi stationed anthropologists inside homes and had them watch what kids did while they were online. The company has even hired an archaeologist to unearth consumer insights. Saatchi likes to take credit for the ethnographic turn, but a number of factors were at work, including the fact that such methods had already taken root with adults.

One reason researchers turned to the naturalistic was that traditional methods were yielding fewer insights. As one marketer explained: "I would say that the reason Procter stopped asking women about laundry every minute was because there's only so much you can ask about laundry. There's only so much you can know. It stopped getting useful and newsworthy. I mean: 'What's your favorite cereal?' 'Lucky Charms.' 'Why do you like it?' 'It's good.' 'Why is it good?' 'It's got the marshmallows.' 'Why do you like the marshmallows?' 'They're sweet.' 'Is there anything else you like about it?' 'The milk turns gray.' " Others think that cost factors have been decisive. A top executive from one agency recounted the history behind today's methods. Forty years ago, the major advertisers, such as Procter & Gamble, surveyed thousands of consumers annually. Then they figured out they could reduce those samples to the hundreds and achieve success at a lower cost. As budgets grew tighter, the hundreds dwindled down to tens, and now ethnographers have seized the moment, arguing that insights gained from intensive studies of even a few people can supplant all that expensive research.

Paco Underhill is one of the field's pioneers. Underhill was introduced to the public by a Malcolm Gladwell write-up in the *New Yorker* and then went on to write his own book, *Why We Buy.* He began his career in academia, a student of William Whyte, the distinguished sociologist and chronicler of everyday life. But before long, Underhill had begun using his research skills to dissect consumer behavior. Armed with a video camera and a keen set of eyes, he eventually accumulated hundreds of thousands of hours of tape of consumers in stores, restaurants, parks, and on the street. His firm, Envirosell, currently records about 20,000 hours of in-store behavior annually. In the process, he has become the chronicler extraordinaire of numerous lucrative consumer insights. These include the law of the invariant right turn—the observation that we always turn right upon walking into a store; the butt brush—the fact that women are very unlikely to make a purchase just after being accidentally bumped in the behind; and the decompression zone—the place where we inevitably stop, a few steps into a retail space, to take stock and figure out what to do next. Over the years, Underhill has developed an in-depth understanding of impulse buying, which, given its importance in our economy, is of undisputed value to companies. He has consulted extensively for retail chains, and you can see his handiwork in the layout, display, and signage in places such as the Gap and Starbucks. Although Underhill is not a child expert, his firm has worked for Nickelodeon, Disney, and other companies that do a significant child business.

His methods have also caught on more widely. Marketing snoops, with cameras, notebooks, and videotapes, can be found in toy stores, clothing shops, and supermarkets, hanging out in the aisles and watching what kids do. They're in playgrounds and on the streets. They're even inside classrooms. Schools have sold rights to probe kids as young as age seven. Noggin, a joint venture of Nickelodeon and PBS, set up shop in an elementary school in Watchung, New Jersey. In return for $7,100, the Noggin people gained access for six months, coming in weekly. Noggin representatives conducted focus groups, designed homework assignments that elicited consumer information, even sat inside classrooms, to amass background research prior to launching their new venture. As one of these marketers explained to me, they worked to establish "rapport and friendship" with the kids. In a *New York Times* story on these practices, Robert Reynolds, president of Education Market Resources, raised a key aspect of these arrangements. Most companies will not be granted entrée into schools, so they need intermediaries like his firm, which allows the client companies to be hidden from view. His company does not mention the names of its clients, which include Kentucky Fried Chicken, Nabisco, Kellogg's, and Nike. Once inside the school, the marketers turn their information-gathering tasks into what Reynolds termed "an educational process."

Kid specialty firms have gotten into the business of naturalistic observation in a big way. One such company is the Strottman Group, based in southern California. In 2002, Strottman pioneered an in-store videotaping method, in the style of Underhill. Its major innovation was the use of a hidden camera that kids themselves carried around. The Strottman study was done in grocery stores in California and Atlanta and involved twelve boys and girls, ages six to seven and eight to nine. Each kid was equipped with a headband with a lens built into it, which was then connected to a camera hidden in a backpack. They were sent into a store and asked to pick any twenty things they would like to buy. The camera recorded everything the children did, such as what they looked at, which aisles they lingered in, what they picked up, and what they ultimately chose to put in the cart. The study was conducted with what at Strottman are called "rookies," that is, kids who had not yet been interviewed or briefed by the firm. (They were also unaware of the purpose of the study.) After the shopping trip, each child reviewed the footage with staff and discussed what he or she was doing and what was going on in his or her mind.

Following its original presentation at an industry conference in 2002, the Strottman study garnered a lot of interest, and the group planned to expand its use of the method to other types of retail environments. Because the technology is fairly easy to replicate, it's likely that other firms will also jump on this bandwagon. A major part of the appeal is that the cameras are hidden, so the taping can be done without store managers' knowledge. The process of getting managers' permission is often complicated, and it's part of why kid researchers haven't used cameras in stores more often.

Another practitioner of naturalistic research is Rita Denny, a principal of the Practica Group and one of the most insightful researchers I interviewed. Practica does not take on children's business, but did do work with tweens to help craft the government's antidrug advertising. Denny explained that her approach goes beyond videotaping for the purpose of finding unrecognized behaviors, and it goes beyond the psychological perspective that characterizes most market research. As an anthropologist, Denny is interested in culture and the way in which products fit into the larger cultural context. She studies images and metaphors that consumers usually do not articulate but that lie behind motivation and action. Most important, her work is designed to tease out the deep symbolic meanings that consumers attach to products. It's a more complex framing than most of what goes on in the industry.

The tween study Denny and two colleagues worked on for the National Office of Drug Control was designed to explore the culture of drugs among tweens. Rather than merely focusing on a psychographic orientation, which might find that kids who take drugs are risk loving, or lack self-esteem, or are depressed, this work elaborated the broader context in which kids experience drug use. Practica's portion of the research involved sixth- through eighth-grade students defined as mainstream, living in suburbs or inside city lines in New York and Chicago. Participants were screened in order to assemble a group with a somewhat open proclivity toward drugs. The kids were asked to find two to three friends to do the interview with them, and the sessions took place wherever they felt most comfortable. This was usually in their bedrooms, but could also be in family rooms, a coffee shop, or anywhere else. They brought together eight groups in each city, with one to three kids per group. Each mother, kid, and friend received $75 for participating. The interviews lasted for two to three hours and were videotaped by whoever was conducting the interview. Before they met, the researchers asked the kids to record details about their worlds, friendships, families, and daily lives. They distributed cameras and asked the children to create a diary. By the time the sessions rolled around, there was already a self-reflective process and a relationship in place.

Through this research, Denny and her colleagues found important flaws in the government's antidrug messages. It is widely believed that many of the ads have been ineffective, lack credibility, and are seen as uncool or even ridiculous by kids. The Practica researchers have insight into why that's the case. For example, they discovered that kids feel adults are obsessed with drugs and that using drugs is considered a normal part of being an adult, so they feel there's hypocrisy in the messages to avoid drugs. This research also found that drugs have become "thoroughly and deeply implicated in the process of self-construction" for American kids, in large part because of their role in separating from adults. The secrecy surrounding drugs, the dangers associated with them, and the forbidden fruit quality are a draw for many kids. So when adults counsel kids to "just say no," that is in many ways equivalent to a "don't grow up" message.

This study is a good example of how much valuable insight can be gleaned when a talented researcher uses these methods. In this case, the researchers suggested the government should reorient its message to challenge the pervasiveness of the drug culture and provoke tweens to reject the idea that drugs help to create a more "real self." They urged the Office of Drug Control Policy to include tobacco and alcohol in antidrug messages, because kids view these substances as drugs and find their absence hypocritical. Such an approach would match the target audience's worldview, and thus gain credibility. Unfortunately, the Bush administration, a recipient of considerable sums of money from tobacco, alcohol, and big pharmaceutical companies, rejected these insightful suggestions.

Denny, Prescott, Gilding, Coughlin, Underhill, and others I've met and interviewed are just a few of the many researchers who are involved in these naturalistic research methods. Firms have set up Manhattan townhouses where the kids come for overnight parties and marketing professionals eavesdrop on their conversations. Companies rent out warehouses to bring kids together. All manner of on-site research is now available to clients who want to get in on the latest research tools marketers have to offer.

The New Child Labor: Kid as Expert

Levi Strauss not only pioneered closet peeping; it was also one of the earliest companies to employ children in innovative ways, taking them on as official consultants. One such child was Manhattanite Josh Koplewicz, who began his work for the company when he was ten. Josh had gone to a focus group and impressed the marketing folks so much that they wanted to hear more. Josh was apparently extremely sophisticated, with a keen fashion sense and fashion interest at an early age. He's now a history major at Brown University and a hip-hop deejay at clubs in New York and elsewhere.

After the focus group, Josh was interviewed by a Levi executive armed with a reported one hundred questions that plumbed his opinions in excruciating detail. The company liked his answers enough to hire him. As a consultant, he would look at clothes that were in various stages of production and design, accompany executives into stores and give his opinions on the merchandise, and hold forth on upcoming trends. The company would call periodically with an assignment and instructions to reply within twenty-four hours. Josh reports that "they were pretty blunt." If he didn't comply with their request, they made it clear he would be fired. They'd send a disposable camera, a notebook, and a tape recorder, and ask him to comb the city. He was on the lookout for cool kids he could interview and whose outfits and accessories he would record. Company executives then appeared at Josh's apartment, where they'd go over his findings. They'd also go through his own clothes, looking in his closet and his drawers, and at his room. They probed him about what he liked and why, as well as his interpretations of what others were doing. Levi Stauss paid him $200 to $1,000 per assignment. It was big money for Josh, but dirt cheap for the company.

What began as a brilliant idea by a couple of Levi Strauss executives has now mutated into a massive recruitment effort by firms around the country. Agencies are hiring children to provide insight and feedback, and to carry out research. For example, the Strottman Group hires what it calls "kid engineers" and "1317 teens" (for ages thirteen to seventeen) on staff and on an on-call basis. Strottman's Sharon Fogg, who oversees the program, estimates that the company maintains an ongoing relationship with about 750 kids, ranging in age from six to seventeen. The children are screened through an enrollment process, which includes parental permission forms and the completion of a profile detailing the kinds of products they like and use. This information is then entered into a confidential database that the firm accesses when specific jobs come up. Most of the company's business is with packaged goods, soft drinks, and fast foods. About half the jobs are on the premises, and half involve going to stores, fast food restaurants, and the like. The kids are paid for their time, but Fogg refused to be precise about how much they get. It's "more than $15 or $20 but less than $50," and sometimes they get to keep the products they are working on. The amount of work varies, but they might be asked to come as often as once a week. As the child graduates from engineer status, he or she can move up to the tween and teen groups and stay with the firm for years.

In the early days, Fogg recruited her own family and employees' kids, grandkids, nieces, and nephews. As they ran out of family members, she began attending outdoor civic events and giving presentations. Now, her colleague Ron Coughlin explained, "we have a very aggressive recruiting program through schools." They work only with private and parochial schools, because the safeguards and regulations at public schools are too complex—"the reality is that they [the children] are working," says Fogg. She presents the program to the boards of the schools and then to parent meetings, offering cash or other compensation to the school in return for their participation. In her spiel, she promises that the children will gain self-esteem because "someone" is listening to them, and that they will be thrilled to see products they've worked on being advertised on television. She promises the kids will have fun, get to be creative, and "never do the same thing twice." In 2003, the firm embarked on an ambitious recruitment effort, through the Boys and Girls Clubs of America, which had agreed to facilitate access to the 3,700 children in the organization. Fogg reports that she's never been asked in advance by school or organizational officials about the kinds of products the kids will be working on, whether alcohol or cigarette advertising would be part of the work, or about violent toys or video games or sexist portrayals.

Variants of the practices Strottman is engaged in have become commonplace throughout the industry, and kids are now involved at all marketing stages, from product design to final ad copy. Doyle Research in Chicago has used children extensively to develop new product ideas. It runs Kideation sessions in which kids are brought together to a facility to brainstorm and "create." The Heinz E-Z Squeeze bottle, a favorite industry success story, is reported to have come out of one of these sessions. Companies also run their own programs to integrate children into planning. Microsoft developed the "Kid's Council," where kids give the software giant ideas. The company offers a small honorarium and some giveaway merchandise, and the children must sign a contract forgoing any royalties on products that come from their ideas, a practice one kid consultant described as "a little unfair." Nickelodeon and MTV have ongoing efforts of this sort. In 1995, Nickelodeon started the Zoom Room Panel of two to eleven year olds. It has also conducted an online panel for more than a decade that brings together eight to fourteen year olds from around the country on Wednesday evenings from 7 to 8 P.M. to provide information and opinions to the company. Each week it convenes twenty-five kids from the larger panel, and kids can participate for up to two years.

As I did this research, I puzzled about why people are so willing to cooperate with market researchers. I wondered why the parents let perfect strangers into their homes and expose their private spaces and behaviors. When I asked, the marketers pointed to the money. "It starts with the money," Mary Prescott said. Others agree: "I think the money is what makes people go," explained one woman in the field. Even among the upper middle class, for whom a $40 fee isn't significant, the parents reason that it's a lot for a child, who, after all, will be keeping it. Not everyone is willing to share their lives with strangers, but Prescott notes that "between reality TV and the Osbournes, everyone knows what marketers are doing." My informants report that becoming a subject in market research or even a consultant may be a way for ordinary people to get their fifteen minutes of fame. Prescott reports that among the many in-home research visits she's done, she has never once not been asked back.

For the children, the reasons are somewhat different. They do like the money. But Sharon Fogg, Laura Groppe, and others are adamant that the kids participate because they are thrilled to have someone who is actually listening to them and acting on their advice. These marketers portray a world in which parents and teachers are not paying attention or empowering kids. GIA reports back to the girls to let them know how the client companies responded to their information. Alissa Quart, who interviewed a number of teen consultants for her book *Branded: The Buying and Selling of Teenagers,* came to a similar conclusion. Of course, not all kids are enthusiastic about marketing, but it's clear that marketers don't have to twist arms to get adult or child participation. A moderate amount of cash and an attentive ear seem to do the trick. That's a testimony to how accepted, trusted, and normalized market research has become in our society.

Inside the Child Brain

At the entrance to G Whiz Marketing, a New York firm specializing in Generation X marketing, is a large colored x-ray of a brain, with a starlike light emanating from middle of it. It's an unsettling image, implying that G Whiz is succeeding at what so many advertisers dream of: getting access to kids' deepest thoughts. The logo suggests even more than share of mind, the mantra that has replaced share of market as the goal for kid advertisers. It implicitly promises a kind of power to permeate the brain.

Some researchers have become explicit about that goal as they combine scientific discoveries about the brain with new computerized technologies, to craft ever more effective and irresistible messages. One practitioner in this area is Langbourne Rust, now an independent consultant who sells his time helping companies figure out what captures children's attention. Rust did his undergraduate psychology training at Harvard University and then earned a doctorate in child development at Columbia University's Teachers College. His dissertation involved painstaking observation of preschool children to figure out those attributes of toys, books, and educational material that attracted boys and girls differently. His research involved spending countless hours in classrooms, collecting large quantities of data, recording every move the children made at prespecified intervals of time. He then subjected the data to statistical analysis to ferret out patterns and regularities, and ultimately to identify the design and other product attributes that most attracted children's attention and interest. As with many other child researchers, he was trained originally to help children, and his funding came from the nonprofit sector.

After graduate school, in the early 1970s, Rust landed a postdoctorate fellowship at the Children's Television Workshop, producers of *Sesame Street* and *Electric Company.* It was an ideal place to pursue his intellectual passions of attraction and distraction. CTW was interested in what made the kids pay attention to one character, story line, or musical sequence and not another. Rust's breakthrough came while his boss was on vacation, and he had some free time. He took the so-called distracter data (measurements of when kids are paying attention and when they're not) that CTW had been analyzing in an ad hoc way and subjected them to his more rigorous theoretical framework. When his boss returned, he had formulated a memo that became the basis of a set of creative guidelines for *Electric Company* and later for *Sesame Street.*

In the early days, this type of data collection was done by hand. The field evolved to filming kids and using researchers to watch and code the films. Now, the process is fully computerized, and much cheaper, so far more data can be analyzed. In addition, the potential to predict consumer behavior accurately is considerably greater. Rust now has his own product, the EyesOn Copytesting System, and he consults for companies whose missions are to get kids to drink more soda, eat more potato chips, buy more toys, and spend more money. His technology measures children's every move while they watch ads or programs. How many times do they blink? How intent is their gaze? The computer records every look, cough, and turn of the head. And in a nod to real-world viewing situations, the setup includes two monitors—one with the ad, another with alternative material. These data are then analyzed in order to determine the appeal of whatever the kids were watching.

Rust's particular system is unique, but the broad approach of subjecting kids' viewing behavior to quantitative analysis is common. There are many companies that test commercials and programs. Some specialize in kids, and others do both adults and kids. One company, with its AccuPoll system, claims a unique expertise in child-parent interactions. With such sophisticated testing available, companies can be assured that their commercials will at least capture kids' attention, if not their hearts.

But the field is moving far beyond eye-tracking to techniques that have been dubbed "neuromarketing." Neuromarketing involves using brain science to determine how to sell to consumers. The BrightHouse Institute for Thought Sciences in Atlanta is paying people to have MRI brain scans done while they look at pictures of different products. Harvard Business School professor Gerry Zaltman pioneered this technique in the late 1990s, but he has since dropped the MRI component and has patented another method called ZMET, which he claims gets inside the subconscious. ZMET, which is enormously influential in the field, has been used with teens and children. Which companies are involved? BrightHouse's Adam Koval is tight-lipped: "We can't actually talk about the specific names of the companies, but they are global consumer product companies. Right now, they would rather not be exposed. We have been kind of running under the radar with a lot of the breakthrough technology."

One planner I met in New York has a more eclectic approach. He regularly consults with university brain scientists, hypnotizes consumers, and is hard at work developing an emotional field theory that can "tap into the human mind . . . [into] the brain functions which control emotion. . . . When I send out a virus, I'm trying to do it in a way so that it will be more receptive. I'm not calling for some Orwellian vision of the future," he says, but "we'll be able to . . ." At this point his voice trailed off, perhaps because he was contemplating a lucrative future of irresistible ads.

These efforts are reminiscent of earlier decades when marketers such as Ernest Dichter thought they could unlock the secrets of consumers' brains and learn to manipulate their buying behavior. Dichter became legendary in the field, doing thousands of "depth" interviews with consumers and helping companies sell more coffee, dishwashing liquid, and other products. Dichter himself was a controversial character whose claims overstated his capabilities. But his dream, which was to get inside consumers' heads, is the same as that animating today's neuromarketers. What's new about today's efforts is that a far more sophisticated scientific understanding and inexpensive new technologies have raised the odds on marketers' being successful.

How much of this is happening in the kids' market is hard to say. Experts I've talked with say they don't know of MRI scans being used on kids. But there are kid marketers who keep up with and rely on the new brain research to advise companies. Dan Acuff has been one of them. His firm, Youth Marketing Services, specializes in applying psychology and new brain science to marketing, and his book, *Why They Buy,* has been widely read. He boasts an 80 percent success rate for his "proprietary and revolutionary system for determining the viability of products and programs." His clients are a who's who of the big kid marketing firms: Nike, Disney, Kraft, Coca-Cola, Nickelodeon, Warner Bros., Microsoft, General Mills, Pizza Hut, Nestlé, Johnson and Johnson, ABS, CBS, Mattel, Hasbro, Pepsi, M&M, Fisher Price, Chuck E. Cheese, and Scholastic. Unlike most other texts in the field, *Why They Buy* is very strong on ethical concerns, including the importance of age appropriateness and the dangers of violent products and media.

Much of Acuff's work has been done in partnership with media psychologist Robert Reiher, who employs the concept of the triune brain, with its reasoning, emotional, and instinctive components. Reiher explained to me that he is very concerned about how advertising can manipulate viewers' attention mechanism and "downshift" the brain, that is, activate the emotional midbrain and the instinctive reactive centers. Such downshifting makes it virtually impossible for critical thinking and effective reasoning to occur while watching an ad. In combination with age-inappropriate content, Reiher believes that downshifting can have a negative impact on brain development in children. In his view, "The 'muscle' of metacognition is the key to the higher thought processes and this can be compromised by high-powered entertainment experiences that keep the brain engaged in the emotional and instinctive modes of processing." Reiher worries that what the people using MRI scanning techniques and other advanced brain technologies are doing is trying to discover more effective brain downshifting techniques.

Reiher remains committed to the positive potentials of entertainment, but he has been disappointed by his experiences in the field of children's marketing. He had hoped to get across a message about the potential misuse of brain science, and to encourage more ethical behavior by marketers, in terms of the products they choose to represent and the approaches they use. He felt that his discussions fell on deaf ears and that for the most part, marketers were interested in using brain science and media psychology to sell more stuff. He is now very concerned about the abuse of the information that he provided and the misuse of the material in the book he worked on with Acuff.

Conventional Research

These efforts are in addition to a barrage of traditional research. Companies are still organizing consumer panels with kids; conducting telephone, written, and online surveys, and mall questionnaires; doing thousands of focus groups; testing commercials; and the like. Nowhere is this effort more refined than at Nickelodeon, whose phenomenal success is partly based on a research effort that seems almost obsessive. At any one time, Nickelodeon probably has about twenty studies in process. It holds about 250 to 270 focus groups annually. It does ongoing telephone interviews. It conducts in-home research, in-store observations, research at preschools, research at parks and in malls, and online research. According to Donna Sabino, Nickelodeon does "virtually every type of research." Sabino estimates that Nickelodeon alone probably talks to 5,000 to 10,000 children a year. This volume and scope of research is unprecedented in children's marketing. Every episode of *Blue's Clues* is tested at four different stages in the production process to assess kids' reactions and make sure that once it airs, it'll be a success.

Nickelodeon isn't the only company that's out there asking. The major polling firms, such as Harris, Roper, and Yankelovich, have youth products such as the Roper Youth Reports, Harris Poll's Youth Pulse and Youth Query (with more than 10,000 respondents annually), and Yankelovich's Youth Monitor. There are firms that maintain large Internet-based surveys of kids. Smaller outfits have specialized indices, such as the Gepetto

Group's Trend Tracker and its new index of which brands are cool. JustKid Inc., Child Research Services, C&R Research, and many other firms maintain a variety of research tools and publications. Alloy engages in continuous online research. Major companies that sell to kids, such as McDonald's and the toy companies, do a lot of their own research as well as relying on what's available in the vast marketplace of information for hire. The list goes on and on. Children are under the microscope as never before.

As with many other trends in the great push to sell stuff to kids, schools have gotten sucked into the business of for-profit research. In addition to the six-month effort conducted by Noggin, journalists have uncovered examples of market researchers' being let into schools to conduct focus groups and interviews during school hours. I found evidence of extensive use of school time to conduct quantitative surveys on thousands of children. Marketers like school-based surveys because they can reach a broad cross-section of kids far more cheaply and easily than with any other method. In addition, when surveys are sanctioned and organized by school officials, participation rates are far higher than with other methods such as telephoning. They're also preferable to online research, which, although cheap, is still not able to produce a population representative of the actual distribution of children. This is partly because children are disproportionately poor and low income, and homes with Internet access are still skewed toward the middle and affluent segments of the population. So schools remain a highly prized and efficient venue for studying and investigating kids.

One example of a school-based survey is KidID, which is done on a regular basis by JustKid Inc., a small Connecticut firm. The most recent wave included 4,002 children in grades 4 through 8. This is a long survey that asks a variety of questions about kids' behaviors, attitudes, and preferences. It asks about their hopes and dreams, how they view their parents, what kinds of things they think are cool and would like to have. One might wonder how a for-profit firm such as JustKid Inc. gets permission from school boards, administrators, and teachers to administer its surveys. One answer is that schools are given money to participate. Researchers were reluctant to go on the record about how much they pay, but one admitted that her firm pays schools "generously"—about a thousand dollars for each study it conducts. In these days of squeezed school budgets, that's not a trifling sum. Interestingly, many schools don't care about who the clients sponsoring the survey are, and they're willing to allow surveys for for-profit companies. But some schools do care, and in those cases, researchers use an insidious strategy to entice school officials—the lure of a "good cause."

One company conducting in-school surveys was founded by a genial and highly skilled man named Michael Cohen. Formerly called Applied Research and Consulting and now renamed the Michael Cohen Group, this firm has done socially valuable work; for example, it was involved in an extensive survey of trauma among New York City children after September 11. At the same time, that good work provides the entrée for his activities on behalf of companies that aren't in the business of doing good work for kids but making money off them. Cohen worked for many years at Public Broadcasting on the *Sesame Street* program. Sesame Workshop is a prime example of a wholesome halo company that has been widely respected by school administrators and teachers. While at PBS, Cohen developed many contacts around New York and an impressive reservoir of trust and credibility that has paid off in tremendous access to schools. He now puts that access to work for the for-profit clients by pairing up nonprofit and for-profit companies in one survey instrument. He approaches a school with a worthy research subject, the one the nonprofit is interested in. It's noncommercial and oriented to kids' welfare, something a principal could justify devoting class time to, especially when monetary compensation is attached. With the socially worthy topic taking the lead, the interests of the commercial client or clients are kept in the background. Questions on particular brands or spending habits are buried in the back of the survey, attracting less notice. According to Cohen, school officials are typically not too concerned about the consumer and brand aspects of the surveys, so discreetly including those questions has not been too difficult. He says the flashpoints are topics they think parents may be angry about, such as queries about the quality of parenting. Surprisingly, although many schools ask to see copies of the surveys in advance, not all do. This gives researchers tremendous latitude and suggests that many principals are asleep at the switch. So too are school boards that are sanctioning the use of valuable classroom time for market research with no educational value. These practices are a costly subsidy from the taxpayers who fund the schools to the private companies that are reaping the benefits of the research.

Ethical Lapses

The proliferation of new research methods poses a variety of ethical issues, many of which have not been seriously thought through or dealt with. This is not to say that there are no standards or protocols. In focus groups, parental permission through a signed form is standard for children under the age of thirteen. Permission forms from both kids and parents are the norm for the thirteen-to-seventeen age group. Of course, not all firms adhere to these guidelines, and asking parental permission does not ensure that children are protected. Parents have a financial incentive to use their kids in these ways and have the right to force them to participate even if they'd prefer not to. And even if the children enjoy it, one has to ask whether it's really in their interest. Watching the bedraggled crowd at one focus group site as the evening (a school night) wore on, I wondered why this phenomenon has stayed out of public view. We don't let eleven year olds staff fast food joints at 8:30 on weeknights. Why hasn't there been any discussion of their work at the local focus group facility?

Permissions are also typically used only in certain circumstances. For videotaping and observation in retail stores or other public places, permissions are not obtained. Some in-home researchers reported that they don't use permission forms at all. If they're taping, they will let the subjects know, but that's about it. They don't even ask for videotape release forms. In school situations, what's called passive consent is often used, in which parents must inform the school that they do not want their child to participate in a research exercise or survey. If they fail to do so, their consent will be assumed. This method does not ensure that the parent has actually received and read the notice that went home and is willing to allow his or her child to participate.

Ethical issues go far beyond permission slips. One of the most troubling practices is the lack of control over what happens to videotapes once they are shot. Although the vast majority of the hours and hours of tapes that are currently being produced never see the light of day, tapes have begun appearing beyond the confines of the conference room. They are shown to clients and have become a staple at industry conferences and presentations. When subjects sign release forms, they have little idea about how those tapes may be used. Some researchers destroy tapes when a project is finished, but not all do. As one marketer noted: "I remember giving them waivers, and the people who are facilitating are like, 'You know what? We just need you to sign this. Don't worry, you're not going to turn on the TV and find yourself there. We'll be showing you in conference rooms.' The other thing is they're getting hundreds of dollars, so they kind of get over it."

Most researchers have not thought seriously about the complex issues raised when people's everyday and private lives are taped and shown widely. Rita Denny is one of the few who has. Denny has a personal rule of thumb she uses when doing videotaping. She tries to figure out whether there's anything in the tape that would leave the subject vulnerable to any type of exploitation. If there is, she won't allow the tape to be shown to others. For example, she felt that some of the scenes she recorded in the drug study crossed the privacy boundary and decided not to give the tapes to the Office of Drug Control. When she wanted to show clips from the footage at an academic conference, she obtained an additional round of permissions from the interviewees.

Denny and her colleagues stand out partly because they were educated in academic institutions where ethics are part of graduate training and where all research projects involving human subjects must be approved through institutional review boards with strict and well-defined guidelines. As an anthropologist, Denny has had extensive exposure to the thorny issues of privacy, confidentiality, and the myriad ways one might think about consent. Anthropology is a field where accusations of exploitation have been raised repeatedly, so researchers with training in it are especially sensitive to these concerns. But her sensitivity is in stark contrast to the lack of training of most market researchers. The majority have no graduate education and have never had to submit their proposals to institutional review boards. The ethical guidelines they work with are minimal and have not been formulated in a serious manner.

The research practices I studied raise other issues as well. In-store studies are typically carried out without the permission of store personnel, who may not be keen on allowing taping or other data-gathering in their aisles. In the Strottman hidden camera supermarket study, the researchers went into some of the stores without permission. Ron Coughlin explained that "stores can be pretty nasty about it, if an adult were in there." He hopes that with kids, store managers will be less likely to have a harsh response. But if the gamble didn't pay off and a manager decided to call security personnel or the police, the child might have been in for a rough experience. That's not something that they're warned about when they sign a permission slip. Furthermore, the widespread practice of doing in-store research without prior permission ignores the privacy of other customers in the store, who may be taped and have their behavior analyzed without their knowledge. That's one reason store managers are reluctant to allow such taping.

I encountered other troubling aspects of the research process, such as the use of one child to recruit others. In these cases, full disclosure to both children and parents is much harder to ensure. The researcher cannot be certain about how a situation is being described and the preconceptions friends are coming with. The recruiting child also has a financial incentive to get others to participate, which raises the potential for exploitation. Furthermore, in many cases, there are no attempts to get informed consent from participants. For the in-home slumber parties organized by the Girls Intelligence Agency, host parents are required to sign a permission slip, but none of the guests or their parents are. There is no mechanism to check that they have been apprised of what is going to occur. The guests and their parents may not know what products will be discussed, which television shows or films will be shown, and what types of subjects will be raised. It's even possible that invited girls and their parents are unaware these are marketing events.

Parental surrogates such as athletic coaches, clergy, and community workers have also been drawn into commercial research efforts and typically operate without prior approval by parents. These practices tend to be concentrated in inner-city areas, which are prime locales for trend spotting and cool-hunting. Firms give shoes, clothes, and other products with instructions to the coach or clergy to elicit the kids' opinions on the products. The kids and parents may have no prior knowledge of what's being planned, with no chance to opt out. The parents may be left with a new and expensive consumer demand on their hands, without the means or inclination for satisfying it.

Another ethical issue is the question of who is benefiting financially from the information being elicited from children. At the moment, the gain is accruing almost solely to the client companies and research agencies. The sums given to children are extremely small in comparison to the value of the information. When a couple of kids in Chicago gave Doyle Research the idea for a squeeze bottle for Heinz ketchup, the company made millions on it. The kids got the standard fee. Microsoft gives kids the chance to contribute ideas that may be worth billions. But the software giant is quite clear that the kids won't get a cent from those revenues. Josh Koplewicz may have been happy with his five dollars an hour; Levi Strauss was laughing all the way to the bank. Nike has it even better. When it goes "bro-ing," it has gotten away with paying nothing at all. It's a form of financial exploitation we tolerate because it's kids, rather than adults, whose ideas, creativity, and labor are being shortchanged.

CHAPTER SEVEN

Habit Formation

Selling Kids on Junk Food, Drugs, and Violence

> I think there are some [products] out there that are downright offensive and disgusting, that just offend me with what pure unadulterated, unapologetic crap they are. But we have products to sell and money to be made and there's definitely a market for these things.
>
> —Amanda Carlson, former food marketer

Without a doubt, 2002 was an annus horribilus for one segment of the children's marketplace—the packaged goods, soft drink, and fast food purveyors increasingly known by the moniker "Big Food." Just before the year began, the surgeon general issued a report, to great media fanfare, that obesity had reached epidemic levels. In Massachusetts, new data showed that one-third of all low- and middle-income children aged two to five were already overweight. Media accounts pointed the finger at supersized portions, high-calorie fast foods, and snacks. These were logical targets, given that a supersized Extra Value Meal had risen to 1,550 calories, three times the McDonald's meals of the 1950s.

Lawyers who had successfully taken on Big Tobacco declared that junk food was next and filed the first of what is likely to be a long series of lawsuits addressing deceptive marketing, failure to label, and the addictiveness of high-fat, high-sodium, high-sugar foods. In June, the United Nations convened a widely publicized emergency meeting to discuss new evidence linking french fries and cancer. And books on food gained a wide readership. Eric Schlosser's *Fast Food Nation* continued to sit atop best-seller lists, amid speculation that the book was contributing to McDonald's domestic woes. Marion Nestle's *Food Politics* revealed the enormous political clout wielded by Big Food in its attempts to dominate

Americans' food choices and habits. At year's end, *Fat Land* hit the shelves with more bad press for the industry. The first half of 2003 proved to be even worse, with a torrent of publicity on soft drink marketing in schools and other industry practices. By the summer of 2003, more than thirty state legislatures were considering bills that would require fast food labeling or restrictions on junk food sales in schools.

The Scope and Scale of Food Advertising

Processed food is at the center of children's consumer culture. Sex and violence have received more headlines, but food and beverages account for the bulk of advertising dollars and are the most frequently advertised product categories. Kids are treated to a steady diet of enticements for sugary food, fatty food, salty snacks, fast food, and solid and "liquid candy" (a.k.a. soft drinks). A 1999 content study by Margaret Gamble and Nancy Cotugna of the University of Delaware found that among the 353 ads shown on Saturday morning children's television, 63 percent were for food products. And those foods weren't broccoli. In fact, after surveying twenty-five years of Saturday morning food advertising, and nearly 1,400 food ads from 1972, 1976, 1987, 1994, and 1997, the authors reported that with the exclusion of some public service announcements, "there have been no food advertisements for fruits and vegetables . . . in the past 25 years." Furthermore, this study found that the nutritional content of advertised products is getting worse. Among cereal ads, which made up almost 40 percent of the total, the proportion in the high-sugar category increased between 1991 and 1996. Other research has found that 20 percent of all fast food restaurant advertising includes reference to a toy premium.

While much of the research has been on after-school and Saturday morning, children are increasingly watching prime-time television, which now accounts for the larger portion of children's television viewing time. A 1998 content analysis of television ads during the top-ranked prime-time network shows watched by children aged two to eleven found that food accounts for 23 percent of all ads and that 40 percent of those were for fast food items. Analysis of the nutritional content of the advertised items found that they deviated sharply from recommended guidelines in the U.S. Department of Agriculture's food pyramid. Excluding fast food ads (which fit into a number of categories), the study found that 41 percent of the foods fell into the fats, oils, and sweets category. A similar percentage were in the grains category (bread, cereal, rice, and pasta), and about half of these products were high in either fat or sugar. The authors concluded that "the diet advertised on prime-time television is indeed the antithesis of the recommended diet."

Other venues, such as print ads, movies, and the Internet, exhibit similar patterns. An accounting from the May 2002 issue of *Nickelodeon* magazine, the most popular kids' magazine in the country, found that of its twenty-four ad pages, eighteen and a half were for junk foods. Five and a half were for candy and gum, and the remaining thirteen were devoted to products such as Pop Tarts, Tang, Jell-O Sticks, and sugary cereals. This breakdown is typical. The Pepsi-Cola company, which claims not to advertise caffeine drinks to kids under age thirteen, had a two-page Pepsi spread in the August 2001 *Nickelodeon* issue complete with a stick-on label for kids to personalize their can. (Nickelodeon's target audience is six to fourteen year olds.) Junk food placements are also common in programs and movies. The most extreme example may be *Foodfight!,* a feature-length movie created to hawk candy and junk foods, complete with characters such as Twinkie the Kid and Mr. Pringle. Foods appearing in the movie include branded candies (M&M's, Skittles, Tootsie Rolls), Coke, RC Cola, sweet and salty snacks (Cheetos), syrups, cakes, and sugared cereals.

Food advertising pervades children's Internet sites. Online games are created around food products to keep kids interacting with brand logos for extended periods of time. Many kids' sites contain junk food advertising or links to the major food brands. Nick.com is currently featuring Hostess's Twinkie the Kid Surf and Skate Challenge. Nabisco's site features a variety of games such as the Super Snack 500, a racing game with a car festooned with cookies and cracker logos; the Bull's Eye Saloon, where the challenge is to throw darts at various snack products; and the Chip Blaster, in which the object is to shoot chocolate chips into Chips Ahoy cookies. The McDonald's site has coloring books and games, with a small warning at the top of the screen, "Hey kids, this is advertising." Hershey's site features its Kidztown. Food dominates in-school advertising, with examples such as Channel One, sponsored curricula from fast food and grain-based companies, incentive programs, and vending machine ads. Nationwide, schools are reported to receive $750 million a year in marketing dollars from snack and processed food companies.

The food industry is estimated to spend $33 billion a year in direct advertising to promote its products, and increasingly those dollars are targeted to children. Seventy percent of the dollars are for convenience foods, candy and snacks, alcoholic beverages, soft drinks, and desserts.

Fruits, vegetables, grains, and beans comprise only 2.2 percent. McDonald's, the world's largest fast food restaurant chain, reportedly spends $500 million a year on ads, of which approximately 40 percent is targeted to children. A 1998 study by Campbell Mithun Esty found that food items dominate kids' favorite ads. Of the ten most popular ads that year, five were for junk foods (Pepsi, Coke, Snickers, McDonald's, and Hostess) in addition to the perennial favorite: Budweiser.

Confessions of a Former Food Marketer

In late 2002, I met Amanda Carlson, who had just left a position at one of the world's top advertising firms, whose substantial kid business is heavily centered on Big Food. Carlson is a smart, lively, and hip young executive who had an almost meteoric rise at her agency as a specialist in youth marketing when such expertise was greatly in demand. Although she is still engaged in the children's side of the business, her exodus from food has made her less defensive about how the industry encourages kids to eat junk food than many of the people I encountered. She was willing to talk freely about her own feelings as a food marketer and how manufacturers and advertisers are responding to their critics.

In some ways, the foodspace, to use an industry term, hews closely to the model of timeless needs I outlined in Chapter 3. Themes of kid empowerment and antiadultism are used to sell ostensibly mundane items such as snacks and cereal. Carlson described the agency's approach for one sugary snack: "It's empowering because it's a snack that's really very kid-proprietary, it's not for adults . . . sometimes it's licensed so it has shapes that only kids would like. There's also an element of separation in there because it separates me from you: This is my snack. It's a little irreverent. It's something your mom might not want you eating, so that gives you power."

Dual messaging is also common in food marketing. Ads directed at kids try to hook them on the fact that it's a high-energy fun food; mother-directed messages emphasize that the product is vitamin fortified or oat based. This two-pronged strategy has been successful in cereal, beverages, and snacks. Trans-toying, or the transformation of ordinary products into play objects, is more prevalent in food than any other category. Child development expert Diane Levin dubbed it "eater-tainment." In a brilliant example of trans-toying, Kentucky Fried Chicken offered kids a meal inside a computer laptop package.

But the foodspace also has unique dimensions. One distinction is the enormous efforts devoted to product innovation, in the form of adding and subtracting ingredients and changing features and colors. In cereals, a popular trend has been to add candy and other sweets. Examples include Post's Oreo O's, Reese's Peanut Butter Puffs, and Mickey's Magix—a collaboration between Kellogg's and Disney that contains colored Mickey Marshmallows and pixie dust that turns the milk blue. Heinz created green and then mystery color ketchup. Parkay sells blue margarine. There's also General Mills Glow in the Dark Yogurt and Kraft's Blue's Clues macaroni and cheese with eight pasta shapes and blue paw prints. Carlson worries that the process of innovation has careened out of control: "I think people might be going crazy. People were trying to invent peanut butter that has popping things in it, that makes you do better in school and gives you energy."

Carlson agrees that a competitive process is at work. "Particularly now, with marketing and media being so prevalent, so much more than it was before. It has to impact what kids are thinking and we have to keep—I don't want to say upping the ante, because I don't think that's fair. I do think kids do require more stimulation now because they're so used to it and because they're so savvy, they're less easily impressed." But she believes the companies could go in another direction: "I don't know that we have to keep getting more and more extreme, and the flavors have to go more sour or the games have to be more violent, or anything like that." In her view, it's partly a failure of imagination. "I feel like people are running out of ideas." At the same time, kids are expecting more. One anecdote, recounted at KidPower 2002, had a mother offering her child a package of licorice and the kid replying, "What's it do?"

The trend in product innovation has been to increase calories, and especially sugar content. This is now virtually textbook strategy. I witnessed a case involving a company that had almost no presence in children's food and had hired a kid-oriented consulting firm to help it establish one. The targeted meal was breakfast. One of the consultants gravitated quickly to the idea of satisfying children's cravings, offering slogans such as "Get the crave," "Need the crave." The crave, of course, was for sugar. The company had already mapped out the range of types of food consumed at breakfast, and the consultants immediately identified the "indulgent" or sweet breakfast as the way to break into the kid market, with product innovations that involved adding sugar.

Sugar has also become enmeshed in a complex interaction between cultural meanings and marketing messages. This dynamic was revealed to me during a series of tween focus groups for a sugared beverage. With one group of boys, what began as an unremarkable conversation about the after-school "snack opportunity" became very spirited as they started discussing sugar, hyperactivity, and energy. They were keenly aware of the effect of these drinks on their metabolism. "I wanna get hyper!" "I wanna bounce off the walls when I get home." They also made the link between hyperactivity and caffeine. "I want Coke, 'cause it has caffeine!" "Yeah. Yeah." Sugar- and caffeine-induced hyperactivity has become a highly desired state. While the children repeatedly articulated a desire to be "healthy," their understanding of what that meant was rudimentary at best. Water, the most healthful alternative to sugared drinks, never arose. Milk, which has been marketed as a nutritious option, was absent from the conversation. The choices in the world of Big Beverage are between carbonated and noncarbonated, grape and cherry, caffeine and noncaffeine.

While adult attempts to clamp down on hyperactivity by kids may be part of what attracts kids to that state, there has also been a concerted campaign by soft drink companies to create a buzz around high energy and hyper. Pepsi's Mountain Dew, with its Code Red brand, has risen like a Phoenix from the ashes of rural America to become a hot youth drink. Its themes of extreme sports, extreme activity, and extreme cool communicate that this drink is about excess. What's behind the code is the fact that this and copycat brands have more sugar and caffeine than other soft drinks.

Looking at the bigger picture of food marketing to children and teens reveals that the companies are skirting dangerously close to a subtle association with drugs. Caffeine is recognized as a drug with addictive properties, and messages that stress its ability to give energy or "jolt" the consumer are straightforward. There are similarities with sugar. While the current social understanding is that it's a food rather than a drug, this has not always been the case. In the past, sugar has been considered addictive. In eighteenth-century Ireland, for example, working-class mothers who started buying sugar for their tea were publicly criticized in a discourse reminiscent of that which raged around crack-addicted American mothers in the 1980s. They were accused of taking needed household income to feed their sugar addictions, neglecting their children, and ruining their families because they were caught in the grip of this powerful, dangerous substance. Today, researchers are investigating the habituating properties of sugar. A Princeton research program has found that rats fed high-sugar diets produce excessive amounts of opioids, a pleasurable brain chemical also stimulated with drug use, and that when they are taken off the sugar, they show clear signs of withdrawal. While addictiveness has not yet been conclusively shown in the literature, sugar dependence has been.

In 2003, information emerged that food companies know more about this than they've been letting on. The *London Telegraph* reported that "scientists working for Nestlé and Unilever have been quietly investigating how certain foods, such as chocolate biscuits, burgers and snacks, make people binge-eat, thereby fuelling obesity." The fast food industry is also reported to have done work on humans, testing to see whether its products trigger overeating. One theory is that the combination of fat and carbohydrates present in many processed foods is especially potent in creating opioids, which reduce feelings of satiation and lead some people to want to eat more. According to one industry scientist, quoted in the *Telegraph,* "We have created a bio-chemical Monster."

If the idea of food as drugs sounds far-fetched, consider the findings of Wynne Tyree, director of research at JustKid Inc.: "Kids say they use sugar like adults use coffee—to give them a boost. Since coffee isn't allowed, and they have no other means to 'get them going' or 'give them energy,' they use soda, chocolate, candy and sugary fruit drinks. It gives them the jolts they say they need throughout the day." Tyree reports that this has come up many times in her research for a variety of food brands and categories. Consider the marketing of Cheetos. The company likens its product to an addictive drug and warns that consuming it leads to "signs of cheese-crazed behavior" and becoming "officially hooked." The only cure: "A never-ending supply of that cheesy crunch you crave." The message to kids is that these products help them stay awake, provide energy, and keep them going so that they can do sports, hang out with friends, and be cool. These themes are shared with the marketing of drugs such as caffeine, alcohol, tobacco, and some dietary supplements.

Decades of studies show that food marketing to children is effective. In the 1970s, Marvin Goldberg studied differences between children who saw and did not see television advertising and found that sugared cereals were more likely to be present in the homes of the former. H. L. Taras and colleagues found that for children aged three to eight, weekly television viewing time is significantly correlated with requests for specified advertised products as well as overall caloric intake. More recently, Dina Borzekowski and Thomas Robinson's research on low-income preschoolers found that even brief exposure to ads led the children to choose advertised food products more often. And a study of fourth and fifth graders found that more television viewing is related to poor nutritional habits, even controlling for social and other factors. These results accord with parental experience. According to one industry poll, parents report that television ads are the most important factor influencing their children's desire for foods and brand recognition of foods. Eighty-one percent of parents feel that there is too much food marketing, compared to only 14 percent who think current levels are fine. Parents are also critical of the nutritional content of kids' food. Thirty-nine percent rate it as "fair," 28 percent consider it "poor," and 26 percent of parents say it's "horrific."

Food advertising is contributing to major changes in eating habits. Snacking among children has increased markedly over the past two decades, and the fraction of calories that comes from snacks, rather than meals, has risen by 30 percent. Snacks tend to be of nutritionally poorer quality than meals, and this trend has contributed to the dramatic deterioration of children's diets I reported in Chapter 2. Marketing has also boosted sugar consumption, especially through soft drinks. Pepsi has even licensed its logo on infant bottles. The roughly 45 grams of added sugar in each drink is about the total daily recommended limit for added sugar, leaving no room for cereals, pizza, cookies, snacks, candy, bread, or any other foods with added sugar. The fraction of calories consumed outside the home, with their higher fat and sugar content, has also risen markedly, to about a third of the total. By the mid-1990s, fast food comprised 10 percent of kids' daily caloric intake, up from 2 percent twenty years earlier.

Over time, these developments took their toll on Carlson's feelings about marketing food. "We'd leave a meeting, I don't know, I'd feel icky . . . I don't want to sell [sugary cereal—brand omitted] anymore." She saw the writing on the wall for the grain-based companies her agency served. "I really think it's on its way down. I feel like there's going to have to be a backlash." Concerned about her conscience and her career, she preferred to work on products she could feel good about. Others I interviewed expressed similar misgivings. One researcher recalled working for Duncan Hines and receiving a carton of its Dunkaroos product as a gift. Not only did she not want her children eating them, she confessed, but she considered the product so offensive she didn't even want it in the house. She dumped the box at her synagogue.

From Faux Food to Political Hardball— The Companies Fight Back

The industry insiders I asked reported that their clients are worried. They've also started to act, after years of ignoring the obvious failings of their products and questions about their marketing strategies. So far they've chosen to replicate the sophisticated, multipronged strategy employed by Big Tobacco after its products came under scrutiny. Of course, Philip Morris owns Kraft and Nabisco, and R. J. Reynolds is the former owner of Nabisco. The tobacco strategy had a number of elements: phony product alteration (such as low-tar variants), denial of the causal role of tobacco in cancer, massive campaign donations to prevent legislative action, PR touting consumer choice and individual responsibility, and corporate philanthropy. Big Food is already deep into the same modus operandi, with the introduction of more faux substances and small content adjustments, a public relations strategy built on denying the link between food and fat, campaign donations, attacks on children's health advocates, and gifts to nonprofit organizations. They're active on many fronts, but they are failing miserably at what is ultimately a simple task: the production of healthful food.

The product innovation is at an early stage; however, adjustments thus far appear to be marginal. McDonald's has announced a shift to a less unhealthful, but no less caloric, oil for its fries. Frito-Lay reported that it will reclassify some of its products from "snacks" to "indulgent snacks." Kraft gained the bulk of the headlines in 2003 with a major announcement that it would reduce fat, sugar, and portion sizes for some of its products, as well as cease its multimillion-dollar in-school marketing efforts. But the headlines may have suggested more than the company intends. Spokesman Michael Mudd promised that "we're not going to do anything radical. This is about making small, incremental changes."

The history of health-induced product alteration does not provide a basis for optimism. Low-fat variants were created by adding sugar, and low-sugar options involve adding potentially dangerous chemicals. The *New York Times* reported in late August 2003 that Kraft and other Big Food companies are interested in AMP, a recently patented compound that blocks bitter taste. Amanda Carlson discussed her frustrations with this mentality: "The part that always bothered me was that the solution was always in fortification or some kind of food science, where they construct some faux substance that would lower the fat or lower the sugar or whatever. That just seemed wrong. I mean, you're replacing something that's going to make you fat with something that's going to give you cancer or whatever. I know that's dramatic, but I think that was the way they're looking at it. . . . One of my soapboxes when I was working on food was we need a healthy alternative to the healthy alternatives. A Nutrigrain bar, there's nothing healthy about that. But that's supposed to be a healthy alternative because it's got fruit and grain in it. But it's packed with sugar."

Meanwhile, Kraft has reassured investors with promises to continue focusing on fast-growing sectors such as snacks; to step up marketing to African Americans and Hispanics, two groups with especially high rates of overweight; and to "aggressively" pursue growth in overseas markets. Big Tobacco is carrying out a strikingly similar program.

The second leg of the strategy is public relations to deflect attention from the products themselves and the influence of advertising. One refrain is that the relationship between calories, fat, carbs, and obesity is complex and depends on individual factors. This is similar to the tobacco industry's claim that it's personal risk factors, rather than smoking, that causes cancer. It's a bogus argument. Although it's true that individual metabolisms matter, so too does caloric intake and nutritional quality. A key element of the deflection strategy has been to emphasize inactivity and lack of exercise, rather than food, as the causes of obesity. Coca-Cola has distributed step-counting pedometers in schools, and Pepsi has founded the PepsiCo/Cooper Aerobics Center with fitness guru Dr. Kenneth Cooper. However, research from Harvard's Children's Hospital suggests that soft drinks are especially problematic when it comes to weight gain, because children do not compensate for the extra calories by cutting down on other foods. Calories consumed through the drinks increase the daily total. This two-year study of eleven and twelve year olds, which controlled for exercise, other food intake, and media viewing, discovered that each additional soft drink consumed per day increased the likelihood of a child's becoming obese by 60 percent. Consumption of soft drinks by kids has almost doubled in the past ten years, according to the study's author, Dr. David Ludwig. Estimates now suggest that more than half of the average American child's daily calories come from sodas, juices, and other high-calorie drinks.

In early 2003, responding to the barrage of adverse publicity, Coca-Cola signed a million-dollar agreement with the American Academy of Pediatric Dentistry to promote "education and research." The arrangement was immediately criticized on grounds that it constituted a conflict of interest, but opposition was muted partly because some academic pediatric dentists were forbidden by their universities to comment on the arrangement. Later in the year, Coke scored a bigger coup. A gift of an undisclosed amount to the National Parent Teacher Association yielded Coke's being named as a PTA sponsor and John H. Downs, Jr., Coke's top lobbyist, being named to the organization's board of directors.

The Bush administration has sided squarely with Big Food against its critics. Secretary of Health and Human Services Tommy Thompson got public attention when he spoke out against obesity, but behind closed doors, he urged members of the Grocery Manufacturers Association to "go on the offensive" against their critics. Part of that offensive has been to downplay the connection between food and obesity, defining the problem as inadequate exercise. The administration engineered a taxpayer giveaway for a lifestyles ad campaign called VERB, run by a private-public partnership between HHS, the Centers for Disease Control, and what Commercial Alert's Gary Ruskin has dubbed the "obesity lobby." The money goes to companies that are heavily involved in marketing junk foods, such as the advertising agencies that work for McDonald's and media giants that rely on food advertising revenues. Channel One, with its high volume of candy, soft drink, and snack ads, received $2.8 million in government funds in the first year. The majority owner of Primedia, the parent company of Channel One, is Kohlberg Kravis Roberts, whose Henry Kravis gave $250,000 to the Republican party in April 2002, just months before the program was announced. The VERB campaign itself is so confusing and devoid of content that I've wondered whether it's an intentional failure. Other critics have noted the cyberlinks between its Web site and junk food advertising.

The restaurant and beverage companies have also founded a political front group, the Center for Consumer Freedom, which espouses extreme right-wing views. The center ran print and radio advertising ridiculing the public health agenda and the scientists and medical professionals who are trying to help Americans achieve healthier eating habits. It has targeted the Center for Science in the Public Interest, which has been effective in raising these issues publicly. Big Food is giving millions of dollars to Republican and Democrat candidates and their parties. Industry has also tried to suppress information it fears will be damaging. In late 2003, the Sugar Association tried to prevent publication of a World Health Organization report on obesity, and threatened lobbying to block WHO funding if the report was not changed. Some months later, the Bush administration secretly tried to derail a WHO antiobesity initiative, denying the link between weight gain and junk food, fast food, and soda consumption, and objecting that the WHO has identified certain "bad" foods. The administration's document also questioned the scientific basis linking "fruit and vegetable consumption to decreased risk of obesity."

In the end, the industry claims sound hollow. When confronted with the epidemic of childhood obesity and their role in it, McDonald's and its advertisers say their product should be part of a healthy, balanced diet. But with an actual marketing goal of twenty visits per customer per month, company actions speak louder than words.

Who's Responsible, Parents or Advertisers?

The industry line is that responsibility for children's eating habits lies squarely with parents and that skyrocketing obesity is due to parental abdication. Amanda Carlson articulated a common view: "Your parents aren't home after school for the most part. . . . Kids can eat whatever they want. They open up the fridge. . . . It could be last night's dinner. It can be another full meal. No one's going to stop them. And they just sit around and eat."

Although there may be something to this "home alone" theory of obesity, it's only a small part of the story. First, it's not relevant to younger children and to the majority of school-aged children, who are in fact supervised by adults after school. It also conveniently ignores the provision of junk food inside schools. And it fails to confront some of the glaring hypocrisies in the industry position. For example, the corporations say that proper nutrition is the responsibility of the consumer, but they are currently fighting, and have historically fought, the food labeling necessary for informed consumer choices. Their opposition to the WHO report on kids and obesity is partly because it talks about labeling. They promote education but have subverted government attempts to provide unbiased nutrition information. Industry pressure on the USDA to revise its food pyramid stands out mainly because it was widely written about in the media. Analyses of what's being taught in the flood of nutrition curricula created by the nation's candy, beverage, and fast food companies suggest it's biased, inadequate, and self-serving.

A second industry theme is that parents can "just say no." Paul Kurnit takes the view that "if you don't want your child to eat pre-sweetened cereals, don't buy them. If you don't want your child to eat at McDonald's, don't take your kid to McDonald's. I mean, on some level it is truly that simple." Carlson concurs: "They [the parents] should set the guidelines. They should set precedents. They should be good examples, which they're not, in terms of how to eat healthfully."

A careful look at industry practices suggests things aren't as simple as Kurnit and others claim. The soft drink companies have demanded exclusive access in schools. The chains dominate highway rest stops, airports, malls, and other public places, so fast or junk food is usually all that's available. Agriculture and food lobbies have pushed through food disparagement laws in twelve states where they're politically powerful. (These laws make certain statements about food products illegal.) Oprah

Winfrey was sued by a group of Texas cattlemen under their "veggie libel law" after she did a show on mad cow disease. Biotech giant Monsanto has been suing small dairies that inform consumers that their milk is produced without bovine growth hormone. The company has been vigilant in its attempts to oppose labeling, and for good reason. Since 1994, when Monsanto's recombinant BGH was approved, it has been outlawed in every other industrialized country and has been linked to premature puberty and cancer.

These are blatant attempts to curb free speech and restrict consumer choices. Advertisers are also engaged in a subtle and duplicitous effort that parents and the public are less aware of. It's a strategy developed partly through the intrusive research they've conducted inside American kitchens that involves the companies' attempts to break down parental opposition to marketed foods. Amanda Carlson recounted the results of one in-home study: "The kid opened the pantry and I saw that the Oreos were at kid level. The box was totally open. . . . There was a mom who was standing there baking cookies saying, 'I want my kids to have something good and healthy.' She was taking out a stick of butter and the sugar. But to her, because it was wholesome and from her, that was a perception of healthy. . . . There were incredibly rich insights in there. . . . It's one thing to have the Oreos, but to have such clearly unlimited access . . ." There were two marketable "take-aways" from that ethnographic encounter. First, the agency learned that it could promote open access even for a product as sugary as Oreo cookies. And second, the deeply symbolic and contradictory nature of mothers' views about nutrition was reinforced. For many parents, the symbolism is more about intention than actual ingredients. Baking from scratch is nutritious because love is wholesome. Food has deep subconscious associations for people, and marketers are figuring out how to capitalize on those. On the basis of this and other research, Carlson ended up arguing that former taboos such as promoting open access for a cookie product were no longer valid and that her company could profit from breaking down mothers' resistance.

This type of research has also helped advertisers figure out ways to exploit parents' desires for healthful food for their children. Carlson explained that the marketers are "using words like *health . . . wholesome.* Teddy Grahams are probably wholesome. . . . You have the goodness of graham. . . . There's definitely a halo. I mean, parents will look at Lucky Charms and say, 'Well, it's oats.' They look at Go-gurt that has twelve grams of sugar and say, 'Well, it's yogurt. It's got that bacteria in it that's good for you.'" Taking advantage of these emotional contradictions has contributed to a pervasive loosening of parental rules around food. Faced with the barrage of food advertisement, too few parents have been able to hold their ground.

Parental resignation on food is also occurring because parents feel assaulted on so many other fronts. Carlson believes that parents "are fighting forces like their kids want to have it, their kids are driving them crazy. They have to go to work. They're more worried about their kid going to school and smoking pot than what they're drinking. And it's like . . . if this is going to shut you up and make you happy . . ." Johann Wachs feels that "today's parents don't have the time or the energy. They pick their battles extremely carefully and they decide what is really worth fighting over." Some of the parents I interviewed articulated similar sentiments. Food is a tough battle in the midst of other influences that seem more immediate and pernicious. One mother, who is simultaneously trying to rein in wrestling, inappropriate lyrics, excessive Gameboy time, television, and junk food, explained: "You can't fight every fight. So food's the one that lost."

Tobacco, Alcohol, and Drug Marketing

One reason parents have so much to contend with is that alcohol and tobacco companies continue to advertise to young people. Even after the tobacco settlement, FTC criticism of alcohol advertising practices, and strong evidence of underage consumption, the manufacturing corporations, in collaboration with the media companies, continue to expose kids to their ads. They're well aware that their futures depend on turning today's children into tomorrow's customers.

The companies say they aren't specifically targeting youth, but intentions are hard to measure. In any case, the fact that ads for beer, alcohol, tobacco, and drugs proliferate in venues that attract large numbers of children is more important than the companies' stated intentions. NFL games feature a steady parade of beer ads, as do Major League Baseball broadcasts and car racing. If you take a kid to a live sporting event, there's a good chance he or she will see tobacco, as well as drug and alcohol advertising. Television and movies expose kids to high levels of covert advertising, because the vast majority of programming contains smoking and alcohol use.

In late 2002, a study by the Center on Alcohol Marketing and Youth

uncovered evidence to show that kids are not only viewing large numbers of alcohol ads, they're often more likely to see certain ads than adults, the companies' ostensible targets. Over the study period, a quarter of the advertising time purchased by alcohol companies was scheduled for programming that was more likely to be seen by youngsters than by adults. The companies are in clear violation of the voluntary guidelines they agreed to not to air ads when underage viewers comprise more than half the audience (the so-called 50 percent rule).

But even if the companies were in compliance, the guideline is ineffective. Underage youth, defined as those aged twelve to twenty, comprise just 15 percent of the population, and only about 1 percent of the 14,359 cable and network programs surveyed by Nielsen Media Research are excluded under the 50 percent rule. Furthermore, many youth watch adult programming, a conclusion confirmed by the finding that in 2001, 89 percent of youth were exposed to alcohol advertising. Networks on which beer and alcohol are advertised most heavily are among those most favored by teens and children—ESPN, Comedy Central, and BET. Alcohol ads are also very common in popular youth magazines such as *Rolling Stone, Glamour, InStyle, Car and Driver,* and *Sports Illustrated.*

While much of the policy discussion has been about the twelve-and-over group, analysis of some of the ads suggests they're appealing to even younger children. The Budweiser brand has made heavy use of cute animal characters, such as the dog Spuds MacKenzie and the clever talking frogs and lizards campaign. Kids love animals, and they especially love Bud's creations. A 1998 survey done by Kidcom, the children's marketing arm of Campbell Mithun Esty, found that the favorite commercial of kids aged six to seventeen was a Budweiser frog spot, with another Bud commercial coming in second. Bud's subsequent "Whassup" campaign also became the favorite ad for boys aged eight to twelve. In 1999, more ten to seventeen year olds recognized the Budweiser frogs and lizards (67 percent) and Joe Camel (69 percent) than knew the name of the vice president of the United States (62 percent). Beer companies such as Anheuser-Busch and Coors deny intentionally targeting kids, but they continue to overexpose kids in a variety of media outlets.

Children are also exposed to alcohol, tobacco, and illegal drugs in television programs, films, and music videos. A major content study found that alcohol and tobacco appeared in more than 90 percent of the 200 most popular films from 1996 and 1997 and illicit drugs appeared in 22 percent. Of the 669 major adult characters featured in the 200 movies, 5 percent used illicit drugs, 25 percent smoked tobacco, and 65 percent consumed

alcohol. Seventy-nine percent of G and PG films include tobacco use, and 76 percent include alcohol. A subsequent study of the 250 highest-grossing movies released in the late 1990s found that 85 percent of them showed tobacco use. In fact, smoking and alcohol use are more prevalent in film and television than they are in the real world. One reason is that the tobacco companies have historically spent money to put cigarettes in films, a practice that is now illegal. Brown and Williamson paid Sylvester Stallone half a million dollars in return for his smoking in five feature films. Lark cigarettes appeared in *License to Kill,* courtesy of a payment by Philip Morris. Notably, research conducted since the settlement has found an increase in depictions of tobacco use in movies, including a dramatic rise in PG-13-rated films, which now show more smoking than R-rated films. I asked a number of advertising executives whether tobacco companies are still paying actors to smoke on camera, and the opinions I received were mixed. But one statistic bears further investigation: 80 percent of the smoking found in movies involves the four most heavily advertised cigarette brands. Television also depicts addictive substances at high rates. In the most popular prime-time shows of the 1998–1999 season, illicit drug use was shown or mentioned in 20 percent of episodes. Tobacco appeared in 22 percent of episodes and alcohol in 77 percent. Rates for popular teen shows were nearly as high. While only 9 percent of the ads aired during popular prime time are explicitly for alcoholic beverages, alcohol use occurred in 60 percent of ads for other products that aired during the shows most watched by teens.

Many of these beer and malt beverage ads have insidious themes. Sexy babe ads are still with us, of course, in ads such as Coors' Twins spots for beer and football. A Coors ad from its Rock On campaign uses the slogan "Who Needs Sleep?" showing young people at rave parties. I guess the message is that they're using substances that make sleep unnecessary, and beer is the drink of choice to bring one down after the all-night party. Another spot, asking questions such as "Why do we party?" and "Why do we act like fools?" shows a wild and crazy party with women making suggestive tongue movements and half-naked guys with *Coors* written on their stomachs. Against such messaging, "Just say no" and "Parents: the antidrug" don't stand a chance.

The companies are also using street marketing campaigns, which inevitably reach the underaged. Sky Vodka hired Look-Look, a trends research firm founded by DeeDee Gordon, the subject of Malcolm Gladwell's widely read *New Yorker* profile, and the original "cool hunter." Look-Look conceived a campaign to propagate the urban myth that Sky

Vodka didn't cause hangovers. Sales among young people rose almost instantly. Other street marketing tactics used by alcohol companies include paint wraps on subway cars in metropolitan areas, postering, and T-shirt giveaways, all of which bring children into contact with the product.

Tobacco companies have continued to advertise to young people despite the 1998 tobacco settlement prohibition. The companies' print advertising to youth reached record levels after the settlement as they stepped up ads in youth magazines. They are pursuing other venues as well. In 2001, a group of child advocates and public health organizations requested an investigation into millions of Philip Morris textbook covers distributed in schools, which *Advertising Age* described as looking "alarmingly like a colorful pack of cigarettes." Knowledgeable advertisers I interviewed believe that Philip Morris's current "antismoking" ads are a sophisticated campaign to encourage smoking. The ads use the company name, raising the possibility that they are trying to build name recognition and a positive brand image.

Within the industry, a conspiracy of silence surrounds the de facto advertising of these products. In response to a question about underage viewing, one planner I interviewed confirmed his colleagues' denial: "It's like poverty or the homeless or inner-city difficulties . . . they don't want to hear about it because when you hear something like that, then that means you have to take some personal responsibility." The agencies continue to derive large streams of revenue from alcohol and tobacco companies, although tobacco work is now politely kept out of view. Posters of prized print ads for many products adorn the hallways of the agencies, but there are no tobacco examples. An embarrassing moment during my visit to one agency occurred when a cigarette commercial produced for use outside the United States popped up on a tape. The executives quickly switched to a less controversial product. I found only one agency that had a policy of refusing tobacco money, Arnold Advertising. It was earning millions producing antismoking advertising funded by the settlement and was therefore prohibited from taking on tobacco clients.

A considerable body of evidence shows that children and adolescents are more likely to smoke, drink, and use drugs when they're exposed to ads or programming depicting these products. A recent study of nearly 5,000 students in grades 5 through 8 by James Sargent of Dartmouth Medical School looked at the factors that lead kids to try a first cigarette. The most important variable affecting smoking was the amount of time spent watching Hollywood movies. This was true even after controlling for parental smoking and attitudes, personality traits, self-esteem, and propensity to take risks. This is a major finding because the study carefully controlled for other explanations and because it is the first population survey to test the link between movie viewing and smoking. It has broader importance as well, because tobacco is a gateway drug for illegal drug use.

Other studies show the effectiveness of media and advertising in promoting alcohol consumption. A major study just released by the National Bureau for Economic Research found that exposure to alcohol advertising substantially increases high school students' likelihood of drinking, and the effect is particularly strong for girls. (A follow-up by the same authors found similar effectiveness for tobacco advertising.) Similarly, watching music videos has been shown to raise alcohol intake. In a California study of ninth-grade students, Thomas Robinson found that each extra hour of MTV watched per day was associated with a 31 percent increased risk of starting to drink over the next eighteen months, controlling for a variety of factors. Overall television viewing also mattered. Each additional hour of television watched per day led to a 9 percent higher likelihood the student would start to drink during the following eighteen months.

Exposure to drug advertising has become a part of children's everyday lives. In addition to the illegal drugs that appear in films, television shows, and popular culture, advertising of prescription drugs has soared. Children see drug ads on television, at sporting events, and in other public spaces. Prescription drugs have also become a regular feature of school life, as nurses dispense them to kids. Tweens have intimate knowledge of many types of drugs; many know the differences between Prozac and Ritalin. The surge in drug ads is recent, so we don't know whether or how children's long-term desires for drugs will be affected by viewing these ads. Will they be more likely to use illegal drugs? Will they consume excessive levels of prescription drugs? We have entered uncharted territory.

Ads and direct marketing of performance-enhancing supplements have already become widespread, and athletes' use of legal and illegal supplements, such as steroids and hormones, has filtered down to the high school level. During my research, I heard predictions that advertising dollars for over-the-counter drugs and health and diet supplements may be on the verge of a substantial increase. Citing kids' concern with athletic performance, as well as how they look and feel, savvy marketers are beginning to see the potential in this as-yet-undeveloped market.

Taken together, the proliferation of commercial messages encouraging drug use has contributed to a cultural normalization of drugs, as Rita Denny and her colleagues found in the qualitative study I discussed in the previous chapter. Drugs are so taken for granted in our culture that the kids she studied put most of them in what anthropologists call an unmarked category, meaning they're considered benign, assumed, and unremarkable—part of the cultural background. That unmarked category includes over-the-counter drugs, drugs that are advertised heavily such as Prozac, as well as another group comprising alcohol, tobacco, and marijuana. Those are precisely the drugs that the government and many adults want kids to "mark." By contrast, the drugs considered marked and dangerous (as in they can kill you) were heroin and inhalants. Part of what led Denny to these conclusions was a striking bit of play acting that happened in one group, where the kids took a box of Altoids mints, crushed them, and then snorted them, as if they were cocaine. Their demonstration displayed a strong imagination, or perhaps even experience, with the details of illegal drug use.

Denny believes that her research reveals both the normalization of drugs and their lure and fascination for kids. Kids "have to negotiate drugs in this culture. There's no way around that." Part of growing up is learning details about drug use, such as the slang that users prefer when referring to drugs, the mechanics of use, and an inside track of knowledge from movies, music, and friends. Drug use by musicians, actors, athletes, and other celebrities becomes part of the lore of the drug culture that ordinary kids participate in. In the words of Denny and her colleague Patty Sutherland, "Drugs were relentlessly discussed, officially and unofficially, by young and by old." In their view, if adults want to make a dent in illegal drug use by kids, they're going to have to address the larger culture of drug use that pervades society.

Selling Violence

The marketing of violent products and their connection to violent behavior has been widely described, analyzed, and debated. The frequency and severity of media violence continue to increase, and the cultural cultivation of a "taste for violence" among American youth has become a serious problem. In addition to movies and television, about which a great deal has already been written, music videos have become a major source of exposure. A 2001 *Pediatrics* study found that more than half of all concept music videos involve violence, usually against women. One-fourth of all MTV videos portray violence, and attractive role models are the aggressors in more than 80 percent of these videos. Violence is also pervasive in boy-oriented toys. At the International Toy Fair in 2002, one of the hot trends was action figures, most of which are violent, being newly targeted to preschoolers. Examples of violent toys, and valuable commentary on them, are available from the Lion and the Lamb Project and Teachers Resisting Unhealthy Children's Entertainment (TRUCE).

Video games now dominate revenues in the toy category. By 2002, spending on these games topped $10.3 billion, and violent video games are the most popular type. A Center for a New American Dream poll found that what the survey called "inappropriate video games" have become the number one item that children ages twelve and thirteen say they want but their parents don't want them to have. While the research on gaming is not nearly as extensive as for television and movies, the findings are becoming more conclusive. Thomas Robinson found that reductions in video game playing time among youth led to significant decreases in a number of measures of aggression. A study of college students published in 2000 found that the amount of time they spent playing video games was positively related to aggressive behavior and delinquency, especially for men. Academic achievement was negatively related to gaming. Two recent Indiana University Medical School studies have provided another interesting, if not yet altogether interpretable, finding. In these experiments with adolescent males, brain responses differed if the game was violent. The study also found that among adolescents who have been diagnosed with disruptive behavior disorder, playing violent video games stimulated brain activation patterns differently from playing nonviolent but exciting games. David Grossman, a national expert on violence, takes the argument further, pointing out that the video games children are playing are the same killing simulator tools the military uses to desensitize its soldiers.

Technological changes in gaming are coming fast and furious, nearly outpacing the ability of researchers to keep up. New developments have made on-screen violence far more graphic and less fantastic. There are games that allow kids to scan in the heads of friends, family members, or people they don't like to sit atop victims' bodies. Other technologies translate players' body movements into action on the screen. Some games allow reprogramming so that the environment of the game becomes one's home or neighborhood. Although video games have a ratings system, it is not well publicized, nor do most stores restrict the sale of violent games to kids. In its 2000 report on marketing violence to youth, the FTC found that 70 percent of all Mature-rated games (for ages eighteen and up) were targeted at kids under seventeen years of age.

A recent meta-analysis using all the existing studies provides the strongest evidence to date for a link between violent games and aggressive behaviors and thoughts. University of Iowa psychologist Craig Anderson found that playing violent games leads to a large increase in aggressive behavior, aggressive cognition, and aggressive affect (or feelings) and a decrease in prosocial behavior. These results were confirmed for girls and boys, and for adults.

Violent toys and media have become a contentious issue. In July 2000, on the basis of what was said to be thousands of studies, the major medical associations and the U.S. Congress issued a joint statement confirming a causal connection between the viewing of media violence and violent behavior. The statement attributes at least some of the rising violence in our society to the impact of media and games. The studies in question used a variety of samples, time periods, and methodologies, including some compelling research designs. A small number of researchers disagree, on the grounds that too much of the evidence shows correlations rather than causes, although that is truer of earlier studies than later ones. And they note that many of the studies measure overall television viewing rather than explicitly measuring exposure to violent content. This leaves open the possibility that it's not violent content but the act of watching itself that is responsible for the subsequent aggression. Even allowing for these objections, my reading of the evidence is that the case for significant effects for some, although not all, children has been well made.

The critics are on stronger ground when they claim that children need some violent content as a way of working through their fears and passions. This is a classic interpretation of the function of fairy tales and other works of culture. Gerard Jones, comic book writer and author of *Killing Monsters: Why Children Need Fantasy, Super-Heroes, and Make-Believe Violence,* makes this argument in the context of contemporary violent content. He writes that many children use violent content constructively, as an important emotional outlet. And he argues that we need a more sophisticated understanding of the links between content, emotion, and behavior. Echoing a sentiment shared by many, myself included, he claims that fantastic violence has positive functions. This is an important point and is not disputed by many of the activists and scholars who have opposed media violence. Nevertheless, with the escalation in the frequency and graphic nature of violence, length of exposure, and the proliferation of mediums, it's likely that we're well beyond the point where media violence serves a useful function. Too much of what is marketed today appears gratuitous rather than constructive, and its role in perpetuating a disturbingly violent culture needs to be seriously addressed. Unfortunately, that task is being made harder by skewed media coverage. A 2001 study by Brad Bushman and

Craig Anderson found that as the scientific evidence of the effects of media violence on aggression has mounted over the past twenty-five years, media accounts have steadily grown more skeptical and increasingly likely to discount the scientific research. This contributes to a climate of denial and complacency.

Violence is only one of the documented impacts of television and other electronic media. There are other reasons to be wary of contemporary media. A large number of studies have uncovered negative effects, such as the association between television viewing and lower cognitive skills, reading competency, brain development, and academic achievement. A growing literature explores the link between viewing and obesity, as well as documents increases in eating disorders after the introduction of television. The American Pediatrics Association recommends that children under the age of two not watch television at all and that all patients be given a "media history," because of the significant effect that heavy viewing has on well-being. (Because this research has been written about so extensively, I will not reproduce the arguments here, and refer the reader to the sources given in the endnotes.) I will just note that my own statistical findings lend further support to this literature by connecting viewing with declines in psychological well-being.

The marketing of addictive products, the promotion of unhealthy eating habits, and cultivating a taste for violence are especially abhorrent practices when children are the targets. Addictions often begin during youth, and some researchers suspect that changes in brain chemistry occur that make early dependency very difficult to break. Eating habits learned in childhood frequently continue throughout adulthood. That's part of why Happy Meals and Lunchables are not harmless. Another worrisome trend is that the gambling industry has turned its attention toward kids, remaking its hotels into kid-friendly places and producing slot machines with children's themes, such as Monopoly. Some of the machines have been denied licenses, but reports are that the industry has been busy locking up licensing agreements with kid icons. Like drugs, gambling is becoming pervasive, and the boundaries between kids and adults are likely to come under increasing strain.

Manufacturers and marketers of all these products understand the importance of establishing early demand. There's even an industry term for it—the *future market*—and it's about turning kids into lifelong customers.

CHAPTER EIGHT

How Consumer Culture Undermines Children's Well-Being

On a wintry morning in February 2002, I rang the bell at the modest house of Pat Dunn and her husband, George. Pat answered the door in her dressing gown, evidently surprised to see me. I was there to talk about her stepson Greg, a sixth grader at one of the six elementary schools in Doxley, a pseudonym for a Boston suburb. Greg had participated in a survey I was conducting in the Doxley schools, and I wanted to interview Pat about how she navigated Greg's relationship to consumer culture. She was willing to proceed if I didn't mind the mess or her attire. Our conversation was one of the most interesting I had.

Greg is an avid consumer. He loves professional wrestling, Gameboy, Nintendo, television, movies, junk food, and CDs (especially those with parental advisories). Since he came to live with Pat and George, they've had a succession of incidents, most of which resulted in Greg's losing privileges to one or another of these things. He isn't allowed to do wrestling moves on his younger sister, but he does, and he loses the right to watch wrestling. He's supposed to do his homework, but he has lied and said he doesn't have any so he can spend his time playing a new Gameboy. He's supposed to tell the truth, but he stole Pat's Snickers bar and denied it. He knows he's not allowed to have CDs with parental advisories, but he went behind Pat and George's back and asked his mother to buy them for him. So they were confiscated.

Pat described what seemed like endless conflicts about consumer culture. As the conversation wore on, I also learned about Greg's problems. He's overweight, so they're trying to reduce his consumption of fast food and processed items. He had a tendency to fly into rages and has been diagnosed as bipolar, but now he's on medication and is doing better. He's keeping up in school, but only by diligent attention and spending more time than most of the other kids. Lying to the teacher and his parents about homework he'd rather not do hasn't helped.

Pat was one of twenty-five mothers and three fathers I interviewed in Doxley. Greg was the most extreme case of a problem kid heavily immersed in consumer culture. But I heard similar stories from other families. One boy was "drawn like a moth" to television and had to be strictly regulated in the amount of time he spent with electronic media. One mother talked about how her generally obedient son would lie to her when he wasn't following the rules about media or the Internet, rules she'd instituted after she was shocked to find her older son involved in conversations about sex and drugs through instant messaging. One couple described their son Doug as the "ultimate consumer." He wanted to buy every product he saw advertised on television. Doug was now in sixth grade, and they were fighting constant battles. He would stay on the computer all day if they let him. He has a weakness for fast food. He has a lot of trouble holding on to money. His mother even described trying to sneak out to the store without him to avoid conflicts about buying stuff. As the conversation progressed, I discovered that Doug is overweight and finds physical activity difficult. He has had a tendency to be distracted and hasn't always done well in school. I interviewed one mother whose son I recognized because he had trouble filling out the survey on his own and I had to help him. As she described his social and academic problems, I remembered that he had checked the top category for weekly television viewing—more than thirty hours. Another mother described a younger daughter who went through a stage where she didn't want to go to school; she wanted to watch TV and eat all the time. She went on antidepression medication at age three and was doing better, but she still gravitates to the TV.

A majority of the parents I interviewed were not grappling with such serious problems, but many of those parents described restrictive regimes in which media usage and content were strictly monitored and regulated, use of the Internet was limited or forbidden, and fast food was a special treat. Some of these mothers watched their children's engagement with consumer culture like hawks, carefully scrutinizing every suggestion at the video store, conferring with other mothers about sleepovers and movies. Others maintained strict controls over allowances and spending money, mandating set-asides for charity and the savings account, and forbidding some purchases even when children saved up their own money. The most restrictive mothers generally described their children as healthy, well functioning, academically and socially successful, and not all that resistant to the rules and prohibitions.

In the weeks and months after the interviews, my thoughts reverted frequently to the conversations about the problem kids, who were mostly boys. The case of Greg stood out. But each time I thought about him, I also dismissed his experience because he had medically diagnosed problems. His passions for consumer culture were a symptom, not a cause, I reasoned. I was determined not to fall into the trap of falsely laying blame on those influences. When I wrote the first draft of my book, I ignored Greg, Doug, and similar children on grounds that they were atypical.

But my survey results suggested otherwise. They implied that the link between the children's problems and their heavy involvement in consumer culture wasn't symptomatic. Involvement in consumer culture leads to problems. I reached these conclusions on the basis of a sophisticated statistical model that allows differentiation between mere correlation, or association, and underlying causes. Furthermore, the model also found that there is no relation in reverse—kids with psychological problems are no more likely to be attracted to consumer culture than are other children. The conclusion of these results is that we shouldn't discount Greg, Doug, and the other troubled kids. They are classic examples of the kinds of damage that heavy consumer involvement can lead to. Conversely, the stories of well-adjusted kids are testimony to the diligent efforts of their parents, who carefully ration their exposure to the culture.

In the preceding chapters, I have referred to many studies and whole literatures—investigations of the impact of television, studies of whether food marketing affects caloric intake and obesity, and research that documents how smoking in movies leads young kids to smoke, among others. Altogether these findings provide a wealth of information about how consumer culture affects children. But virtually all the existing research looks at particular aspects and products of consumer culture rather than commercialization as a general phenomenon. And most of it focuses on electronic media. I felt that new work was needed to create a better understanding of the whole picture. I wanted to link media use, advertising, and children's involvement in the larger consumer marketplace and then test to see whether that involvement has palpable effects on well-being. To my knowledge, this is the first study of its kind. Its results are not encouraging.

The Survey on Children, Media, and Consumer Culture: Setting the Scene

The Survey on Children, Media, and Consumer Culture has now been taken by 300 children between the ages of ten and thirteen, in and around Boston, Massachusetts. These children come from varied socioeconomic and racial backgrounds, and span the spectrum from avid spenders and TV watchers to kids who are mostly isolated from commercial culture. Three hundred may sound like a small number in comparison to national polls, which typically start at a thousand, but within the psychological literatures that are most closely related to this study, 300 children is actually a large sample size. Most important, it's far bigger than is needed to establish statistical reliability and confidence in the findings.

The children who participated in the survey were nearly all fifth and sixth graders. I chose this age group because they form the core of the tween market and are a key target for marketers. In contrast to younger children, fifth and sixth graders tend to be significantly involved in consumer culture and have developed some independence in terms of tastes and consumer choices. In the interviews, parents frequently described newfound interests in clothes, labels, and popular music. This age group has also been identified in classic developmental psychology models as distinct. They are thought to have moved beyond the purely self-centered acquisition stage of "I want this" and "Give me that," which characterizes younger children. Fifth and sixth graders are capable of taking written surveys and providing more accurate information than younger children. This age was also appealing because the academic literature on their relationship to consumer culture is very limited. In contrast, teens have been studied more intensively. Because teens and children are so different, I decided not to add the older age group.

The questionnaire consists of 157 questions and covers five major topic areas: media use, consumer values and involvement in consumer culture, relationships with parents, demographic variables, and measures of physical and mental well-being. The measures of well-being were mainly previously established scales, or what psychologists call screens, for depression, anxiety, and self-esteem. The survey was administered in two phases and two locales—one suburban, the other urban. The first phase took place during the fall and winter of 2001–2002, with 210 children in three schools in the suburban town of Doxley, located about thirty minutes outside Boston. It's an old town with a rural feel, but throughout the area, upscale subdivisions are springing up, filled with large brick colonials. Like other Boston suburbs, Doxley has experienced a housing boom over the past ten years, fueled by an influx of professionals seeking proximity to the high-tech companies that ring Interstate 495. Household income in the town is very high, at $90,000, compared to a statewide median of $50,502, and a similar nationwide level. Housing prices are high as well. In 2002 the median house cost more than $350,000, almost twice the price a decade earlier. Doxley boasts excellent public schools but without the prestige premium exacted in some of the neighboring towns.

The second phase of the survey occurred just about a year later (2002–2003) in two Boston schools and included ninety-three children. These are not neighborhood schools but special schools that serve children throughout the city, the bulk of whom are African Americans or Latino/as. Many are also low income. One is a charter school, the other a pilot school whose stated academic focus is science and math. (At the charter school, the children who participated were those with higher math achievement.) The children live mainly in the neighborhoods of Dorchester, Mattapan, Roxbury, and Boston proper. These locales provide a sharp contrast to Doxley and have far more low-income residents and less home ownership. One characteristic shared by both sites is that the parents are highly educated and place a high value on education for their children. None of the schools, in either Doxley or Boston, was paid to participate, but did so because the school officials believed that the research was asking important questions.

Table 5 presents background information on the children. The sample was somewhat more male, at 53 percent boys and 47 percent girls. Racially, the makeup is 57 percent white, 16 percent African American, 3 percent Latino/a, 10 percent Asian American, and 6 percent multiracial. In addition, 8 percent of the children identified with the "other" racial category. Twelve percent had moved to the United States in the past two years. Between the two sites, the racial composition of the children varies significantly. In the suburban site, 79 percent are white, compared to only 10 percent of the Boston sample. As expected, there are other differences between the two samples. In Doxley, 83 percent of the children reported that their parents were married, and only 12 percent reported that their parents were divorced. By contrast, in Boston, 47 percent of the parents were currently married, and 19 percent were divorced. Only 60.5 percent of the Boston children reported that they live with their fathers, in comparison to 90 percent in Doxley. And although parental college graduation rates are very high for both samples, they are near universal in Doxley, where over 85 percent

Table 5
Describing the Sample (percentages of respondents)

Characteristic	All Respondents	Doxley Respondents	Boston Respondents
Gender			
Male	52.8	53.7	57.1
Female	47.2	46.3	48.9
Race/Ethnicity			
White	56.8	78.7	9.6
African American	15.9	1.0	47.9
Latino/a	3.4	0.5	9.6
Asian American	9.8	12.9	3.2
Multiracial	6.4	2.5	14.9
Other	7.8	4.5	14.9
Educational attainment			
Mother graduated college	79.5	89.6	57.1
Father graduated college	76.9	85.0	58.1
Parents' marital status			
Married	72.2	83.4	46.7
Divorced	13.9	11.7	18.9
Single	8.1	2.0	22.2
Widower	2.7	2.9	2.2
Does mother hold a job?			
Yes	76.3	69.5	91.3
No	23.7	30.5	8.7
Mother full- or part-time job?			
Full-time	59.6	46.8	80.0
Part-time	40.4	53.2	20.0
Does father hold a job?			
Yes	94.7	96.0	91.6
No	5.3	4.0	8.4

of the children reported that their mothers and fathers had graduated from college, compared to about 57 percent of the Boston children. Many of the parents also hold postgraduate degrees, but during the survey administration, the children displayed high rates of uncertainty about their parents' educational credentials beyond college, and almost half reported "don't know." These responses were nearly the same in the two groups. The survey also included questions about parents' work status. In Doxley, 70 percent of the mothers are employed, but fewer than half (47 percent) work full time. In Boston, 91 percent hold jobs, and 80 percent of those are full time. Overall, 95 percent of the fathers are employed. Twenty-two percent of the children agree that their mother "works really long hours," and 45 percent said the same about their fathers. The survey did not ask about financial status because children are unlikely to know much about their parents' income, wealth holdings, or debts. Instead, following a common research practice, we used parental education to stand in for socioeconomic class. (Because I collaborated with others on the data analysis, I use the pronoun *we* to discuss the statistical results.)

While the inclusion of two very different locales yields a varied group of children, it is important to recognize that in neither Boston nor Doxley did we have a true random sample. School-based surveys reproduce the particularities of the population of children who attend them. For all the participating schools, there is a bias toward parents who place a high value on education. And while the sample includes a wide socioeconomic range, there are more children on the high and low ends of the spectrum than exist in the population. However, this does not present a problem for the kind of study I have conducted, whose purpose is to identify relationships among and between variables, for example, between consumer involvement and depression. That's because if there is a true relationship between those two variables, it should be valid through the whole population, including both the segments of the population I have surveyed and those I haven't. Therefore, conducting the analysis at a particular subset of schools does not introduce worrisome biases. The fact that the results were replicated in two very different types of environments also gives confidence in their wider applicability. Of course, the more groups one can replicate findings with, the more confidence one has. But the fact that the children do not form a nationally representative sample does not undermine my findings. However, it does mean that what we call descriptive data, such as the average number of hours the children spend with media, the average score on the psychological outcome variables, and the average level of consumer involvement, cannot be assumed to match any national or even Boston average. Those are the kinds of descriptive pieces of information for which a truly representative sample is necessary.

Consumer Involvement Among the Children

Consumer culture is a sprawling entity that is hard to define and measure. This study attempted to quantify something we called "consumer involvement." But there's no single piece of information that summarizes how involved a child is in consumer culture, and every measure has drawbacks and ambiguities. Having a lot of possessions could indicate that a kid is highly materialistic and focused on things, or it might just mean that he is wealthy. One child may care desperately about the label on her jeans, but be content with owning only one or two pairs, while another accumulates many cheaper outfits. Who is more "consumerist"? Agreeing on a survey that you feel deprived means something very different at the top and bottom of the income scale.

Because it's impossible to find one or even two summary measures that can accurately capture what we were interested in, we started with a broad range of consumer attitudes, values, and activities. The children were asked to respond to eighteen statements, or what psychologists call "items," such as "I like to watch commercials," "Brand names matter to me," and "When I go somewhere special, I usually like to buy something." The items and the children's responses are contained in Table 6.

The children display a wide range of consumer involvement, both among and between the two sites, and also among the eighteen items. The average answer is right in the middle, between the consumerist and non-consumerist range of the scale. However, this average masks wide variation. On some items, most of the children report a strong consumerist orientation. Eighty-eight percent agree or strongly agree that "I usually have something in mind that I want to buy or get," 85 percent say that they "care a lot about my games, toys, and other possessions," 76 percent say that they "like shopping and going to stores," and nearly all of them (92 percent) say that they "want to make a lot of money when I grow up." On other issues, the answers were split more evenly. Fifty-two percent agree and strongly agree that they like clothes with popular labels, 40 percent say that brand names matter to them, 42 percent say that "being cool is important to me," 47 percent wish their parents gave them more money, and 44 percent agree that they don't care too much about what they wear. Finally, some statements evoke low levels of consumerism. Only 35

Table 6
Consumer Involvement Scale: All Respondents
(All data are in percentages of respondents.)

	Strongly Agree	Agree	Disagree	Strongly Disagree
I feel like other kids have more stuff than I do.	4.1	28.6	44.6	22.8
I wish my family could afford to buy me more of what I want.	13.4	20.0	33.8	32.8
I have pretty much everything I need in terms of possessions.	28.6	49.5	17.5	4.4
I wish my parents gave me more money to spend.	21.3	26.0	40.9	11.8
When I decide who to be friends with, I don't care what toys or stuff the person has.	63.7	29.0	5.0	2.0
I usually have something in mind that I want to buy or get.	43.1	45.1	9.8	2.0
I want to make a lot of money when I grow up.	63.3	29.3	5.4	2.0
I care a lot about my games, toys, and other possessions.	40.1	44.8	12.8	2.4
When I go somewhere special, I usually like to buy something.	36.5	51.4	10.0	2.0
I don't care too much about what I wear.	9.1	35.2	29.5	26.2
Brand names matter to me.	13.0	27.3	33.1	26.6
I like clothes with popular labels.	20.0	32.2	32.2	15.6
Being cool is important to me.	12.9	28.9	39.5	18.7
It doesn't matter to me what kind of car my family has.	29.6	41.2	18.2	11.0
I like shopping and going to stores.	39.9	36.5	14.9	8.8
I wish my parents earned more money.	13.4	21.9	32.9	31.8
I like collecting things.	28.7	43.2	22.3	5.7
I like watching commercials.	8.4	16.2	28.3	47.1

Table 6a
Consumer Involvement Scale: Doxley Respondents
(All data are in percentages of respondents.)

	Strongly Agree	Agree	Disagree	Strongly Disagree
I feel other kids have more stuff than I do.	3.5	35.6	45.0	15.8
I wish my family could afford to buy me more of what I want.	10.1	22.1	37.2	30.7
I have pretty much everything I need in terms of possessions.	28.1	50.7	17.2	3.9
I wish my parents gave me more money to spend.	17.8	23.3	47.5	11.4
When I decide who to be friends with, I don't care what toys or stuff the person has.	66.0	29.6	2.9	1.5
I usually have something in mind that I want to buy or get.	37.9	47.3	12.3	2.5
I want to make a lot of money when I grow up.	55.7	35.0	7.9	1.5
I care a lot about my games, toys, and other possessions.	34.5	50.7	13.3	1.5
When I go somewhere special, I usually like to buy something.	29.8	57.6	10.7	2.0
I don't care too much about what I wear.	9.3	37.7	32.8	20.1
Brand names matter to me.	7.9	27.2	35.6	29.2
I like clothes with popular labels.	10.0	33.3	38.8	17.9
Being cool is important to me.	9.5	31.5	41.0	18.0
It doesn't matter to me what kind of car my family has.	31.7	45.5	14.9	7.9
I like shopping and going to stores.	34.7	38.1	17.8	9.4
I wish my parents earned more money.	7.9	23.7	34.7	33.7
I like collecting things.	29.6	43.8	23.2	3.4
I like watching commercials.	7.9	15.8	31.0	45.3

Table 6b
Consumer Involvement Scale: Boston Respondents
(All data are in percentages of respondents.)

	Strongly Agree	Agree	Disagree	Strongly Disagree
I feel like other kids have more stuff than I do.	5.4	13.0	43.5	38.0
I wish my family could afford to buy me more of what I want.	20.9	15.4	26.4	37.4
I have pretty much everything I need in terms of possessions.	29.8	46.8	18.1	5.3
I wish my parents gave me more money to spend.	28.7	31.9	26.6	12.8
When I decide who to be friends with, I don't care what toys or stuff the person has.	58.5	27.7	9.6	4.3
I usually have something in mind that I want to buy or get.	54.3	40.4	4.3	1.1
I want to make a lot of money when I grow up.	79.8	17.0	0	3.2
I care a lot about my games, toys, and other possessions.	52.1	31.9	11.7	4.3
When I go somewhere special, I usually like to buy something.	51.1	38.3	8.5	2.1
I don't care too much about what I wear.	8.5	29.8	22.3	39.4
Brand names matter to me.	24.2	27.5	27.5	20.9
I like clothes with popular labels.	41.5	29.8	18.1	10.6
Being cool is important to me.	20.2	23.4	36.2	20.2
It doesn't matter to me what kind of car my family has.	24.7	31.5	25.8	18.0
I like shopping and going to stores.	51.1	33.0	8.5	7.4
I wish my parents earned more money.	24.7	18.3	29.0	28.0
I like collecting things.	26.9	41.9	20.4	10.8
I like watching commercials.	9.6	17.0	22.3	51.1

percent say that they wish their parents earned more money, 33 percent say they feel other kids have more stuff, 25 percent like to watch commercials, and 71 percent say that the kind of car their family has doesn't matter to them.

Overall, the Boston children displayed a higher average level of consumer involvement than those from Doxley. The Boston children were more likely to enjoy shopping; more of them care a lot about their possessions; they were more likely to care about brand names and having clothes with popular labels; they say being cool is important to them; and they were more likely to have something in mind that they want to buy or get. They are more likely to wish their parents earned more, and far more of them (80 percent versus 56 percent) strongly agreed that they want to make a lot of money when they grow up. However, there are some items where the differences were reversed. Although the Boston children come from less well-off families, they are less likely to feel that other kids have more stuff than they do and just about as likely to report that they have everything they need as the suburban sample. They are also slightly less likely to care about what they wear, or to like collecting.

Having collected these data, our next task was to figure out whether these eighteen items together comprise a reasonable measure of consumer involvement. Answering that question involves conducting what is called a factor analysis—a statistical technique that tests whether the items fit together in a systematic way. Factor analysis analyzes the relationships among all the items and assesses how closely answers to one item correlate with answers to the others. Do children who like to shop also care about designer labels? If a child wishes her parents earned more money, does she also want to earn a lot when she grows up? If the answers are similar across the items, then we can group them together into a common factor. This means that we are justified in believing that the different statements are measuring one psychological or social construct.

The factor analysis revealed high levels of common answers among the items. Sixteen of the eighteen grouped together into one single factor measuring consumer involvement. (The two items that were dropped were "I like collecting things" and "I like watching commercials.") There was also evidence that some of the items were more closely related to each other than others, which means that they form what are called subfactors. The three that we identified loosely measure "dissatisfaction," "consumer orientation," and "brand awareness." The items are ordered in Table 6 to replicate these scales. Items 1–5 represent dissatisfaction, items 6–9 are consumer orientation, and items 10–14 are brand awareness. The remaining two items, numbers 15 and 16, are not closely connected with any of the subscales. In addition, because we suspected that some of the questions might have significant differences by gender (for example, that girls care more about clothes or popular labels, and boys are more likely to be collectors), we did all of the confirmatory factor analysis separately for boys and girls. To our surprise, we found only minor differences by sex and therefore combined the boys and girls in subsequent analysis.

Patterns of Media Use

The survey included a series of questions about television, video games, computer, movies, and magazines. As expected, the children of Doxley and Boston are involved with a variety of media. We found that almost two-thirds (63 percent) of the children watch television every day, and the median estimate of weekly television viewing time is six to ten hours per week (see Table 7). This is far lower than national estimates of twenty-five hours, but that's not surprising given the strong academic orientation of most of the children in the survey. We also found major differences between the two sites, with the striking finding being the low levels of time Doxley kids spend watching television. In interviews, Doxley parents explained that their children's television time was curtailed by the heavy demands of homework and extracurricular activities, as well as by their own restrictions. Only 17 percent of Doxley children report watching more than fifteen hours of television a week, compared to 39 percent of Boston children. And only about a tenth of Doxley children report watching more than twenty hours a week, compared to a third of Boston children. Fifty-six percent of Doxley kids watch TV every day versus 78 percent of the Boston children. (Table 7 also shows data on the frequency of watching at particular times of day.) We asked only one or two questions about what children were watching and found that 19 percent in Doxley and 57 percent in Boston watch MTV or VH1 regularly, and quite a few watch every day. We also found that 45 percent of the children report watching R-rated movies, including a substantial number who watch them fairly or very often.

Table 8 presents data on other types of media use. Here the differences between the samples were less consistent. Doxley kids spend more time playing on the computer, while Bostonians are more avid moviegoers, watch more videos, buy more CDs, and spend more time watching video games. Magazine reading is roughly the same.

Table 7
Television Viewing: All Respondents

Number of hours spent per week watching television	0	1–2	3–5	6–10	11–15	16–20	21–30	30 +
	2.7%	12.1%	25.0%	20.1%	16.1%	6.7%	8.1%	9.1%

	Never	1–2 Times per Month	Once per Week	2–3 Times Weekly	4–5 Times Weekly
Watch television after school	14.6	13.2	13.5	24.0	34.7
Watch television before school	34.9	13.2	10.5	15.3	26.1
Watch television during dinner	46.5	20.8	7.4	11.3	14.1
Watch television after dinner	12.0	15.8	13.4	27.8	31.0

	Rarely/Never	Occasionally	1–2 Times per Week	Every Day
How often do you watch MTV/VH1?	57.1	11.8	18.9	12.2

	Yes	No
Watch television every day	63.0	37.0

Table 7a
Television Viewing: Doxley

Number of hours spent per week watching television	0	1–2	3–5	6–10	11–15	16–20	21–30	30 +
	2.9%	12.3%	28.9%	24.0%	15.2%	7.4%	6.4%	2.9%

	Never	1–2 Times per Month	Once per Week	2–3 Times Weekly	4–5 Times Weekly
Watch television after school	16.2	17.3	17.8	26.4	22.3
Watch television before school	37.8	13.9	12.4	16.4	19.4
Watch television during dinner	50.0	27.3	6.7	9.3	6.7
Watch television after dinner	11.2	19.4	17.9	29.1	22.4

	Rarely/Never	Occasionally	1–2 Times per Week	Every Day
How often do you watch MTV/VH1	63.9	17.3	10.9	7.9

	Yes	No
Watch television every day	56.0	44.0

Table 7b
Television Viewing: Boston

Number of hours spent per week watching television	0	1–2	3–5	6–10	11–15	16–20	21–30	30 +
	2.1%	11.7%	17.0%	11.7%	18.1%	5.3%	11.7%	22.3%

	Never	1–2 Times per Month	Once per Week	2–3 Times Weekly	4–5 Times Weekly
Watch television after school	11.0	4.4	4.4	18.7	61.5
Watch television before school	28.7	11.7	6.4	12.8	40.4
Watch television during dinner	38.9	6.7	8.9	15.6	30.0
Watch television after dinner	13.6	8.0	3.4	25.0	50.0

	Rarely/Never	Occasionally	1–2 Times per Week	Every Day
How often do you watch MTV/VH1?	42.6	0	36.2	21.3

	Yes	No
Watch television every day	78.3	21.7

Table 8
Other Media Use: All Respondents

Number of hours spent per week	0	1–2	3–5	6–10	11–15	16–20	21–30	30+
Watching videos	13.0%	35.7%	32.0%	11.7%	3.0%	1.7%	1.7%	1.3%
Playing on the computer	14.3	39.5	22.1	11.6	5.4	1.7	3.4	2.0
Playing video games	23.8	26.5	19.8	10.4	7.0	5.4	2.3	4.7

	0	1–2	3–5	6–10	10+
Magazines read regularly	29.3	48.3	18.7	2.3	1.3
Movies watched per month	5.1	32.0	35.4	16.5	11.1

	Rarely/Never	Occasionally	1–2 Times per Week	Every Day
Watch R-rated movies	55.6	27.9	10.1	6.4

Table 8a

Other Media Use: Doxley Respondents

Number of hours spent per week	**0**	**1–2**	**3–5**	**6–10**	**11–15**	**16–20**	**21–30**	**30+**
Watching videos	14.1%	42.2%	30.6%	9.2%	1.9%	1.0%	.5%	.5%
Playing on the computer	14.4	37.6	21.3	13.4	5.9	2.0	4.0	1.5
Playing video games	25.5	28.9	18.6	9.8	7.4	5.9	2.5	1.5

	0	**1–2**	**3–5**	**6–10**	**10+**
Magazines read regularly	28.2	50.0	19.4	1.5	1.0
Movies watched per month	3.4	35.0	39.9	15.3	6.4

	Rarely/Never	**Occasionally**	**1–2 Times per Week**	**Every Day**
Watch R-rated movies	66.2	23.5	7.4	2.9

Table 8b

Other Media Use: Boston Respondents

Number of hours spent per week	0	1–2	3–5	6–10	11–15	16–20	21–30	30+
Watching videos	10.6%	21.3%	35.1%	17.0%	5.3%	3.2%	4.3%	3.2%
Playing on the computer	14.1	43.5	23.9	7.6	4.3	1.1	2.2	3.3
Playing video games	20.2	21.3	22.3	11.7	6.4	4.3	2.1	11.7

	0	1–2	3–5	6–10	10+
Magazines read regularly	31.9	44.7	17.0	4.3	2.1
Movies watched per month	8.5	25.5	25.5	19.1	21.3

	Rarely/Never	Occasionally	1–2 Times per Week	Every Day
Watch R-rated movies	32.3	37.6	16.1	14.0

Assessing the Children's Well-Being

The central question to which the study was addressed is how the children's involvement in consumer culture affects their well-being. We collected four measures to assess how they are doing: depression, anxiety, self-esteem, and psychosomatic symptoms. For the first three, we used scales with well-established track records in the psychological literature. The psychosomatic symptom questions are original to this survey. In all four cases, we conducted factor analysis to ensure that the measures held together as single constructs, and they did. Throughout, we relied on the children's own answers about their feelings rather than assessments from adults.

Tables 9 and 10 show that most of the children report being happy and well adjusted, and the scores for well-being are within normal levels. Consider the case of depression (Table 10). The students were asked to respond to seventeen items, which asked about how often they are sad and how often things bother them. The range of possible scores is from 17 (least depressed) to 51 (most depressed). Our average was 21.7, indicating a low average level of depression. Boston students scored 1.3 points higher than their counterparts in Doxley. Findings for anxiety, which tends to be correlated with depression, were similar, although this variable is scored in reverse, so that higher scores indicate less anxiety. We also asked about how often they felt bored, had an upset stomach, or had a headache, because children with more psychological distress experience these problems more frequently. The fraction saying they have these symptoms "most of the time" ranged from 3.7 percent for upset stomach, to 7.7 percent for boredom, to 11 percent for headache (Table 9). The fourth psychological variable we collected is self-esteem. This is measured by a thirty-six-item scale with five subscales: general or "global" self-esteem, peer self-esteem, family self-esteem, body self-esteem, and academic self-esteem (Table 11). The children also displayed a generally healthy sense of self-esteem.

Parents and Children

I have argued that a major thrust of contemporary marketing to children is the interposition of the marketer between the parent and child. Marketers create utopian spaces free of parents and employ insidious dual-messaging strategies. Ads position the marketer with the child against the

Table 9
Psychosomatic Outcomes
(All Respondents)

	Never	Almost Never	Sometimes	Most of the Time
How often do you feel bored?	5.7%	30.9%	55.7%	7.7%
How often do you have an upset stomach?	12.3	46.7	37.3	3.7
How often do you have a headache?	9.7	37.8	41.5	11.0

Psychosomatic Outcomes
(Doxley)

	Never	Almost Never	Sometimes	Most of the Time
How often do you feel bored?	4.4%	32.8%	56.4%	6.4%
How often do you have an upset stomach?	13.1	51.9	32.0	2.9
How often do you have a headache?	10.7	42.4	38.0	8.8

Psychosomatic Outcomes
(Boston)

	Never	Almost Never	Sometimes	Most of the Time
How often do you feel bored?	8.5%	26.6%	54.3%	10.6%
How often do you have an upset stomach?	10.6	35.1	48.9	5.3
How often do you have a headache?	7.4	27.7	48.9	16.0

parent. These strategies raise the issue of whether marketing depictions of parents and children have any effects on real life relationships. Do children who are more exposed to antiadultism develop more negative attitudes to their parents? Does nag factor marketing make kids feel their parents are an impediment to acquisition? Or are these portrayals just good fun that kids don't take too seriously and adults shouldn't either?

From my interviews with Doxley parents I knew that there were plenty of kids who were fighting with their parents about consumer culture. I heard about rewards and punishments, privileges granted and denied, trust and lies. I was curious whether high media use and heavy psychological

Table 10
Depression and Anxiety (All Respondents)

	Number of Items	Mean	Range
Children's Depression Inventory	17	21.7	17–43
Children's Anxiety Scale	16	27.1	16–32

Note: The Children's Depression Inventory is a 17-item scale, with higher scores indicating more depression. Anxiety is a 16-item scale, which is reversed-scored, that is, higher scores indicate less anxiety.

Table 11
Self-Esteem (All Respondents)

	Number of Items	Mean	Range
Global Self-Esteem	8	16.9	11–29
Peer Self-Esteem	8	14.3	8–32
Family Self-Esteem	8	12.6	8–30
Body Self-Esteem	4	7.2	4–16
Academic Self-Esteem	8	13.9	8–29

Note: Lower score indicates higher self-esteem. Higher score indicates lower self-esteem.

involvement in consumer culture made those fights more likely and undermined good relationships between children and parents.

To test that theory, we asked the children to describe their feelings toward their primary parent and used those answers to create a "parental attitude" scale. (The primary parent was defined as the "person who mostly takes care of you . . . your mother, father, or another adult.") The first four statements measure whether the child feels the parent responds to his or her needs and come from an existing scale. Four new items were specifically oriented to common portrayals of parents in consumer culture: "She is not at all cool," "She doesn't understand what kids need to have these days," "She is boring," and "She is not too much fun to be around." Factor analysis found that all eight questions fit together (see Table 12).

Table 12
Parent-Child Relations (All Respondents)

	Strongly Agree	**Agree**	**Disagree**	**Strongly Disagree**
She (he) . . . makes me feel better when I am upset.	51.5%	38.0%	6.4%	4.1%
She (he) . . . listens to what I have to say.	46.8	39.3	10.2	3.7
She (he) . . . is too busy to talk to me.	6.5	9.6	36.2	47.8
She (he) . . . wants to hear about my problems.	52.7	33.7	9.5	4.1
She (he) . . . is not at all cool.	8.3	14.6	35.8	41.3
She (he) . . . doesn't understand what kids need to have these days.	13.7	14.3	32.8	39.2
She (he) . . . is boring.	6.5	6.2	32.2	55.1
She (he) . . . is not too much fun to be around.	7.5	5.4	29.2	58.0
	Never	**Sometimes**	**Often**	**Very Often**
How often do you fight or disagree with your parents?	34.6	50.2	10.2	5.1

As expected, the children have positive views of their parents. Nearly 90 percent reported that their parent makes them feel better and wants to hear their problems, and roughly 85 percent say that their parent listens to them and that she (or he) is not too busy too talk. However, for the four questions that hew more closely to portrayals of parents in consumer culture, some of the results are less positive. Twenty-three percent report that their parent is not cool, and 28 percent agree that she doesn't understand what kids need. There were also differences between the two samples. The Boston children were more likely to be strongly positive about their parent. For example, 62 percent of the Boston children strongly agreed that their parent made them feel better, in comparison to only 47 percent in Doxley. Almost half of the Boston kids strongly disagreed that their

Table 12a
Parent-Child Relations (Doxley)

	Strongly Agree	**Agree**	**Disagree**	**Strongly Disagree**
She (he) . . . makes me feel better when I am upset.	47.1%	42.6%	5.9%	4.4%
She (he) . . . listens to what I have to say.	40.7	44.6	11.3	3.4
She (he) . . . is too busy to talk to me.	6.4	8.9	40.1	44.6
She (he) . . . wants to hear about my problems.	48.5	39.2	7.8	4.4
She (he) . . . is not at all cool.	7.6	14.1	42.9	35.4
She (he) . . . doesn't understand what kids need to have these days.	13.4	16.3	35.1	35.1
She (he) . . . is boring.	7.5	5.0	35.3	52.2
She (he) . . . is not too much fun to be around.	6.9	3.9	36.3	52.9
	Never	**Sometimes**	**Often**	**Very Often**
How often do you fight or disagree with your parents?	28.4	53.4	12.3	5.9

mother "doesn't understand what kids need to have these days," in comparison to only 35 percent of Doxley children.

We found similar distinctions when we asked the children about how often they fought with their parents and how often they disagreed about how much time they should spend watching television, or using other media, about time on the computer, and how much disagreement they had about "whether or not to buy you things you want." The Boston children revealed very low levels of fighting overall. Forty-eight percent said they "never or almost never" disagree or fight with their parents, compared to only 28 percent of the Doxley kids. Boston kids were also much less likely to disagree about media use or what their parents would buy them.

Table 12b
Parent-Child Relations (Boston)

	Strongly Agree	Agree	Disagree	Strongly Disagree
She (he) . . . makes me feel better when I am upset.	61.5%	27.5%	7.7%	3.3%
She (he) . . . listens to what I have to say.	60.4	27.5	7.7	4.4
She (he) . . . is too busy to talk to me.	6.6	11.0	27.5	54.9
She (he) . . . wants to hear about my problems.	62.2	21.1	13.3	3.3
She (he) . . . is not at all cool.	10.0	15.6	20.0	55.4
She (he) . . . doesn't understand what kids need to have these days.	14.3	9.9	27.5	48.4
She (he) . . . is boring.	4.4	8.8	25.3	61.5
She (he) . . . is not too much fun to be around.	8.8	8.8	13.2	69.2
	Never	**Sometimes**	**Often**	**Very Often**
How often do you fight or disagree with your parents?	48.4	42.9	5.5	3.3

From Correlation to Causality

One of the longstanding issues in social science research is that much of its analysis shows that two factors are related to each other, or what is called correlated, rather than that one causes the other. A common research technique for establishing correlation is regression analysis. As a first step, we estimated a variety of regression models to test whether the well-being measures were correlated to consumer involvement. As expected, we found that they are. The children who are more involved in consumer culture are more depressed, more anxious, have lower self-esteem, and suffer from more psychosomatic complaints.

Although regression analysis is common, its findings of correlation are limited. One worry is that the causality is actually the reverse of what the model is assuming. For example, we hypothesized that children with higher levels of consumer involvement are more likely to get depressed and anxious. The causality is going from consumer involvement to depression and anxiety. But perhaps the connection is reversed, and children deal with their anxiety by accumulating stuff because they find it soothing. Maybe depressed kids seek out television because they don't have the energy for other activities or because it helps them forget their emotional pain. We all know about the hyper kids who can't tear themselves away from the video console, or image-obsessed teens poring over fashion magazines. Much of the discussion on media and consumer culture has gone around and around on just this issue. Chicken or egg?

To resolve questions of causality, we used a more sophisticated statistical technique called structural equation modeling, which allows us to infer causality. With the structural model, we specify all the possible causal relationships in advance, and then the computer estimates them all and tests to see which are best supported by the data. It also takes into account all the other variables in the model and all the possible directions of causality that they present. It's a powerful tool that allows analysts to make statements about causes.

To construct our model, we considered each of the possible causal relationships among the four basic variables: media use, the consumer involvement scale, the parental attitude scale, and for each model, one of the well-being variables (anxiety, depression, self-esteem, or psychosomatic complaints). We tested to see whether children who watch a lot of media develop more consumerist values, or whether the kids who already have high consumer involvement opt for more screen time. Similarly, we asked whether children who already have poor psychological functioning gravitate toward consumer culture, or whether involvement in consumer culture causes poor functioning. We tested to see whether media use directly affects psychological outcomes—for example, if watching more television leads to more depression or anxiety. This might occur because there are physiological effects of viewing, such as the lowering of metabolic rates or reduced exercise levels. Or it might be that program content, which depicts high levels of conflict, violence, and crime, causes people to be more fearful or anxious. Or perhaps the reverse is true: children who are already depressed and anxious might seek out television as a way to relax and calm their fears. Finally, we tested whether consumer involvement causes more negative attitudes toward parents and also the reverse—whether children who already have negative relationships with their parents are more likely to become heavily involved in consumer culture. We tested to see whether poor relationships with parents affect psychological well-being and, conversely, whether children with poorer psychological health become more negative about their parents.

We included what are called background, or "control," variables. These are typically not variables of great theoretical interest, because they represent previously established relationships. For example, research has shown that many psychological outcome variables differ by sex, race, and socioeconomic status. So we included measures of sex, age, race, parents' marital status, and parents' education level. In the pictures below, they are represented as control variables. (As is standard in analysis of this type, we also tested other control variables but did not include those that were not statistically related to our outcome measure.)

Statistical Results: Consumer Involvement Undermines Children's Well-Being

The estimates provide strong support for our hypotheses. High consumer involvement is a significant cause of depression, anxiety, low self-esteem, and psychosomatic complaints. Psychologically healthy children will be made worse off if they become more enmeshed in the culture of getting and spending. Children with emotional problems will be helped if they disengage from the worlds that corporations are constructing for them. The effects operate in both directions and are symmetric. That is, less involvement in consumer culture leads to healthier kids, and more involvement leads kids' psychological well-being to deteriorate. These results are depicted in Figures 1 to 4—one for each psychological outcome. Each of the arrows in the diagram indicates a statistically significant causal relationship from one variable to the other. The number above the line is the estimated coefficient for that relationship. The effects are large in magnitude, and they are what we call "robust." That means that the results are reproduced in virtually all the different models that we tested. (In order to establish the robustness of a result, researchers typically estimate many different models, adding and subtracting variables, using different parts of the sample, and so on.) In the many regression equations and structural equation models we estimated, the results for consumer involvement were very consistent.

By contrast, we did not find a significant effect in the reverse direction, and hence no solid arrow appears in the figure. Being depressed or anxious or having low self-esteem does not cause higher levels of consumer involvement. This result was consistent across all the models and different specifications. These are the results that led me to stop discounting the

Figure 1
Causal Model of Psychosomatic Outcomes

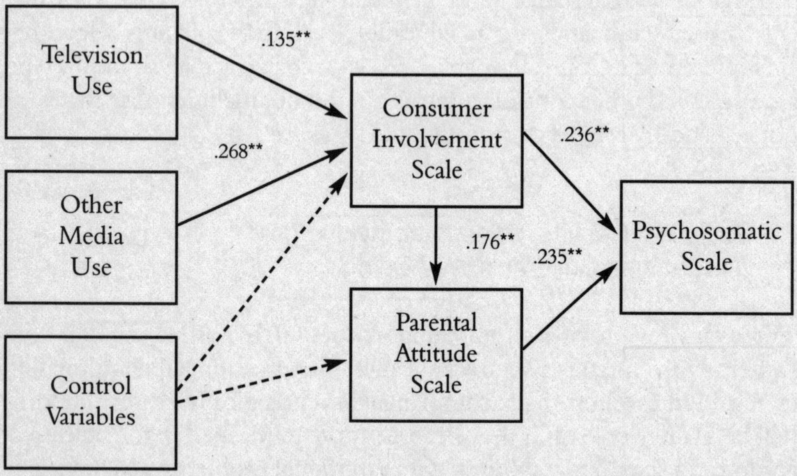

Note: The number presented is the standardized regression coefficient. Sample size equals 300.

**Indicates that the p-value is less than .05, and thereby statistically significant.

experiences of Greg, Doug, and the other children with problems and to realize that consumer culture was more damaging than I had imagined.

A second finding is that media use matters, but its effect flows through consumer involvement. The model yields the commonsense finding that children who spend more time watching television and using other media become more involved in consumer culture. Television induces discontent with what one has, it creates an orientation to possessions and money, and it causes children to care more about brands, products, and consumer values.

But media use does not operate directly on either psychological functioning or attitudes toward parents. There is no direct causal arrow between media use and depression or between media use and parental attitudes. Rather, when we use media, we process the effects through a cognitive and psychological structure. Furthermore, and very much counter to my prior expectations, we do not find that media use is caused by any of the variables we included in the model. Depression and anxiety do not

Figure 2
Causal Model of Depression

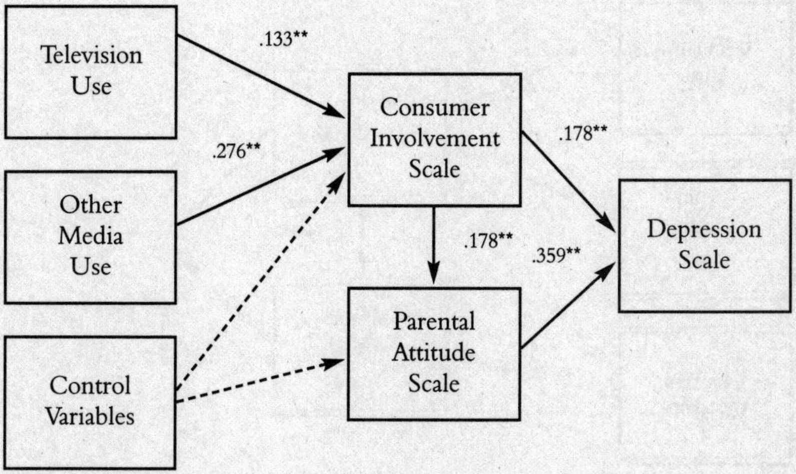

Note: The number presented is the standardized regression coefficient.
Sample size equals 300.

**Indicates that the p-value is less than .05, and thereby statistically significant.

lead to more screen time. Children who are more alienated from their parents do not seem to seek refuge in televisions, computers, or video games. In this sample at least, psychological distress is not driving media use.

Relationships between parents and children are also an important part of the story. Higher levels of consumer involvement result in worse relationships with parents (as measured by both the parental attitude scale and the likelihood of fighting or disagreeing with parents). That's the first causal link. The second is that as children's relations with their parents deteriorate, there is an additional negative effect on well-being. Relating poorly to parents leads to more depression, anxiety, lower self-esteem, and more psychosomatic complaints. Consumer culture packs a double wallop, operating through both this direct and an indirect channel. Surprisingly, there are no effects in the reverse direction. Poor psychological outcomes such as depression and anxiety do not cause relations with parents to deteriorate, nor does a poor relationship with parents lead to higher consumer involvement.

Figure 3
Causal Model of Anxiety

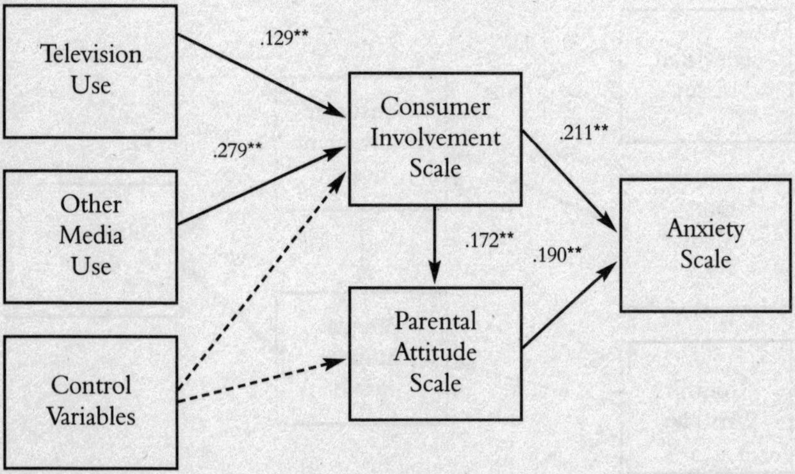

Television Use
.129**
Other Media Use
.279**
Control Variables
Consumer Involvement Scale
.172**
Parental Attitude Scale
.211**
.190**
Anxiety Scale

Note: The number presented is the standardized regression coefficient.
Sample size equals 300.

**Indicates that the p-value is less than .05, and thereby statistically significant.

This finding has an important footnote, however. Although our estimates for the whole sample of 300 children found a significant causal relationship between consumer involvement and relationships with parents, other analyses led us to suspect that this finding was due to the fact that Doxley kids represent two-thirds of the sample. So we estimated the model separately for the two groups, and our suspicions were confirmed: that link is absent for the Boston sample.

The descriptive data show that the Boston children articulate extremely positive attitudes toward their primary parents. These attitudes may form a protective shield against the negative portrayals of parents in consumer culture and insulate these children from the kinds of conflicts found among the suburban kids. By contrast, although Doxley children are also positive about their parents, they are less so. They report more fighting with their parents about issues of access to consumer culture. It may be that in Doxley, parental attempts to limit their children's media use or involvement in consumer culture lead to a backlash among some of the

Figure 4
Causal Model of Self-Esteem

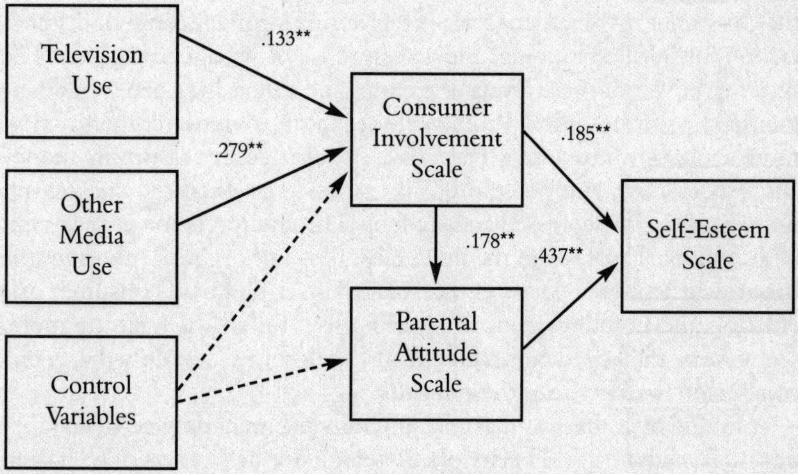

Television Use
.133**
Consumer Involvement Scale
.279**
Other Media Use
.185**
Self-Esteem Scale
.178**
.437**
Parental Attitude Scale
Control Variables

Note: The number presented is the standardized regression coefficient.
Sample size equals 300.

**Indicates that the p-value is less than .05, and thereby statistically significant.

highly consumer-involved children, who resent these restrictions. Quite a few of the Doxley mothers were vigilant about screening out objectionable media, keeping a tight rein on media time, and controlling their children's purchasing behavior. I did not do comparable parental interviews in Boston. However, we do know that in Boston, where media use and consumer involvement are higher, there are also lower levels of parental restrictions on media. For example, among children who report that their parents have television restrictions, the median hours permitted per week are twice as high in Boston as in Doxley (ten versus five hours). There may also be differences between the two sites in attitudes toward consumer culture more broadly. Middle- and upper-middle-class white parents have historically had especially ambivalent and critical attitudes to children's consumer culture, in part because of its low cultural status. Perhaps parental disapproval of commercialized culture in Doxley may be part of what is driving a wedge between parents and their children.

Interpreting the Results

These statistical findings do not tell us exactly how consumer involvement affects psychological outcomes, only that it does. Nevertheless, it may be useful to speculate on how the relationship operates. One possibility is that the consumer involvement scale is registering strong feelings of dissatisfaction, unfulfilled longing, and a keen sense of social comparison. The negative power of these kinds of feelings and values has been well documented by psychologists. People who are more envious of others, worry more about how much they have, have stronger desires to acquire money and possessions, and place more importance on financial success are more likely to be depressed and anxious. This interpretation is consistent with additional analyses of the three subscales. The dissatisfaction subscale had much stronger effects on the outcome variables than consumer orientation and brand awareness. Desiring less, rather than getting more, seems to be the key to contentment and well-being. Certainly that is one conclusion to draw from these results.

A second hypothesis is that consumer involvement detracts from other beneficial activities and behaviors. Research on the impacts of television find that its negative relation to reading scores is partly due to the fact that it undermines reading practice, especially for children who have not yet mastered the skills. Perhaps something similar is going on with consumerism. Children who are more consumerist may be less oriented to socializing with their peers, siblings, and parents, and they may have poorer social connections overall. They may be less engaged in satisfying, creative, and educational activities such as reading, unstructured play, or physical activity. They may have less rich fantasy lives, as some of the literature on television suggests. Perhaps the mechanism is mainly that consumer culture becomes a substitute for what keeps kids happy and healthy. The data we have do not allow us to test this hypothesis directly. To do so, we'd have had to collect information on how children use their time. In retrospect, it would have been useful to do so. But the survey was already long, and accurate time-use data are difficult to acquire, especially with children. One piece of relevant evidence from our data is that high levels of consumer involvement reduce children's self-esteem in the areas of peer and family relationships. This is what we'd expect if consumer involvement pushes out strong social connections.

American children are deeply enmeshed in the culture of getting and spending, and they are getting more so. We find that the more enmeshed they are, the more they suffer for it. The more they buy into the commercial and materialist messages, the worse they feel about themselves, the more depressed they are, and the more they are beset by anxiety, headaches, stomachaches, and boredom. The bottom line on the culture they're being raised in is that it's a lot more pernicious than most adults have been willing to admit.

Materialism and Psychological Distress: The Evidence Accumulates

The literature that comes closest to this perspective is from psychology and investigates how materialist values are related to well-being. There are now scores of studies, using a variety of methodologies and sample populations. An excellent review of this literature by one of its leading scholars, Tim Kasser, is *The High Price of Materialism.* Materialist values are typically measured by asking people about their degree of agreement with a series of statements about money, possessions, and consumption. For example, Kasser and Richard Ryan, of the University of Rochester, collected data on financial aspirations (having a high-paying job, being financially successful, buying things just because you want them), social goals (being famous, admired), and appearance (keeping up with fashions, achieving the right look). Other measures, such as Marcia Richins and Scott Dawson's widely cited materialism scale, focus on desires for success, how central consumption is to people, and happiness. Russell Belk's scale rates envy, possessiveness, and nongenerosity. Kasser has also asked people to state their own goals and then coded the answers according to how materialist they are.

After evaluating the extent of materialism across a sample of the population, many of these studies relate it to psychological outcomes. Kasser and Ryan found in an important study that people with higher financial aspirations scored lower on measures of self-actualization and vitality. They also had lower levels of community affiliation. Subsequent work found even more associations. Materialism is correlated with lower self-esteem. It is correlated with higher rates of depression and anxiety. Materialism is related to psychological distress and difficulty adapting to life. People who value money and conventional success are less likely to experience positive emotions, such as happiness and joy, and they are more likely to experience negative ones, such as anger and unhappiness. Materialism is also related to elevated levels of physical symptoms, such as headaches, stomachaches, backaches, sore muscles, and sore throats. These results have been found in samples of men and women, teens and adults, across income groups, and for students and nonstudents. And they hold up across countries, as this type of research has now been replicated in many places around the globe. The clear conclusion of all this work is that the more strongly a person subscribes to materialist values, the poorer is his or her quality of life.

A number of the materialism studies have involved teens. Findings include the fact that adolescents who have more materialist values are more likely to engage in risky behaviors, such as smoking, drinking, and illegal drug use. They are more likely to suffer from personality disorders such as narcissism, separation anxiety disorder, paranoia, and attention deficit disorder. And they are less likely to be doing well in life realms such as school, jobs, and extracurricular activities. Materialism is also correlated with carrying weapons, skipping school, and vandalism.

One of the issues this research raises is whether materialism causes these negative outcomes or is merely associated with them. Perhaps distressed people adopt materialism as a value system. For example, some of the research finds that teens who are economically deprived or whose parents display low levels of nurturing behavior exhibit higher levels of materialism. Researchers argue that when people's basic needs are not met or they are exposed to conditions of insecurity, they become more materialistic. And as they take on more materialist lifestyles, they are less likely to do the life-affirming things that create true well-being. Kasser has attempted to get at the causality issue in a study with Ken Shelton, drawing on a field of research called terror management. They asked half the participants to write about their own death (the terror condition) while the control group wrote about music. Those who were assigned the former task later exhibited significantly higher rates of materialist values. What Kasser and others conclude is that there is a circular effect in which materialism and poor functioning are self-reinforcing. That kind of complex interaction means that the simplistic terms on which marketers typically defend their activities are often off the mark. It is to that debate that I now turn.

CHAPTER NINE

Empowered or Seduced?

The Debate About Advertising and Marketing to Kids

> A line has been crossed . . . advertising and entertainment and all mediums are blurred now. I think we are reaching a point of an overall degrading of values. . . . And it seems like people get desensitized, and then they have to cross yet another line.
>
> —Richard Goldstein, creative director, major New York ad agency

As marketers have become more brazen, parents, educators, and health professionals have begun to fight back. This is not the first time advocates for children have tried to rein in marketers. In the 1970s, television advertising was the focal point, because it was the major avenue for reaching children. In 1974, the Federal Communications Commission explicitly recognized children's vulnerability to ads and enacted regulations that prohibited host selling and program-length commercials, mandated separators between ads and programs, and restricted advertising time to nine and a half minutes per hour on the weekends and twelve minutes on weekdays. Action for Children's Television, a public interest group, argued that the 1974 regulations were inadequate and pressed the Federal Trade Commission to enact a ban on all advertising to children. In 1978, after considerable deliberation, the FTC issued a report that concluded children under age seven "do not possess the cognitive ability to evaluate adequately child-oriented television advertising." However, by 1981, the agency was unwilling to take on industry, and in any case, Congress stripped it of its ability to do so. At about this time, the FCC reversed its stance on program-length commercials, which remain legal.

The next decade and a half was relatively quiet, but opposition began to surface in the second half of the 1990s. This time, critics took aim at a wider range of practices than television commercials. Ralph Nader, a long-standing opponent of corporate marketing to children, published *The Parents' Guide to Fighting Corporate Predators* and founded Commercial Alert, which has become a major catalyst for activism, organizing professionals and parents on a variety of issues from school commercialization to junk food marketing. George Gerbner warned that corporations were becoming our children's "story-tellers" and the dominant transmitters of culture. Consumers Union opposed the growing commercialization of schools, as did the Center for the Analysis of Commercialism in Education and the Center for Commercial-Free Public Education. In August 1999, the Center for a New American Dream launched its Kids and Commercialism Campaign, just in time to help parents cope with the annual marketing blitz associated with back-to-school sales. Some months later, a group called the Motherhood Project, associated with the right-wing Institute for American Values, put together a broad-based statement titled "Watch Out for Children," which attacked the larger consumer culture being sold to youth. Not long afterward, a new coalition called Stop the Commercial Exploitation of Children developed, on the success of a series of events countering the industry's Annual Golden Marble Awards for the best children's ad.

Major national organizations such as the Children's Defense Fund, the National Education Association, and the American Academy of Pediatrics have also entered the debate about kids and consumer culture. The American Psychological Association began studying whether it should amend its code of ethics to prevent members from conducting marketing research on children. The issue reached the political mainstream in the 2000 elections, as Senate candidate Hillary Rodham Clinton declared that "too many companies simply see our children as little cash cows that they can exploit." Clinton called for a ban on ads to preschoolers and in public elementary schools. The debate heated up and one industry publication declared that "marketing to kids is now officially under the gun." As I've described, 2002 was a watershed year for opponents of food marketing. By 2003, the annual KidPower conference was taking note. "We are accused of manipulating and exploiting kids," the conference brochure intoned. "The kid industry is under attack for selling products to children that are presumed to make them greedy, violent and fat." Organizers added a session that would enlighten participants about "how worried" they should be about growing criticism in the press and the spread of advertising bans now in place in some European countries.

Under attack from many sides, industry has mounted three lines of defense. The first is that they are empowering kids. The second is that advertising to kids is necessary for the economic health of the industry. The third is that parents are the guilty party.

The New Discourse of Kid Empowerment

The core of what I call the new discourse of kid empowerment is the idea that ads and products help children to feel powerful. It says that kids need to feel independent and master their environments to feel in control of their parents. Lisa Morgan argues that "kids want to be in control in a world where they create their own rules . . . we always try to put them into situations where they . . . demonstrate mastery of a specific situation." Gene del Vecchio contends that "kids have very little control over the world in which they live. Therefore, they love to gain any measure of control over their sphere of existence. . . . Control touches a strong need that children have to be independent." Del Vecchio and others argue that a sense of control can be achieved through learning how to operate a toy, having the opportunity to choose among products, even something as simple as choosing among color variations, or watching an ad in which children triumph over adults.

Is it true that ads can create positive psychological outcomes? If a kid buys a pair of Nike shoes and feels better about himself or herself because of them, then Nike's ads may enhance self-esteem. But the messages are a double-edged sword because they also do the reverse, undermining self-worth. Sometimes the reality doesn't meet the promise. Sometimes kids desperately want a product because they're convinced it's essential to their happiness but there's no money to pay for it. As the nation's children are increasingly likely to live in poor and low-income households, this gap between desire and means is likely to grow. Many psychologists already find this a worrisome trend. Allen Kanner and M. E. Gomes have argued that many young people are suffering from feelings of deep inadequacy brought on by an inability to keep up with consumer culture.

Empowerment is also raised in a defense of the widespread antiadultism of commercial culture. Paul Kurnit defended an ad he produced for the board game Operation in which adults are portrayed as buffoons, saying it "levels the playing field" between children and adults. But there's a fine line between wholesome kid mastery and destructive antiadultism, and many believe that line has been crossed. Social conservatives argue that advertising and the media have become unacceptably disrespectful toward adults, undermining children's proper deference and obedience. However, even those who do not believe that adults have a God-given authority over children find themselves disturbed by some of today's advertising, wondering if the pervasive antiadultism is undermining mutual respect between parents and children. Bob Garfield, the influential columnist of *Advertising Age,* called a Nintendo spot that ridiculed parents an "exercise in craven cynicism and moral abdication." Garfield acknowledged that Nintendo was hardly alone in putting forward the "make-fun-of-grown-ups" message. Nevertheless, he argued, "At some point someone has to take a stand. These people have no right to speak to our children this way, and they had damn well better stop." James McNeal, responding directly to Kurnit, called his position "detestable."

Similar issues arise with direct targeting of children. After the gatekeeper model collapsed in the 1980s, industry went full steam ahead, selling their clients on nag factor kid influence. But the further industry goes down this road, the more it must defend itself against charges that it is having excessive and undue influence on kids. Industry has responded by claiming that children are capable of managing the persuasive pressure of commercial messages and are neither overly swayed nor harmed by them. This has led to the idea that kids are different than they were in the past, as, for example, in the 1970s, when research showed that children had rather limited abilities to understand and withstand advertising. Industry insiders now ignore or denigrate this research on the grounds that it's no longer relevant. They describe today's children as savvy, not able to be manipulated. Martin Lindstrom, a branding expert, thinks that kids have "an advertising filter which is greater than any previous generation. Advertisers and marketers cannot lie, and they cannot deliver crap quality." Wynne Tyree argues that "kids are much more sophisticated than most adults understand, and their sophistication levels are ever increasing at younger ages. There is a lot of evidence that kids are cognitively (and physically) developing more rapidly." Lisa Judson of Nickelodeon contends that "kids have a kind of truth meter. They are able to tell when marketers are being truthful and straightforward and they can tell when marketers are trying to trick them." Geoffrey Roche, an award-winning Canadian creative director, opines, "I don't think there is any way that we, as advertisers, can convince children of anything." Of course, this isn't always to the companies' benefit. One McDonald's advertiser, explaining the dynamics of Happy Meals, explained wistfully that "the kids have become a little more savvy, a little more demanding."

As a consequence, industry spokespeople argue that children do not need protection in their dealings with marketers. Those who are pushing for stricter regulations are put down as know-nothings. Paul Kurnit contends that the people who want to protect kids are "overprotective. . . . It is an issue where we often find that the people who are the most vocal about it have the least understanding of what's going on in kids' lives."

It's hard to dispute the view that children have become more sophisticated and worldly. However, there's little evidence on how that newfound sophistication affects children's ability to resist the persuasive power of ads, and whether growing up faster is empowering in the ways marketers suggest. I've found only one study that evaluates whether children's ability to understand and critically process advertising has grown over time. It's a meta-analysis by Mary Martin of the University of North Carolina at Charlotte that assesses the findings of twenty-one previous studies, conducted between 1972 and the mid-1990s. Martin finds that the ability of younger children to understand ads appears to have increased somewhat since the 1970s, although the correlation is weak and may be due to changes in the way researchers have measured understanding. Furthermore, the crucial question of whether young children can resist the persuasiveness of advertising has not been adequately explored. As I noted in Chapter 3, there's evidence that young children's ability to withstand persuasion is limited. Until there's more research, the industry's claims remain unproven.

The Instrumental Benefits of Ads

The industry's second argument is that advertising is justifiable because it creates other benefits, such as free television, better products, and economic growth and employment. Psychologically, these are the most powerful arguments because they reinforce the utter inevitability of advertising. But their logical power is weak.

Let's start with the claim of free television. First, it's not true. Television only appears to be free. The public funds ads and programs by paying higher prices for advertised products. The fact is that if you're a consumer, you pay for television, whether you watch or not. What's more, nominally free television is a bad thing because it leads kids to watch too much of it. Indeed, given the extensive body of research on the detrimental effects of television, free TV hardly makes a compelling case for advertising. Perhaps the strongest argument for free television is that it's available to low-income consumers who cannot afford other forms of entertainment. But given that low-income children spend so much time watching television and are disproportionately affected by some of the most harmful aspects of consumer culture, such as violence, obesity, and depression, this is a hard position to defend. It would be preferable to subsidize other forms of entertainment or to offer pay-per-view at heavily reduced rates to low-income households.

A second argument is that ads promote competition and indirectly lead to better products. More likely, they do the reverse. Advertising is expensive, and therefore creates barriers that make it harder for new products and companies to enter the market. With today's monopolized industries, the high cost of ad campaigns keeps the giants in control and the newcomers out. If we really wanted to maximize product innovation and improvements, we'd structure the system so advertising was inexpensive and mainly informational.

Finally, the industry has long taken the stance that ads create consumer demand, which creates more production and employment. Without ads, the argument goes, the economy would collapse. But most economists don't agree with this logic. They see advertising as mainly affecting brand choice rather than overall sales. And even if it were true, it's a problematic argument. During my research, I had lunch with a man who was then president of one of the nation's largest advertising agencies. He began our conversation by telling me that he believed advertising had become a terribly destructive force around the world, putting fast food joints everywhere, undermining local cultures and global diversity. As he looked over his career, he had lost faith in his business. So how do you live with yourself? I asked. His answer was that he put food on the table for his many employees. By that criterion, he is willing to advertise tobacco, which his firm does, and other harmful products just to maintain business. When it involves children, this instrumentality is even more questionable. Indeed, there's precious little justification for advertising to children merely to keep agencies profitable. Policy should be based on what's best for kids, not on arguments about how using them in one way or another yields particular outcomes for adults. When we argue that it's okay to use kids for the sake of making money, it's much harder to draw lines to protect their health, safety, and well-being. If society permits advertising to children, it should be because we're confident it isn't harmful, deceptive, or overly enticing.

A few marketers have taken that tack, claiming that advertising is actually good for children, helping them to be savvy consumers, and providing product information. But evidence suggests the opposite conclusion. For example, one study found that youth who watch more ads turn out to be more trusting of them, not less. A controlled study comparing students in Channel One and non–Channel One schools found that the former are more positive about the advertised products than those who don't see the broadcasts. If we want children to grow up with good consumer skills, we need to teach them directly, through media literacy courses, lessons in financial management, and information about how to become an informed consumer.

Findings from a Center for a New American Dream poll I collaborated on in 1999 suggest that relatively few parents buy into the industry's claims. Only 15 percent believe that advertising "is a good way for kids to get accurate information about products," and only 23 percent say that "children today are very sophisticated about advertising and are not really influenced by it all that much." To take the "we're doing good for kids" line seriously, one would need to see evidence for the causality that underlies this view: that kids who watch more ads have higher self-esteem and better friendships, are more content with their lives, and are more positively empowered. I found just the reverse.

Industry Blames the Parent

Industry's final line of defense is that parents always have the option of protecting their children from advertising. They can turn off the television and just say no. When parents let their children watch, they are giving tacit approval. Of course, the proliferation of marketing in schools and other public institutions undermines this claim, but it remains a mainstay in the industry's arsenal of arguments. Recently, the debate has gone further, as marketers blame parents for the excesses of consumer culture. If children have become too materialistic, or obese, or aggressive, it's because parents aren't doing their jobs. "The reason that there's childhood obesity is because caregivers don't have enough time to spend with their children. So what they're doing is giving their kids eight hours of TV a day," says Kenn Viselman, the media producer who brought *Teletubbies* to the United States. Other marketers hold a similar position. Peter Reynolds, CEO of Brio Toys, says, "Parents aren't losing control, they're giving it up. . . . The responsibility of the purchase always lies with the adult. Yeah, seventy-two times a day you're going to be asked, 'Can I have that toy? Can I have that toy?' But if the answer is 'no' seventy-two times a day for three or four weeks, then they stop asking." Paul Kurnit says parents are responsible for the decline of the gatekeeper model: "A decade ago I called it 'the unmanned tollbooth.' Today I call it 'Easy Pass.' " Arnold's Jerrie van Gelder worries that industry critics will lead us down a slippery slope: "If we start to remove the responsibility from the parents . . . I wonder where it stops."

This line of argument is powerful because it possesses an essential truth. Parents should and do bear responsibility for restricting children's access to consumer culture. When they fail to exercise judgment or set limits, the outcomes can be disastrous. I subscribe to this perspective as a researcher and as a parent. I've shielded my own children to a degree some people find excessive. But the undeniable fact of parental responsibility does not imply that it's only parents who should be held accountable. The complexities of life today render that approach far too simple-minded. Looking at the evolution of relationships between children, parents, and marketers, we see how much more entangled and difficult this triangulation has become. In the process, it becomes clear that all three parties need to behave differently.

Some of the more thoughtful advertisers I encountered understand this triangulation well. Wynne Tyree describes the case of food, explaining that the pervasiveness of unhealthful choices "puts moms in a tough position—the battle or the surrender." Tyree believes that mothers have only the best intentions for their children and care about their health. "But moms today, unlike many moms of yesterday, want their kids to be happy as much as they want them to be healthy. This is particularly true of those moms who are more time-constrained and/or work outside the home. Since kids want the sweets, the fats, and carbs, the result becomes a child with a little extra baby fat moms are sure their kids will grow out of." Tyree also recognizes the problem of what social scientists call "path dependency"—that what we do today affects our behavior tomorrow. "There's the problem of kids' palates that never get exposed to healthy foods and thus never develop a taste for them." Introducing young children to unhealthy food, even as treats, can undermine their ability to maintain a healthful diet over the long run.

The industry's critics are not so far from this perspective, explaining that it is increasingly difficult for parents when they are overextended and stressed and advertising comes at kids from so many angles. Harvard University's Susan Linn contends that we have put parents in the position of "playing David to the corporate Goliaths." And neither Linn nor others in the critics' camp are arguing against parental responsibility. They're asking for help. Indeed, one might argue that it is precisely because it is getting harder for parents that there should be more restrictions on marketers. We should be focusing less on who's to blame and more on a workable solution that protects children's well-being.

Parents have mixed attitudes about responsibility and blame. The Center for a New American Dream's poll asked about where the responsibility lies—with parents or marketers. Forty-one percent of parents took the view that "it is getting harder and harder to set limits with kids because so much advertising is aimed at making kids feel they need all of these products in order to fit it." A nearly identical number (43 percent) felt that "blaming advertisers is just an excuse parents give because they do not know how to say no." Interestingly, 12 percent volunteered that they agreed with both of these sentiments, an option that was not offered by the interviewers.

The poll also found that the vast majority of parents willingly accept responsibility for their children. But most don't think they should be forced to fight the battle alone, and there is strong support for restrictions on advertising. Seventy-eight percent of parents are opposed or strongly opposed to showing commercials for brand-name products in school; 64 percent believe Internet providers are not doing enough to protect children from online advertising; and 65 percent believe TV networks should be required to reduce the amount they advertise to children. When asked how they felt "when your child pressures you to buy something as a result of an advertisement," 20 percent said "angry" and 38 percent said "pressured." By contrast, only 6 percent reported themselves "ready to please," and 17 percent were "happy I have the money to buy it." A large majority (78 percent) also reported that they believe "marketing and advertising puts too much pressure on children to buy things that are too expensive, unhealthy, or unnecessary." Seventy percent feel "advertising and marketing aimed at kids has a negative effect on their values and world view," and 87 percent think "advertising and marketing aimed at kids today make children and teenagers too materialistic."

These findings reveal that although more than 40 percent of parents don't primarily blame advertisers, most of those respondents are critical of many of the practices marketers are engaged in. The poll suggests that parents have a pragmatic and balanced view of the issues.

Many advertisers speak with a forked tongue about parental responsibility. To the public they extol it. To their clients, they boast about their ability to exploit parental weakness. Whether it's dual messaging, going around parents by advertising in schools, finding the battles that moms are too exhausted to fight, or encouraging pester power, much of children's marketing has become an effort to break down parental opposition. Food marketers search for a believable (never mind true) nutritional claim. ("Give 'em a vitamin, give 'em calcium," David Siegel of the Wondergroup advises.) Toy manufacturers slap on the word *educational.* Companies anointed with the wholesome halo venture into questionable territory, knowing that parents trust them.

Surveying the commercial landscape, it seems that we've reached the point where it is no longer fair to put the onus exclusively on parents. Those who are trying to limit marketers' access to their kids deserve a reasonable chance of success. They shouldn't have to sequester their kids from so much in the environment. That puts an undue burden on both child and parent. The failure to address these issues also unfairly exposes those children who, for whatever reason, don't have parents setting limits for them. Despite his strong rhetoric about parental responsibility, Peter Reynolds's company markets only to parents, not to kids. "I want to save the children from the parents who don't take responsibility," he says. Such a stance is rare.

Advertising Doubts

When I began my research, I wasn't particularly interested in how those within the industry felt about their work. I just wanted to figure out what they were doing. Perhaps naively, I assumed that most would either believe in what they do or, if they didn't, would have well-developed rationalizations to keep their consciences at bay. I was unprepared for the spontaneous articulation of doubts I encountered. Mary Prescott raised her criticisms in both of our conversations: "I am doing the most horrible thing in the world. . . . We are targeting kids too young with too many inappropriate things. It's not worth the all-mighty buck." And later she confessed that "at the end of the day, my job is to get people to buy things. . . . It's a horrible thing and I know it." Thomas Kouns, of Truth Moderating and Qualitative Research and a former strategic planner at a number of agencies, also identified a problem at the core of the enterprise: "We have a message which says to be worth anything, you have to have the product. . . . Brands are about giving you value, giving you self-esteem. Fundamentally, that's really flawed. It stunts your emotional growth in a lot of ways. . . . We're so culpable, everybody's culpable." Mark Lapham, who founded and then sold his own promotions company, seemed as if he's marking time until he makes enough money to retire and do something he can be proud of. Martin Lindstrom decried the growth of materialism among tweens and worried that we've produced a generation that is not very nice. He described how it feels to "wear two hats." As a marketer, he counsels brands that they need tween strategies. But "from a parent point of view, I think this is a sad phenomenon." A marketer with a flair for the dramatic repeatedly foretold a future in which she'd "burn in hell."

For some, the problem isn't so much advertising as the way it's carried out. Langbourne Rust issued a blanket condemnation of his colleagues' use of nag factor: "It is assumed by most of them that it's all about pester power. We end up creating a world and culture around this idea. And we end up with a culture of kids at odds with their parents—wheedling, whining, and cajoling." Kenn Viselman takes a similar view. Referring to Idell's original nag factor study and the direct marketing that followed it, Viselman noted that "ever since that study came out, the concept of advertising to kids has become more and more widespread. It's become a way of life in our country and it's totally wrong. It's sacrilegious. We should be doing whatever we can to protect our youth, and instead we're just selling them out so we can make a few dollars." I encountered a few marketers who refuse to promote violent products or stress the need for positive approaches, but in my experience, these concerns mainly get lip service.

Rita Denney is one of the few professionals I discussed this issue with who shared the critics' view that advertising to children is inherently unfair. She's also one of the most highly educated and knowledgeable people in the field and holds a Ph.D. in linguistic anthropology from the University of Chicago. She understands a lot about children's development, and this is the basis of her refusal to work on children's products or accounts. "I have a third grader who I've watched grow up with television." Denney explains that it's too hard for her daughter to understand the rules of advertising and that she can't make certain kinds of judgments. "I'm willing to sell anything to adults," she explains. But she draws the line at kids.

The most poignant case I encountered was Susan Davies (pseudonym), a senior executive and a single mother who confessed her longtime ambivalence about the whole enterprise of marketing to kids. She's had to advertise products she doesn't believe in and wouldn't let her own children use. This leaves her feeling morally conflicted and unhappy with her work, so she's left the job a number of times. But she keeps returning because she needs the money. "The biggest issue is finding some peace." This is not always easy because, as she explains, in the advertising business you "can't really be critical of the product . . . you can't have a judgment on the product."

In the end, Davies identified the crux of the problem: the industry lacks sufficient moral accountability. In the agencies, people are afraid to confront the clients. In the companies, there's a similar lack of accountability. And all the while, the pressure to make money is overwhelming the need to do well by kids.

CHAPTER TEN

Decommercializing Childhood

Beyond Big Bird, Bratz Dolls, and the Back Street Boys

As marketers strive to capture the hearts and minds of America's children, evidence of their success is everywhere. Kids bond to brands, have adopted cool as a paramount value, and don't seem to mind that their favorite musical groups are pure marketing creations. They flock to Web sites that are mostly advertising, and they cover their bodies with logos. After nearly two decades of intensive targeting of kids, there's no doubt that industry has devised a profitable formula. It's equally clear the corporations are not meeting children's needs.

Constructing a less commercial childhood experience will not be easy. The media conglomerates, packaged goods and soft drink producers, ad agencies, and other corporations that market to kids have fought hard against reforms. They've used campaign donations, lobbying, and public relations. These efforts have been bolstered by the perception that consumer issues are private matters. A majority of parents express support for expanded protections for children, but translating that support into action will require widespread grassroots activism.

It will also require imagination about what's possible for children. Many adults long to return to a simpler time when children were sheltered and innocent. There is debate about that vision. Social analyst Stephanie Coontz calls the 1950s and 1960s "the way we never were." But it is indisputable that the era of idealized, or modern, childhood, whatever its particulars, was historically unique, even improbable. Its reconstruction is even more unlikely. The world has changed too much.

Marketers and advocates of postmodern childhood are critical of those who look to the past. They contend that the enormous influence of electronic media and corporate culture is here to stay and adopt a mainly uncritical stance toward it. But this realist view falls into the same trap they accuse others of. Just as modern childhood has disappeared, so too will its postmodern variant be transformed. The question is in what ways and to what effects. Global corporations may continue as the primary architects of children's futures. But a different future is possible too. Parents and children might come together to recapture childhood from the global giants and put in place a culture that is captivating, healthy, and empowering.

In the pages that follow, I lay out approaches for decommercializing and reconstructing childhood. Some of the changes I propose involve government regulation of advertising and marketing. Others consider what families can do inside their own homes and communities. I envision broadscale changes, which means we need to act on many levels—within the household, the community, schools, in the media, and government. I am optimistic about the possibilities for change, but mindful that there are no easy answers, no simple road map from here to there. Corporate childhood is too deeply woven into the fabric of everyday life.

Consumer Knows Best

In the standard approach to consumer policy, laissez-faire, or leave alone, is the near-universal prescription. This ideology of noninterference holds that one should be able to buy what one likes, where and when one likes, and as much as one likes, without so much as a glance from others. Consumption is arguably the activity our society deems most purely personal, outside the legitimate interest of society or government. Ironically, it is considered even more private than sex. This classical liberal view rests on a series of assumptions about consumers and markets. These include the idea that buyers have full information about the products on offer, that they are rational and in control of their actions, and that they are capable of acting in their own best interest. Liberalism also assumes that sellers are generally honest, that the marketplace is competitive, and that the consumer choices of one person do not affect anyone else. From these assumptions, economists have developed a formal model that shows that noninterference is the best policy, because it allows consumers the freedom to make their own choices, which results in the highest possible level of well-being. This approach is also common in political theory and business, which deploy similar arguments against efforts to regulate, structure, or influence consumer outcomes.

Of course, laissez-faire is sometimes violated. In response to pressure by consumer groups, governments have addressed problems such as buyer's remorse, unsafe and defective products, and deceptive and unfair advertising. Addictive products such as drugs and alcohol have been controlled or prohibited. Government also has a long history of regulating sexually oriented media and commodities, in deference to a puritanical culture and in contrast to the principles of liberalism. An activist period in the middle of the twentieth century led to federal programs aimed at influencing consumers' preferences in areas such as health, nutrition, and energy efficiency, although there has been a marked retreat from regulation since 1980. But these are exceptions.

With children, the theory is applied at one remove. In classical liberalism, children are not considered capable of rational deliberation and self-representation. (This characterization was also formerly applied to women, African Americans, persons without property, and others outside the circle of propertied, educated white men of European origin who formulated this theory and remain its dominant proponents.) Children are represented by their parents, who are assumed to be well-informed, disciplined consumers. The strong presumption against active consumer policy remains. Parents know best. If they don't like what's on offer, they can turn off the TV, just say no, or ban the offending T-shirt, lyrics, Web site, or caffeinated sodas. Consumer culture is not an imperative, it's a choice.

Prisoner's Dilemmas: The Flaw in the Liberal Argument

The standard approach sets a high bar for government regulation. In doing so, it respects individuals' ability to act for themselves and can forestall elitist interventions. But the conclusions of a model are only as strong as the assumptions on which it is built. In the case of consumer policy, the assumptions don't always stand up well to scrutiny. Consumers can be ill informed, impulsive, contradictory, and shortsighted. But even when they're not, the assumption that each consumer is isolated from everyone else is implausible. Indeed, it has long struck me as one of the most wrong-headed assumptions in all of economics.

In truth, consumption is a thoroughly social activity, and what one person buys, wears, drives, or eats affects the desires and behaviors of those around them. Without a social analysis, it is just not possible to understand the appeal of Nike's swoosh, the desire for a diamond ring, the rage for Harleys, or the taste for sun-dried tomatoes. Nor can one comprehend the rapid rise and demise of Pokémon, the turn away from Britney, or the ubiquity of hip-huggers and chunky silver bracelets from Tiffany. Kids have sensitive antennas to what's in and out, what's cool and hip. They care, often desperately, about how their consumer choices are received by peers.

Once we accept that consumption is social, the argument against intervention is much weaker. One reason is a class of situations that have been dubbed the Prisoner's Dilemma. Named after the original formulation of the problem involving two prisoners, the dilemma involves cases where cooperation and regulation yield a superior outcome for everyone but in which individuals have a strong incentive to act on their own. Consider the example of holding a child back a year solely to gain a competitive advantage in sports or athletics. When the first few parents do it, they may achieve that edge. But once a competitive dynamic starts and everyone eventually does it, the advantage disappears. Individuals can't engineer a return to the original situation, despite the fact that everyone would benefit. Only a regulatory intervention, such as a school policy or a collective approach, can do that. Competitive situations, where what matters is one's relative position, are frequently characterized by these kinds of market failures, as they are called. Willingness to engage in risky behaviors is a related example. Peer pressures often lead kids to do things they wouldn't on their own. Adults recognize that intervention from parents or school officials is in the children's interest.

Consumer competitions often fall into this category. When the appeal of a product is largely due to its prestige or social validation rather than its intrinsic benefits to the consumer, people can be made better off by measures to moderate its consumption. Rapidly changing fashions, teen cosmetic surgeries, upgrading perfectly good video game systems, and upscaling to expensive designer brands fall into this category, because the impetus for participating is often that all the other kids are doing it. If everyone wore cheaper, no-name sneakers, there'd be money saved, and no one would be the worse for it. This is what game theorists call a cooperative outcome, in which the upscaling or the risky behavior is moderated or prevented. Cooperative outcomes have the possibility of making kids safer and more satisfied with what they already have, as well as saving families money. The past two decades of commercialization have intensified consumption competitions, propelled kids toward riskier and more extreme behaviors and styles, and undermined cultural restraints. These changes provide a rationale for action through both government regulation and social cooperation.

Race to the Bottom: The Problem for Companies

Companies also face Prisoner's Dilemmas, as competition intensifies trends such as KAGOY (Kids Are Getting Older Younger), the escalation of violence and sex in media content, and edgy attitude. In the past, industry norms were relatively stable. But those voluntary arrangements have come under pressure. At the advertising agencies, material is screened for compliance with network codes and the Children's Advertising Review Unit (CARU). But the stability that came from having three similar networks has broken down with the entrance of scores of new marketing media and venues. Cable stations are far more permissive, and that has led the networks to loosen up. Advertising executives also complain that when programs feature daredevil stunts or risqué language and behavior, the strict guidelines for ads make less sense and are harder to sustain. Internet marketing is far more loosely regulated and features widespread product placement, host selling, stealthy advertising, and individualized targeting of kids. These practices violate the protective thrust of the CARU guidelines. As standards erode, individual companies are caught in a bind. If the competition is doing it, the pressure to go along is strong. In a visit to one conservative agency, I was privy to a duplicitous scheme to get approval for an ad that was described to me as "definitely illegal" for its failure to distinguish fantasy and reality adequately. I left wondering what was going on at the less scrupulous places.

A related dynamic occurs with program and movie content and music lyrics. Once a competitive dynamic toward more violence, sex, profanity, or shocking content begins, it's hard for individual producers to resist. The onus of opting out has been put wholly on the consumer. But industry has also manipulated the system. Observers have noted that not long after the studios were forced to stop marketing R-rated movies to underage kids, they responded by increasing the levels of violence and sex in the PG-13 category. These pressures on companies suggest that although industry has historically spent a good deal of money and political capital to avoid regulation, there are ways they too might benefit from a more structured and less free-for-all environment.

Federal Regulation of Ads and Media

In the past twenty-five years, the willingness of the federal government to regulate children's advertising and media has eroded significantly. As I have mentioned, Congress tied the hands of the FTC in 1981 and hasn't untied them since. It eventually passed the Children's Television Act in 1990, but its provisions are scanty. The act requires three hours per week of educational programming, but compliance has been variable. In the early years, the networks used reruns of *The Flintstones* and *The Jetsons* to satisfy this public interest provision.

The federal failure to protect children is also attributable to the unwillingness of the FTC to address new developments in the marketplace. In 1992, the FTC was asked to require disclosure for paid product placements in movies. It refused to do so. In 1994, it declined to enact a ban on Joe Camel, despite considerable evidence of the power of this character on youth smoking behaviors and attitudes. In 1999, when the FTC asked eight alcohol manufacturers to report on children's exposure to their ads, it found that only half were in compliance with their own guidelines. But the commission again failed to act. Theorists of regulation call this situation a "capture," in which special interests capture regulators and divert them from acting in the general interest. At the FTC, industry has pressured the agency not to enact regulations but to allow voluntary codes of behavior drawn up and policed by industry. The current chair of the FTC hews strongly to this line. But voluntary codes have failed.

Other voluntary industry schemes are also deeply flawed. The movie rating system has spawned what media scholars call the forbidden fruit syndrome, in which movies become desirable to kids largely because they are off-limits. Parental advisories for music lyrics and the television ratings system are failing in part because they have been shown to be virtually invisible to parents. There's a clear public interest in an alternative to these industry-created and -operated solutions.

This history of regulatory inadequacy suggests that meaningful federal intervention is more likely to come through pressure on Congress. Passing federal legislation is always difficult, especially now, with a conservative Congress, well heeled through corporate campaign donations. Indeed, this book began by describing an advertising ban as "inconceivable" in today's climate. Nevertheless, there are some grounds for optimism. Congress acted decisively to protect children's privacy on the Internet. It has been determined in its efforts to regulate telemarketing. In the past eighteen months, the outlook for regulating food sales and marketing has changed dramatically, as schools and legislatures around the country have responded to the obesity epidemic with uncharacteristic fervor. With enough pressure from parents and advocacy groups, Congress may well be moved to act.

A good place to begin is to require full disclosure in children's marketing. Congress should pass a federal act mandating disclosure for all sponsored product placements in television, movies, videos, books, radio, and the Internet. Consumers of media and their parents should have the right to be told whenever they are being advertised to. Disclosure should be appropriate to the age of the viewer; for example, with small children, the information should be verbal and not merely written. Companies should also be required to disclose situations where they target children through real-life product placement and peer-to-peer and stealth marketing. These are cases in which ordinary people are paid to comment on products on Internet sites, to send e-mails to friends about products, or when the companies pay for Web sites without identifying themselves.

A second form of authorial disclosure has been formulated by Commercial Alert, in its Parents' Bill of Rights, a set of nine legislative steps to reform marketing practices. (The entire Parents' Bill of Rights has been reproduced in Appendix C.) The proposed advertising to children accountability act requires corporations with gross revenues exceeding $25 million per year to disclose the names of the individuals who carried out the research, writing, and production for any ad directed at children under twelve years of age. Disclosure would be required for any employee or consultant who worked at least forty hours on an advertisement or proprietary research study, and disclosure statements would be due one week after an ad airs, at the FTC and on the company Web site. This act would allow parents to affix individual responsibility for attempts to influence their children. One hopes it would also encourage marketers to take more social responsibility for their work. A further provision that should be added is the requirement for industry to develop institutional review boards for all research with children, which follow federal government regulations for protecting research subjects.

Congress needs to address whether advertising to children is warranted at all. As I discussed in Chapter 3, the research suggests that young children find it hard to recognize ads, and those under age eight are unable to resist their persuasiveness. Congress should commission a series of major independent studies on the full range of questions associated with advertising to children, such as the age at which they can identify ads, how they comprehend ads at various ages, and when they become able to understand and resist persuasion. Congress should also request a General Accounting Office or FTC report, similar to those that have been done on school commercialism and the marketing of movies and video games, which catalogues the full range of current marketing practices. After receiving this research, it should hold public hearings around the country and decide whether to closely regulate or even ban advertising to children. The Parents' Bill of Rights advocates a total ban on advertising to children under age twelve, which is the policy adopted by the government of Sweden. Another threshold might be age eight. Food marketing deserves special scrutiny. Congress should carefully consider whether food should be added to the list of products that are currently not targeted to children. This list includes alcohol, tobacco, gambling, R- and X-rated movies, and prescription drugs. A ban on food marketing makes nutritional sense, particularly because of the epidemic of obesity and the widespread failure of children's diets to meet nutritional standards. Furthermore, the government needs to strengthen and enforce regulations concerning currently banned products.

These kinds of disclosure and fairness provisions mainly address the abilities of parents and children to make informed decisions. Prisoner's Dilemmas require another style of intervention—policies that reduce the pressure to join consumption competitions. The standard approach in these cases is to tax the behavior one wants to discourage. Congress should levy a tax on advertising because of its role in changing social norms and stimulating consumer desire. I propose a federal levy of 2 percent on all advertising aired on television, radio, movies, and the Internet whenever more than 25 percent of the audience is in the age-eighteen-and-under category. (I suggest this age range because consumption competitions are also strong among teens and because tween viewing of teen media is extensive.) Such a tax would have two effects: it would reduce the volume of ads and could be used to establish a fund for producing noncommercial children's programming. This would be especially important if advertising to young children is banned or curtailed.

There are other changes to federal tax policy worth considering. The Parents' Bill of Rights calls for an end to the tax deductibility of corporate expenditures on market research and advertising to children under age twelve. Another principle is to make advertising easier to avoid for those who prefer to. My favorite idea is to confine ads to a restricted set of commercial channels. If the industry is right that ads are informative, valuable, and enjoyable for viewers, they have nothing to fear. Those who like ads can watch to their heart's content. Those who don't can avoid the commercial channels. In place of our perverse system of subsidizing content by ads, viewers could pay directly for the media content they want to see. The public, which theoretically owns the airwaves, could charge the media providers an honest fee. That money could provide the funding for expanded noncommercial media, controlled by the public and operating in its interest.

These suggestions rely on identifying ads that are directed at the particular age targets. This has become more complex than it was when kids watched just kids' shows and corporations selling adult products didn't bother with them. Now that corporate strategies for reaching youth are often integrated with adult marketing and kids watch adult programming, it's necessary to lower the 50 percent threshold used to identify underage audiences. Children ages twelve and under make up only about 18 percent of the population. Government guidelines and regulations need to reflect that fact.

Ad-Free Schools

Congress should also enact comprehensive legislation to restrict school commercialism. Advertising in schools violates a fundamental principle of consumer sovereignty: the ability to escape ads and marketing. Schooling is compulsory, unlike Internet surfing or patronizing a fast food restaurant. The problem is compounded by the fact that school advertising frequently involves candy, snacks, soft drinks, violent movies, and other products that undermine children's health and well-being and contradict schools' basic mission. Furthermore, the growth of corporate-sponsored curricular materials threatens fundamental principles of objectivity and knowledge in the classroom. As school districts compete to buy new technology, offer electives, mount expensive sports programs, and raise test scores, Prisoner's Dilemmas lead to pressure to raise revenues from companies.

So far, policies have addressed each commercial intrusion individually. Soft drink vending machine sales have been banned or restricted in some districts and states. Channel One has met opposition at school board meetings. But this piecemeal local response has been an invitation to further innovation by marketers. With determined opposition in the California statehouse, Channel One attempted to build political support by targeting individual teachers and school administrators. Facing criticism at the district level, Coca-Cola made a substantial donation to the National PTA.

The Parents' Bill of Rights calls for a congressional act to ban advertising in schools, with minor exceptions such as school newspapers and yearbooks. All contractual obligations for children to view ads, such as Channel One, and Coke and Pepsi contracts requiring ads on vending machines, would be outlawed. A federal act to decommercialize schools should also prohibit sponsored educational materials, the use of brand names in textbooks, in-classroom ads, displays on school buses and other school property, and corporate-sponsored contests. It would forbid giving market research firms access to children during school hours.

The Need for Social Cooperation

Today's most sophisticated children's marketers operate by insinuating themselves into existing social dynamics. They have nuanced understandings of how peer pressure operates; identify trendsetters, influencers, and followers; and target each group with tailored approaches. Fifty-eight percent of nine to fourteen year olds now say that they feel pressure to buy stuff in order to fit in. In addition to the onus of acquiring particular consumer items, social pressures surrounding media content and personal style are of great concern to parents. At what age should kids be permitted to see PG-13 or R movies, use instant messaging, surf the Internet, or get a tattoo? Industry helps popularize these activities.

These are other versions of the Prisoner's Dilemma, this time played out on the freighted terrain of social inclusion and exclusion. The more that market-driven trends structure peer interactions, parental restrictions put kids at risk for social exclusion. But basing decisions about what to allow on the basis of other kids' or parents' choices may mean losing control altogether. It's one of the trickiest aspects of parenting today.

The cooperative solution entails adults' and kids' getting together to set limits jointly. This reduces the pressure on kids and keeps the standards from changing more than individuals want. Such collaboration is already occurring with drug and alcohol use, commodities most adults feel should be absolutely forbidden. Around the country, parents have formed Communities of Concern and signed the Safe Homes Pledge, promising that they will supervise gatherings at their home to prohibit minors from using alcohol, drugs, or firearms. The community comes together to create structures that ease the peer pressures on kids and protect them from danger.

A related approach is possible for other consumer practices that involve peer pressure. A first step is community dialogue. Schools and PTAs can

sponsor conversations and workshops on topics such as movie ratings, media use, video games, school fashion, spending money—even the customs surrounding birthday parties. As communities come together to work through their attitudes, awareness is created, and common approaches can develop. Sometimes the simple fact of airing a topic contributes to changes in social practices and norms. If the dialogue progresses to the point where people feel more formal action is useful, analogues to the Safe Homes Pledge can be developed. Formalization helps socialize newcomers and maintains standards over time.

Smaller-scale cooperation can also be effective. In my research in Doxley, I found that mothers communicate to control consumption choices. Some call before sleepovers to find out what video the kids will be watching. Those who restrict certain types of content make their rules known. Mothers caucus about group dates to the movies. They confer about the acceptability of particular CDs. In some cases, they talk through options and take common responsibility. Occasionally one agrees to play bad cop. The larger point is that to raise children well, adults need to communicate and cooperate and establish safe and healthy environments for them. It's an old-fashioned value that's being lost as neighborhood interaction and community has declined. We owe it to our kids to get it back.

The Limits of Protectionism

The kinds of legislative and social changes I have been describing are esse tial to decommercializing childhood. But they are defensive steps, ba on a traditional paradigm of child protection. In the long run, we'll n more fundamental changes to do well by children. The limitatior the protectionist approach are revealed by a brief foray into history social theory to consider how contemporary notions of childhood developed.

The idea that children require protection has its roots in child opment theory, which we met briefly in Chapter 3. Development assumes that children progress through a fixed set of natural which are defined by biologically given cognitive and emotional and reach their apex in mature adulthood. It assumes that chil incomplete and immature, in need of improvement, alteration, guidance. Seen in this light, developmentalism, despite its s benign attitude toward kids and social sensitivity, is reveale deeply adult-centric and deterministic theory.

Despite continued popular resonance, the developmental paradigm has come in for considerable criticism from sociologists, cognitive and neuroscientists, and linguistic theorists. It was also dealt a serious intellectual blow in the 1960s by French historian Philippe Ariès in his influential study *Centuries of Childhood.* Ariès argued that prior to the eighteenth century, neither the concept nor the reality of childhood existed in the West. Like so many other naturalized ideas, childhood turns out to have been invented.

The Invention of Modern Childhood

A central theme of the Ariès book is that in the premodern era, children were thought of as miniature adults. They dressed in adult clothing and were fully exposed to the adult world. They were not considered to be sexually or morally innocent, as they are today. Children were integrated into society and much less subject to pervasive discipline and training. Ariès based much of his argument on the depiction of children in paintings rather than more direct evidence, and undoubtedly he made too strong a case. Some of his arguments were wrong, and others remain controversial, such as the claim that parents in the premodern era had limited emotional attachment to their children, and his account of the maltreatment of children and its effects on infant mortality. But his larger point is hard to dispute. The ideas and practices that we call childhood have varied greatly throughout history and across societies. This perspective—that childhood is not a natural or biological condition—is called *social constructionism.*

Social constructionists argue that the coming of modernity created childhood as a new social and cultural category. There are several explanations for why this change occurred. One emphasizes economic trends, such as rising prosperity and declines in infant mortality. As children began to live longer, parents invested more time, money, and emotion in them. This investment is thought to have fostered social attitudes that emphasized the differences between adults and children. A second theory credits the spread of literacy. Neil Postman, in his influential book *The Disappearance of Childhood,* argued that in the oral culture of the Middle Ages, children became adults at age seven, when full speech was achieved. By contrast, a culture based on literacy requires a long period in which children gradually learn to discipline their bodies and repress their physical energies—prerequisites for long hours of reading and studying. This resulted in age-based instruction in primary schools, and with it the spa-

tial and social isolation of children. Over time, children were trained in morality, manners, and habits of discipline. Thus, the rigors of schooling underpinned modern notions of proper childhood.

Whatever the original causes (both prosperity and literacy were probably important), the boundaries between adults and children developed and hardened as modernity spread. Children increasingly occupied a segregated environment, protected and excluded from adults. Of course, the extent to which this occurred was partly a matter of social class. As a number of scholars have pointed out, childhood was mainly a project of the middle class, which could afford to realize its vision. The isolation of children happened earlier and more completely for economically privileged children than for those of the poor. But as the middle class came to comprise a large fraction of the population in the United States, its conceptions of childhood came to dominate.

The separations between adults and children were spatial, temporal, cultural, social, and economic. Children gradually came to be restricted from a variety of social settings, such as workplaces, higher-education institutions, bars, adult entertainment zones, fancy restaurants, venues for arts and culture, health clubs, and other leisure spaces. Even within the home, demarcations developed between adult rooms such as living rooms and parental bedrooms, and children's spaces (family rooms, nurseries, and playrooms). This is one reason that children's own bedrooms became places of autonomy and refuge. Children were restricted to being awake during the day; the night was reserved for adult activities. Children were also shielded from adult violence, cruelty, sickness, death, and, most important, sex. In the process, childhood and adulthood came to be defined primarily in relation to each other. Childhood consisted of a series of exclusions from adulthood—places children couldn't be in, activities they were prohibited from engaging in, things they shouldn't see or know about. Eventually, this exclusion began to be seen in very positive terms, and childhood was conceptualized as an almost idyllic, play-oriented, carefree stage that every child had a right to.

The development of childhood led to new emotional attitudes toward children. In the premodern era, children did not merit special affection or affinity. After the rise of Puritanism in the seventeenth century, adults were more attuned to children's potential for evil and charged with keeping the devil at bay, often through violence. Over time, these attitudes moderated, and adults became not only more loving and humane, but children came to occupy an emotionally unique role in society. As I noted in the Introduction, sociologist Viviana Zelizer has found important changes at the turn of the twentieth century, such as declining tolerance of infant death, increased concern for children's physical safety, opposition to child labor, and the growth of an adoptive market in infant babies. Zelizer argues that children came to be considered sacred, priceless, and irreplaceable. This was also the point at which ideas of innocence and purity came to dominate adults' views of children. The first half of the twentieth century became the highwater mark of modern childhood.

The Disappearance of Childhood and the Empowerment of Children

As modernity evolved into its "post" phase, childhood was bound to change. Those changes have been widely interpreted in the language of a disappearance of childhood because postmodernity has been characterized by more porous boundaries between adult and child worlds. Neil Postman, the original proponent of the disappearance thesis, blames the replacement of print culture by television, which requires no training to master and exposes children indiscriminately to adult themes. Cultural trends have further undermined modern childhood. Parenting norms have shifted to become more egalitarian, and the media typically depicts highly empowered children and childlike adults. Social critic Kay Hymowitz has discussed this culture shift as a "new realism," arguing that "far more than in other cultures and regardless of age, American children are treated as autonomous, self-directing actors." Social conservatives are highly critical of these developments and blame liberal ideologies of permissiveness (the Spock generation), moral relativism, and the breakdown of patriarchal authority. Liberals are ambivalent, torn between the view that children should be respected and that they need more protection.

Marketers, on the other hand, have hardly looked back. They ignore most of the assumptions of the modern period, such as the need to protect children from the adult world and respect for adult authority. (Recall the slogan of children's marketer par excellence, Nickelodeon: Kids rule!) Marketers use the developmental paradigm with their talk of timeless needs and motivations, but they reject its depiction of the child as incomplete and defective and employ a child-centric point of view. Advertisers avoid saccharine portrayals of children and rarely regret the loss of childhood innocence. They've put themselves squarely on the side of hedonism and gratification of desire rather than the modern socialization processes of discipline over bodily urges and suppression of physical energies. Marketers stand for fun over work, license over restriction, expression over repression. They dwell on fantasy and imagination. They profess belief in the autonomy and power of youth. Indeed, they hardly ever use the terms *children* or *childhood.* They believe in kids.

Some years ago, cultural critic Stephen Kline made a similar observation: "The merchants and marketers of children's goods have always paid more diligent attention than educationists to children's active imaginations and incidental cultural interests. . . . The marketers didn't have to assume that children's daydreams, hero worship, absurdist humour and keen sense of group identity were meaningless distractions or artefacts of immaturity. Rather, they recognized that these attributes were the deep roots of children's culture, which could be employed as effective tools for communicating with them." This willingness to accept children on their own terms, without judgment, is surely one of the secrets of marketers' success.

Far from being a tragedy, the demise of the modernist categories is an opportunity that has already spawned a significant increase in children's autonomy and power. In the scholarly literature, the most innovative and compelling writing is about child-centered research, children's rights, autonomy, respect, and empowerment. I refer to the work of sociologists and anthropologists such as Allison James, Chris Jenks, Daniel Cook, James Qvotrup, Viviana Zelizer, and Barrie Thorne and cultural studies scholars Henry Jenkins, Valerie Walkerdine, Henry Giroux, and Angela McRobbie, among others.

But empowerment also creates a dilemma. The environment in which children have been set free is increasingly dominated by a toxic consumer culture. In the short run, that's why we need the kinds of protections I have advocated. But in the long run, we need more than protection. We need to create a different culture—one that is safe, fun, and stimulating for children and adults alike. Here are three examples of the kinds of cultural innovations that could move us in that direction.

Decommercializing Culture: Food, Media, and Outdoor Space

Children today are increasingly dependent on junk food, fast food, and microwave meals, and they are disconnected from growing, preparing, and appreciating food. The family meal, once an important social ritual, is now endangered. In recent years, a food reform movement has emerged, advocating a return to "slow food"—locally grown organic food, seasonal menus, and closer ties between consumers and farmers. Although it has mainly been adult oriented, Alice Waters, owner of the celebrated restaurant Chez Panisse and a pioneer of food reform, recognized that reformers also had to include children. In 1995, she teamed up with the principal of a dilapidated, urban middle school in her community of Berkeley, California, and began the Edible Schoolyard project. The Edible Schoolyard is a one-acre organic garden, and a working kitchen, with a comprehensive curriculum teaching gardening, menu planning, nutrition, eco-literacy, and science. Along with teachers and other volunteers, the children are involved at all stages of growing, harvesting, cooking, and eating. They make butter, grind flour, and learn composting. They care for chicks, plant trees, keep journals, and explore ethical issues through the lens of the garden. They have learned to appreciate fresh, tasty food, and the community it brings, as they work together. In addition to teaching the children practical skills and educational lessons, and yielding nutritional benefits, the project's mission is "awakening their senses and encouraging awareness and appreciation of the transformative values of nourishment, community, and stewardship of the land." It's a far cry from McDonald's. It's also the kind of project that deserves replication across the country.

Commercial media and Channel One are the media equivalents of fast food. What might be the media equivalent of the Edible Schoolyard? In the middle school in my neighborhood, the students produce their own news program, which airs every morning, in preference to the commercial offerings of Channel One and CNN. The students work from a real studio. They read the news, operate the cameras, and serve in the roles of director and producer. The broadcast creates a sense of community and accomplishment and is an extremely popular extracurricular activity.

A more ambitious version of this idea would be a National Kids' Public Media Corporation. It would be a noncommercial, publicly controlled alternative to Disney, Nickelodeon, and the other giants, encompassing television, radio, and the Internet. Funding could be provided by the proposed tax on children's advertising. In contrast to previous attempts to offer quality children's programming, such as PBS, this effort would be run by children, and it would not be dependent on corporate funding. As with the most successful commercial media, its creativity would come from children rather than adults' visions of what kids should learn or the values they should have. Lest such an idea seem impractical, it is worth remembering that marketers have already successfully incorporated children into all stages of their work, from brainstorming to design to choice of product name to sales and marketing. A public media corporation could do the same. Youth would comprise the writers, directors, actors, and film crews. Young people would represent a majority on the board. It would be television, radio, and Internet for and by kids. While solving the problems associated with children's media use requires much more than one new television station, moving away from media whose purpose is to sell products is an important first step.

My third example addresses the need to reclaim outdoor space for children. The story of their relationship to the outdoors is a classic example of the pitfalls of modern childhood. In the nineteenth century and in twentieth-century rural and small-town America, children spent a large amount of time out of doors. They enjoyed nature, developed independence, and managed social dynamics without adult intervention. Boys historically had more freedom outside the home, but children of both sexes enjoyed being out of doors. In the urban areas, outdoor play was curtailed in the early twentieth century, when a movement to curb urban traffic fatalities resulted in laws to prevent children from playing in streets and increased indoor confinement. Outdoor play in rural areas declined for other reasons such as the decline of population, longer trips to school, and the loss of woods and other open space.

Today, urban and suburban children represent the bulk of the youth population, and their access to outdoor space without adult supervision remains restricted. One problem is automobiles, which have become more dangerous because of the growth in traffic volume, average speeds, and the deadliness of automobiles and SUVs. Many parents also fear stranger abduction, but such fears are greatly disproportionate to the incidence of these crimes. In inner-city neighborhoods, the pervasiveness of drug dealing, robbery, accidental violence from gunshots, and other criminal activities have combined to make outdoor space perilous for children. But indoor confinement has reduced children's levels of activity and exercise, undermined their social worlds, and eroded their autonomy. It's an important part of why media and consumer culture is so influential in their lives. These effects have been especially severe for low-income and urban children.

We need a national initiative to make outdoor space much safer for children. Indeed, it's hard to imagine making serious inroads into excessive television viewing or the salience of consumer culture without getting kids back outside. Communities will need to address traffic and safety issues. One step is for local authorities to initiate what are called traffic calming measures, such as slower posted speed limits, speed bumps, and other physical barriers in residential areas. In the Netherlands, where I lived for a time, most residential streets had speed bumps, and many were split in half by pedestrian-only corridors.

To protect children from crime, local police departments can deploy crossing guards at fields and playgrounds during after-school hours and weekends. If that's too expensive, neighborhood volunteers can share responsibility for watching over playgrounds and outdoor spaces, and build community in the process. Technology can also be useful. I interviewed one parent who uses a walkie-talkie system when her children are outside alone. Equipping public streets with emergency phones is another strategy for enhancing safety without reducing mobility. In the endnotes to this chapter, I describe a remarkable Swedish initiative that has virtually eliminated traffic fatalities for children.

These are just examples. But taken together, significant initiatives in the three areas of food, media, and outdoor space could have enormous impact on the quality of children's everyday lives.

Decommercializing the Household: Evidence from Doxley

Many parents are uncomfortable with aspects of consumer culture. The parents I interviewed in Doxley certainly were, although their likes and dislikes, as well as their rationales, varied widely, from the aesthetic to the practical. Some hate television because its content is junky. Some feel that designer labels aren't good value, and others object to trendiness itself. They worry about sex on the Internet, media violence, adult themes in movies, and excessive attraction to video games. Their attitudes are rather typically middle class, an issue I discuss in some detail in the endnote to this paragraph.

Where the families may be less typical is in their success at controlling and limiting those parts of consumer culture that they object to. Granted, they were mostly financially secure and could afford high levels of maternal involvement. They didn't need television as a baby-sitter. But more than economics is at work. Those who were most successful were thoughtful and consistent in their rules and choices. They spent a lot of time with their children. And perhaps most important, these families' lives were full of engaging alternatives to the corporate offerings.

One perhaps unsurprising finding is the importance of restricting television viewing. My data showed that kids in Doxley watch relatively little television. Virtually every household I interviewed had rules about when, how much, and what kids could watch. Some allowed only minimal viewing. Many opted not to get cable. The restrictions appeared to be relatively effective, in contrast to other research findings with a less affluent sample, among whom there were fewer nonemployed mothers. (See the accompanying note for a fuller discussion of this issue.) In Doxley, the keys to success appeared to be consistency, rules tailored to the needs of individual children, and heavy time commitments to homework, sports, extracurricular activities, and outdoor play.

None of the parents I interviewed prohibited television altogether, but some came close. Their experiences are notable because they contradict widely held views that children need TV. One argument is that prohibiting television will backfire, and children will become avid viewers once parents relinquish control. A second is that children need television knowledge to prevent social exclusion. Some media scholars have also argued that the dominance of electronic media is so strong that prohibition deprives children of basic cultural literacy. The absence of these problems in the households I visited was notable, even allowing for the fact that Doxley is a low-viewing environment.

My own experience also supports this view. After our first child was born, we decided not to expose him to television, reasoning that he'd eventually become well versed in electronic media, but that love of reading and the dying print culture would be more difficult to instill. When people challenged me on this policy, as many did, I responded that we would let him watch television when he started asking for it. I agreed with the common view that we were at risk of forbidden-fruit syndrome if we were too rigid. But a funny thing happened: he never asked. We told him that we didn't think television was good for him, and he accepted that. When he entered first grade, we started watching videos sometimes. He's twelve now, and we do allow occasional viewing of sporting events. We've followed the same policies with our daughter. She doesn't ask either.

I include my story because things turned out so differently than I had expected. A decade ago, I put much more stock in the counterarguments, such as the view that kids need television knowledge to fit in socially and that only by allowing television can parents prevent children from wanting it too much. In my case, neither of these sentiments turned out to be correct. I believe my children have been much better off growing up TV free. I think it's enhanced their creativity, taught them how to amuse themselves, and given them many more hours of beneficial and more satisfying activities such as reading, writing poetry, doing art projects, and getting exercise. Of course, to be successful in restricting television for our kids, we had to stop watching it ourselves. So we put our set in a third-floor room, where the temperature is uncomfortable in both winter and summer. Instead of creating a special child-only deprivation, we changed the environment in which we all live. And we're all better for it.

My interview material also suggests that the families who are most successful in keeping the corporate culture at bay are involved with alternatives. Some of the most restrictive mothers are active in their churches. Some of the immigrant families, who tend to be rather strict about commercial influences, come together in each other's homes for regular worship and socializing. I encountered a variety of nonreligious activities as well. One woman started a mother-daughter book club, with discussion of the book and an activity. One household had family movie nights, with row seating, ushers, and popcorn. Another specialized in elaborate but low-budget theme parties—Greek mythology, insects, Peter Pan, and Eskimos (complete with a full-scale igloo). Other popular activities were woodworking, playing board games after school, and unorganized sports. The activities they described typically involved parents and kids together. One family makes a yearly pilgrimage to a mine to collect rocks, another took the kids out of school for nearly a year of travel, a third are avid canoeists and campers. These experiences jibe with anecdotal evidence from the downshifter movement, which suggests that many families are rediscovering simple, inexpensive pleasures. Eco-psychologists have also found that disconnection from nature erodes emotional and spiritual well-being. Fostering children's connection to the outdoors serves as a bulwark against excessive involvement with consumer culture.

These kinds of activities require time and energy. My earlier books addressed the inadequacy of free time and the mounting financial pressures on families. Scarcity of time and money is especially acute among low-income and single-parent households, whose members usually have long hours and inflexible jobs, ever-present financial worries, and high-stress lives. But reducing stress and finding time are crucial to engaging with kids in less commercial ways. National survey data suggest that children wish for more of that from their parents, and noncommercial activities remain popular. For example, in their 2003 poll of kids aged nine to fourteen, the Center for a New American Dream found that fewer than a third (32 percent) reported that they spend a lot of time with their parents. Sixty-nine percent of kids said they'd like to spend more time with them, and if granted one wish that would change their parents' job, 63 percent said it would be a job that gave them "more time to do fun things together." Only 13 percent wished their parents made more money. When asked what they would most like to do with their parents, 23 percent chose the three noncommercial outdoor activities offered: building a snowman or a tree house, riding bikes or doing something outside, and gardening. Twenty percent opted for a movie, 18 percent for a ball game, and 13 percent wanted a visit to a zoo or aquarium.

Reducing corporate influences does not entail exorcising money from children's lives. The ideology of childhood sacredness and innocence is frequently counterposed against the profane adult world of money and desire. The moral panic surrounding Pokémon trading cards, and to a lesser extent Beanie Babies and sport cards, revealed the pervasiveness of attitudes that children's play should be motivated by love of the objects themselves rather than acquisitive or speculative desires. Such an attitude pervades the position of the anticommercial Motherhood Project: "We face a conflict of values . . . between the values of the money world and the values of the 'motherworld'—the values of commerce and the values required to raise healthy children."

While restricting children from the profanity of the money world has a superficial appeal, such sacralization unduly deprives children of their right to be economic agents. Recent ethnographic research shows that children are typically engaged in a variety of productive practices—not only trading cards and toys but also participated in lunchtime food swaps, networks of reciprocal favors, and informal entrepreneurial activities. Indeed, children have far more sophisticated and extensive economic lives than many adults give them credit for. Why should they be deprived of these?

I do not raise this point merely for academic purposes. It is important because it makes a distinction between economic activity per se and the contemporary capitalist marketplace. Big businesses rather than a generic world of money are the forces that children need to be protected from.

In Doxley, I was impressed with how parents were teaching their children to handle money. Most families used allowance systems, and many required that children devote a portion of their allowances to charity or savings, or both. Allowances were also used to teach children the difference between needs and wants and to help them budget for things they wanted. Often kids could save up for items the parents didn't want to buy but wouldn't necessarily forbid, such as video game systems or expensive CD players. Parents developed thoughtful schemes about what they would and would not pay for. Many worried about excessive materialism and tried to teach the value of money by letting the kids manage it. Overall, attitudes toward these money matters were practical, respectful of children's skills and decision-making abilities, and founded on values of balance and prudence. At least among the families I interviewed, the kids were learning valuable lessons about the world of commerce rather than being excluded from it.

I end with an obvious but important point. Parents who are interested in reducing the influence of commercial culture on their children need to walk their talk, especially as children age. Preaching against expensive athletic shoes isn't credible with a closet full of Manolo Blahnik shoes. Restricting television is much harder in households where parents watch a lot. Surveys show that highly materialist kids are more likely to have highly materialist parents. And highly materialist parents are likely to have kids with similar priorities. To transmit values effectively, you need to live them. Parents who desire less commercial lifestyles for their children need to change with them.

Join the Movement to Oppose Corporate-Constructed Childhood

The legislative, cultural, and social changes I have been discussing will be realized only if enough people organize to make them happen. A growing number of groups have begun that work, among them Commercial Alert, Stop the Commercial Exploitation of Children, Obligation Inc., the Center for the Analysis of Commercialism in Education, the Center for Media Education, and the Center for a New American Dream. There are many others. National groups include Daughters and Dads, the Media Education Foundation, Teachers Resisting Unhealthy Children's Entertainment (TRUCE), the New Mexico Media Literacy Project, TV Turn-Off Network, the Alliance for Childhood, and the Motherhood Project. There are numerous local groups, many working on school-related commercialization. (I have put contact information for these organizations in Appendix B.)

Although these groups are vastly outmatched in terms of money and personnel, they have managed some impressive successes, especially recently. Daughters and Dads has taken action against offensive commercials, such as a Campbell's soup ad that promoted the product as a diet aid for young girls. The company pulled the ad. In 2002, Scholastic rescinded its sponsorship of the Golden Marble awards for the best children's commercials after a coalition of children's advocates questioned the very fact of targeting kids in its "Have you lost your marbles?" counter-awards. Thousands of communities around the country participate in TV Turn-Off Week. Anticommercialism efforts have made their way into state legislatures and in California led to the passage of two bills. As the public becomes educated about what's going on, it's easier to mobilize support for restricting corporate practices.

The worlds of adults and children are merging. In my mind, that's mainly a good thing. But the commercial aspects of that integration are not working for children. The prevalence of harmful and addictive products, the imperative to keep up, and the growth of materialist attitudes are harming kids. If we are honest with ourselves, adults will admit that we are suffering from many of the same influences. That means our task should be to make the world a safer and more life-affirming place for everyone. Reversing corporate-constructed childhood is a good first step.

Afterword

April 2005

The months since the publication of *Born to Buy* have been a whirlwind. As I had hoped it would, the book helped to blow the cover off the insidious world of kid marketing. Thousands of parents have been outraged to learn that advertisers are ensnaring their kids in stealthy viral marketing schemes, offering Faustian bargains to cash-strapped schools and seducing our youth with sex, violence, and junk food. I've done countless interviews in the media, have spoken all around the country, and have been working the halls of Congress, where there is some receptivity to protecting our youth. The nation's first bill to regulate the use of children in viral marketing has recently been filed in the Massachusetts legislature. Marketers are having a hard time putting a lid back on the issue, despite pouring huge sums of money into lobbying and phony "consumer groups" that claim marketers should bear no responsibility for their actions. The movement to decommercialize childhood is becoming a national force.

Parental involvement in the decommercialization of childhood continues to be propelled by new studies that demonstrate the ongoing and increasing harms that marketing and consumer culture are causing to children. Soon after *Born to Buy* came out, a new study was released showing that television viewing is linked to attention deficit disorders. Children who watch more TV when they are one to three years old have a dramatically higher incidence of ADHD when they are seven. Indeed, each additional hour watched per day increased their likelihood of developing ADHD by 10 percent. Another longitudinal study of television viewing found that children who watched more television when they were four years old were more likely to engage in teasing and bullying of their classmates at ages six to eleven. These studies are important because they analyze behavior over time, showing how problems surface after early television viewing. And childhood obesity trends and their connection to junk food continue to make headlines. In March 2005, researchers from Harvard Medical School published some dramatic predictions in the *New England Journal of Medicine,* arguing that the current generation of children will experience up to a five-year reduction of their life spans, and that for the first time in two centuries, a generation will have shorter and less healthy lives than their parents did. Gary Ruskin of Commercial Alert has aptly termed many of these problems "marketing-related diseases."

Sexy Girls and the Commercial Culture

It is commonplace to acknowledge that we live in a media-driven culture. This means that commercial images are ubiquitous and that Americans, especially young ones, spend enormous amounts of time in front of screens. Media dominance also means that a single image, repeated endlessly, can take on enormous symbolic power. And so it was when Justin Timberlake ripped off Janet Jackson's top at Super Bowl XXXVIII and some months later, when Nicolette Sheridan of *Desperate Housewives* threw herself at Philadelphia Eagles receiver Terrell Owens. The public was outraged. Investigations, fines, and apologies ensued. It seemed clear that MTV, CBS, and ABC had crossed a line: bare breasts and female sexual aggression caused fury among millions of parents.

Who can blame the networks for being caught off guard? For years, the public has mostly treated the relentless increase in sex, violence, and profanity on television by shrugging its shoulders and tuning in. Shows like *Desperate Housewives* are popular in both red and blue states. The most recent Kaiser Family Foundation annual study found that the fraction of television shows with sexually explicit content rose from 56 percent in the 1997–1998 season to 64 percent in 2002–2003. Prime time is even higher, at 71 percent. And "depictions or strong implications" of intercourse have doubled over this period, now appearing in 14 percent of all shows. Even parents seem resigned to the fact that electronic media have been an expanding pornographic environment.

But there are signs that attitudes are changing. Sex is now what parents are most concerned about in terms of content, especially sex on television, in part because they believe that watching TV sex leads kids to have sex earlier. It's a view that is beginning to be validated by research. A recent study of teens found that watching more sexually explicit television at the beginning of the study predicted more sexual activity a year later. Media reports of widespread casual sex among teens have focused adult attention on these programming trends.

The Janet Jackson and Nicolette Sheridan incidents also hit a nerve because they tapped into the fact that parents are worried about another trend: the premature sexualization of their daughters through their participation in the consumer culture. Unlike television, which at least has a ratings system, a V-chip, and an Off button, the rest of consumer culture isn't as easy to tune out. For example, there's the influx of sexually provocative clothing into the girls' 6x–12 department. As the clothes get skimpier, the mothers get angrier. But as more and more girls appear in revealing attire, it's harder for adults to hold the line. I've heard from two entrepreneurs who have started companies to provide wholesome, nonsexual clothing for girls in this age range. They're up against the biases of department store buyers, who now say that unless the styles are downscaled versions of the adult trends, they won't take them. It's a topic that mothers, teachers, and school administrators are talking about a lot, although there hasn't been much activism yet. One conservative Christian group did highlight jeans maker Guess? for store displays with an unclothed Paris Hilton. Guess's CEO Paul Marciano responded curtly by suggesting that they "just stay home."

Another trend is the spread of sexually explicit music and dancing to very young kids, even preschoolers, who bump and grind and mouth pop lyrics they cannot understand. When they do start to learn what those words and images mean, parents worry even more. Toys have also become far more sexually explicit. Barbie has taken her share of criticism for being a swinger with an unrealistic body type. But for years, her sexuality has been out of date, with the result that it is less accessible for children, because it's not culturally resonant with them. Barbie is being replaced by Bratz dolls, which ooze contemporary "heat," with barely there clothes and explicit date themes. The Bratz & Bratz Boyz Secret Date Collection pairs each Bratz character with a mystery Bratz Boy, two champagne glasses, and "tons of date night accessories." It's marketed to six year olds. Bratz dolls are just one of the products that have been targeted by child development experts and parents' groups for being age inappropriate. The activist group Dads and Daughters has been busy ferreting out other damaging products marketed to girls. They protested the "Hunny Bunny" Playboy bunny Halloween costume from the Hottie Tottie collection, manufactured by Design Costumes. They demanded and got an apology from Self-Esteem Clothing (!) for T-shirts emblazoned with the slogan "Property of Boys Locker Room," which were marketed to teen and tween girls.

The companies that sell this stuff to kids tend to lay the blame on "the culture" rather than their own actions. And there are certainly social trends they bear no responsibility for. The proliferation of beauty pageants for little girls and their ensuing eroticization owes more to parents and kids than it does to marketers. Online "modeling" companies that feature seven year olds in revealing bathing suits with sexually alluring poses aren't owned by Disney. But the major companies are behind music, movies, fashion trends, toys, and products that are fueling early sexualization. In the process, they are helping to create the very culture that they then blame. A major hotel chain in the Caribbean appeals to little girls by offering "spa" services such as massages and facials. Health and beauty aids companies are marketing their products to younger and younger demographics. Emphasis on glamor and appearance keeps filtering down year by year. Child development expert Diane Levin chronicles a phenomenon that has been referred to as "so sexy so soon," which includes five-year-old cheerleaders in Texas chanting about their "manicures" and "appearances," kindergartners drawing highly sexualized pictures, and second graders asking their parents about "blow jobs." I suspect this will be an emerging front line in the sure-to-escalate battles between parents and corporations about children's consumer culture.

The Politics of Food Marketing

The battle about sex is just getting going, but the fight against junk food marketing has really heated up. Marketers are definitely concerned, although so far, what they're losing in the court of public opinion, they're making back with influence in the Bush administration and a Republican Congress. But it's early in this battle, and participants on both sides still seem to believe that junk food could be "the next tobacco."

Big Food has responded on a number of fronts. Politically, it has enlisted the support of the Bush administration to forestall any regulatory or legislative changes at the national level and to shift the focus of the debate from food to exercise. Junk food producers scored a big victory through their influence in crafting the successor to the USDA's food pyramid. Not only is there no specific recommendation to reduce sugar intake, but in the new logo, pictures of food have been replaced by a person exercising. Americans' annual sugar consumption currently stands at an astounding 146 pounds, rather than the previously recommended 32.6 pounds. In the last session of Congress, the food corporations hurried a bill through the House that protects them from liability for consumer harm. It was not taken up by the Senate, but will likely be reintroduced in the current session. Fourteen states have passed similar "cheeseburger" bills, absolving fast food chains of liability for the effects of their products. But New York isn't one of them, and in January a court reinstated a previously dismissed lawsuit against McDonald's that was brought by two obese New York teenagers. Other suits are pending.

Big Food is also pouring money into the battle for public opinion, hoping to salvage its image by savaging public health advocates. The Center for Consumer Freedom, a group originally funded by Phillip Morris, which also receives money from restaurant chains and soft drink companies, has been advertising, editorializing, and lobbying to discredit food industry critics. In January 2005, food corporations formed the Alliance for American Advertising, to protect companies' rights to advertise to children. The alliance, which includes Kellogg, General Mills, and Kraft, has openly questioned the link between advertising and obesity, a reprise of tobacco strategy. In April 2005, the Washington Legal Foundation, a right-wing industry front group, used its customary *New York Times* op-ed page ad to make the same argument: food marketing to kids doesn't affect their food choices. I'm wondering why McDonald's and Coke aren't demanding their billions back from Saatchi, Ogilvy, and Leo Burnett.

These are the bad cops. Phillip Morris is also playing good cop, with a recent announcement by Kraft that was widely interpreted as a commitment to stop advertising a subset of its most unhealthy products to children. It is important because it's a tacit admission both that the foods are unhealthy and that the marketing works. Whether they will actually stop marketing Oreos to kids remains to be seen. McDonald's made big headlines when it pledged to reduce the use of transfats in its cooking oils; two years later, it has failed to do so and is being sued for it. On the other hand, it has phased out SuperSizing. Apparently the bad publicity from the documentary *Supersize Me,* Morgan Sperlock's brilliant exposé of McDonald's, was more than it could spin. Food industry representatives have so far been unwilling to debate or even appear with me. When the Advertising Education Foundation scheduled a panel with me during "Advertising Week," New York's September celebration of advertising, the foundation was besieged by calls from industry insiders asking it not to hold the panel. McDonald's and others were subsequently unwilling to participate, and the panel was canceled. A few months later, an invitation to me to speak at a government, but industry-dominated, workshop dematerialized.

A New Political Environment?

While it's still early to know how these battles will unfold, the political landscape for challenging, and even restricting, marketing to children seems to have become more favorable in the past year. Two bills have been introduced in the Senate that sharply limit junk food marketing to children in schools. Senator Kennedy's Prevention of Childhood Obesity Act would prohibit in-school vending machine sales of foods of "minimal nutritional value" and reward schools that prohibit food advertising and promote water consumption. Senator Harkin's HELP (Healthy Lifestyle and Prevention) America Act restores rule-making authority over children's advertising to the Federal Trade Commission, gives the secretary of agriculture the right to prohibit junk food marketing in schools that participate in federal breakfast and lunch programs, and eliminates the tax deductibility of tobacco ads. Activist groups have been busy publicizing and organizing support for both these bills.

After a few days of lobbying on both sides of the aisle on Capitol Hill in March, I came away cautiously optimistic about the Parents' Bill of Rights and prospects for introducing some of its planks into law. Congress may take up privacy rights in the near future, and children's rights not to have information about them sold without permission may be included. Food labeling requirements for the fast food chains are another legislative step that may be reintroduced. Forward momentum on these important legislative efforts will come as voters contact their congressional representatives. Many are receptive but need to hear from constituents. Commercial Alert is also awaiting word from the Federal Communications Commission on its petition to require full disclosure for ads that take the form of product placement. A similar petition to the FTC was denied recently, but the fact that the FCC is taking a long time to rule may be a positive sign. Commercial Alert has also recently filed a petition with the Department of Agriculture asking it to enforce existing restrictions on the sale of foods of minimal nutritional value in schools. And perhaps the most significant recent political development is the current state of Channel One: near-dead. Its key man in Washington is Republican lobbyist Jack Abramoff, whose alleged misdeeds are at the core of Tom DeLay's ethics problems and who is the subject of a federal grand jury investigation. Additionally, growing discontent from schools over outdated equipment, a dramatic loss of ad revenues, and the resignation of one of its founders have been devastating for Channel One. It's possible it won't survive the year.

At the state and local levels, there is increasing legislative and regulatory action. In the city of Seattle, a comprehensive policy prohibiting all advertising, junk food marketing, and junk food consumption in public schools went into effect in January 2005. It is the most far-reaching in the nation, and activists are hoping it becomes a widespread model for other districts. In Maine, Representative Sean Faircloth has been promoting the "Four Freedoms" relating to obesity, which include the right of citizens to have caloric information on marketed foods and the right to commercial-free public schools. Maine was the first state in the nation to pledge to remove soda and apply the federal minimum nutritional value standard to vending machines at all Maine public schools, including high schools. Faircloth is now working on removing all junk food advertising from public schools and setting strong nutritional standards for all food that is sold in schools. Stay tuned.

Another marketing issue that has created considerable concern among parents is the growing use of children as viral, or "word-of-mouth," marketers. *Born to Buy* exposed a number of companies that are active in this field, such as the Girls Intelligence Agency. GIA founder Laura Groppe and I were subsequently included in a CBS *60 Minutes Weekday* piece. The *New York Times Magazine* devoted a cover story to the phenomenon and included considerable discussion of Procter and Gamble's large "Tremor" unit. (Tremor currently has more than 250,000 youth involved in its viral activities.) Massachusetts legislators have taken the national lead on this issue with the introduction of a bill in the state's House of Representatives that would require parental consent for all marketers that employ or use children under the age of sixteen to carry out viral marketing activities. At the moment, this is a completely unregulated industry segment, but that is likely to change.

Empowering Parents

The can-do attitude of activists, childhood professionals, and legislators contrasts sharply with the stance of most of the mainstream media, especially the electronic community. When *60 Minutes* let me know it would be doing a piece on the GIA, I was pleased. But its tone ended up being all too predictable, and it followed what has now become almost a formula on this topic: expose a cutting-edge, problematic marketing practice; document its spread; include an expert to criticize it; and end by concluding that such commercialization is inevitable. It's the shrugged-shoulders approach. While those of us watching marketers' every move have been successful getting publicity for what we're finding, it's not clear if these media portrayals help or hurt. In some cases, the stories become valuable free publicity for the companies. This explains the marketers' willingness to cooperate, be interviewed, and let producers film them at work. Among audiences, I suspect the disempowerment they engender in many parents outweighs the indignation they create in others. Of course, the media are not monolithic; a number of exemplary newspaper journalists cover these topics, including or such as the *Washington Post*'s Caroline Mayer, the *New York Times*'s Constance Hays, and the *Boston Globe*'s Barbara Meltz.

But I suspect that the mainstream media are out of touch with the emerging mood in the country. The parents who are speaking up about television porn, unhealthy messages to our daughters, and junk food marketing are not interested in shoulder shrugging. We want results. And many of us are finding that if we take the time to make our voices heard, we are listened to. Seattle is leading the way on anticommercialism because one woman was appalled by what she saw in her daughter's school. She started her fight at the kitchen table with a few friends. Now she's a leader on the school board. Another outraged parent, Alabama's Jim Metrock, is on the verge of having put Channel One out of business. These people and countless others around the country show how much one person can do. When my daughter came home from school with an advertising supplement from Toyota inserted into her weekly *Time for Kids,* I contacted the principal right away. I got an apology from the teacher and a promise it wouldn't happen again. Another parent from my town objected to the use of licensed characters to market junk foods in the elementary school lunch program. The program administrator had apparently felt that Chester Cheetah and SpongeBob would entice kids, but after talking to parents, he agreed never to use characters to market food again. When groups take action, the results are even more dramatic. The Campaign for Commercial-Free Childhood got U.S. Youth Soccer to drop its association with ChemLawn. And Coke's top lobbyist withdrew from the National PTA Board after activist pressure.

As I've traveled around the country, I've had the opportunity to hear the views of large numbers of parents. I've been most impressed by the voices of those who argue that we parents have more power than most of us realize. They insist that it's possible to turn off the television, say no to

Coke and Pepsi, and ignore the persistent nagging instigated by marketers. Some of them are a tad self-righteous. And many don't acknowledge that being middle class, or even wealthier, is a big part of why they can avoid using the television as a baby-sitter or ban cheap fast foods from their diet. Or that very few parents can protect their children from in-school marketing by putting them in private schools or home-schooling them. But all that having been said, these parents do have a point. Many more of us can turn off the TV than do. We can boycott those McDonald's-branded preschool toys. And just because our daughter is invited to a spa party or a "shopping spree at the mall" birthday bash doesn't mean we have to let her go. It's important to remember that we shouldn't let our choices be unduly determined by the popularity of a trend. After all, by that standard, we'd be condoning our children's consumption of alcohol, tobacco, and drugs. Instead, we should keep an eye on the expanding scientific evidence of marketing-related diseases and harms, try to keep our children safe from them, and trust that we'll be joined by a growing number of like-minded parents. As that happens, it will get easier and easier to take a stand.

The media's shoulder shrug or our own feeling that we can't do much about the relentless tide of commercialization reveals, at its core, a lack of imagination about what's possible for children. It's a problem, because more than ever before, children need not only their own imaginations but ours as well. They need more people like Alice Waters, who saw, and then created, a fertile, organic garden on the site of a decrepit inner-city playground. And like Raffi, the children's singer whose refusal to go along with advertising at the Vancouver Children's Music Festival led him to create a whole new organization devoted to "child honoring" rather than child exploiting. And like Sean Faircloth, who envisions for the children of one of the poorest states in the nation, during one of our most conservative eras, freedom from corporate greed. As more and more of us replace our resignation with imagination, enlisting our children's energies and vision in the process, we may find we're creating a better world not only for them but for ourselves as well.

APPENDIX A

Data Appendix

Survey on Children, Media, and Consumer Culture

The Survey on Children, Media, and Consumer Culture comprises 157 items and questions, and it's taken with paper and pencil. I developed it. It has eight sections: (1) television and other media use; (2) eighteen consumer involvement items; (3) items on the child's relationship and attitudes to the primary parent, including four items from the Authoritative Parenting Scale; (4) three items on psychosomatic complaints; (5) the thirty-six-item DuBois Self-Esteem Scale; (6) seventeen items from the Children's Depression Inventory; (7) sixteen items from the Revised Children's Manifest Anxiety Scale; and (8) demographic questions. References for the existing scales (depression, anxiety, self-esteem, and authoritative parenting) are given in the endnotes to Chapter 8. The survey takes between twenty and fifty minutes to complete and has been taken by 300 children between the ages of ten and thirteen. The survey was administered in two phases and two locales. The first phase took place during the fall and winter of 2001–2002, with 206 children in three schools in a suburban locale west of Boston, Massachusetts. The second phase occurred in the winter of 2002–2003 in two Boston public schools—one a charter school and the other a pilot school. Children who attend the urban schools come from throughout the city. Demographic and other information about the children is contained in Table 5 in Chapter 8. Copies of the survey instrument are available from the author on request.

Consumer Involvement Factor

The eighteen consumer involvement items were subjected to confirmatory factor analysis using the AMOS program. The CFA revealed that sixteen of the eighteen items grouped together into one single factor measuring consumer involvement. Analysis of subscales found three, which comprised thirteen of the sixteen items. The subscales measure "dissatisfaction," "consumer desire," and "brand orientation." Separate analyses of boys and girls found that differences were not significant.

Estimates

Ordinary least squares (OLS) regression estimates (not reported in text) using SPSS were done for all the dependent variables prior to estimating the structural model. The OLS estimates were very similar to the subsequent structural equation estimates, as one would expect given the unidirectional causality found in the latter. A variety of OLS models were estimated, with robust results for the Consumer Involvement Factor. Structural equation estimates were done using AMOS.

Details on the data and estimates are contained in Schor, Shandra, and Kunovich (2004), available from Schor.

APPENDIX B

Organizations

Commercial Alert
4110 S.E. Hawthorne Boulevard, #123
Portland, OR 97214–5426
Phone: 503-235-8012
Fax: 503-235-5073
E-mail: info@commercialalert.org
http://www.commercialalert.org

Center for a New American Dream
6930 Carroll Avenue, Suite 900
Takoma Park, MD 20912
Phone: 877-68-DREAM
Fax: 301-891-3683
E-mail: newdream@newdream.org
http://www.newdream.org

Campaign for a Commercial-Free Childhood
53 Parker Hill Avenue
Boston, MA 02120
Phone: 617-278-4172
Fax: 617-232-7343
E-mail: ccfc@jbcc.harvard.edu
http://www.commercialfreechildhood.org

Daughters and Dads
34 East Superior Street, Suite 200
Duluth, MN 55802
Phone: 888-824-DADS
Fax: 218-728-0314
E-mail: Info@dadsanddaughters.org
http://www.dadsanddaughters.org

Obligation, Inc.
Barbizon Building
3100 Lorna Road, Suite 311
Birmingham, AL 35216
Phone: 205-822-0080
Fax: 205-822-3336
E-mail: info@obligation.org
http://www.obligation.org

Alliance for Childhood
P.O. Box 444
College Park, MD 20741
Voice and fax: 301-779-1033
E-mail: info@allianceforchildhood.net
http://www.allianceforchildhood.net

American Academy of Pediatrics
141 Northwest Point Boulevard
Elk Grove Village, IL 60007–1098
Phone: 847-434-4000
Fax: 847-434-8000
E-mail: aapnews@aap.org
http://www.aap.org

New Mexico Media Literacy Project
6400 Wyoming Boulevard NE
Albuquerque, NM 87109
Phone: 505-828-3129
Fax: 505-828-3142
E-mail: nmmlp@nmmlp.org
http://www.nmmlp.org

Citizens' Campaign for Commercial-Free Schools
3724 Burke Avenue N
Seattle, WA 98103
Phone: 206-523-4922
E-mail: cccs@scn.org
http://www.scn.org

TV Turn-Off Network
1200 29th Street, NW, Lower Level 1
Washington, DC 20007
Phone: 202-333-9220
Fax: 202-333-9221
E-mail: Email@tvturnoff.org
http://www.tvturnoff.org

Media Education Foundation
60 Masonic Street
Northampton, MA 01060
Phone: 800-897-0089
Fax: 800-659-6882
E-mail: info@mediaed.org
http://www.mediaed.org

APPENDIX C

Commercial Alert's Parents' Bill of Rights

WHEREAS, the nurturing of character and strong values in children is one of the most important functions of any society;

WHEREAS, the primary responsibility for the upbringing of children resides in their parents;

WHEREAS, an aggressive commercial culture has invaded the relationship between parents and children, and has impeded the ability of parents to guide the upbringing of their own children;

WHEREAS, corporate marketers have sought increasingly to bypass parents, and speak directly to children in order to tempt them with the most sophisticated tools that advertising executives, market researchers and psychologists can devise;

WHEREAS, these marketers tend to glorify materialism, addiction, hedonism, violence and anti-social behavior, all of which are abhorrent to most parents;

WHEREAS, parents find themselves locked in constant battle with this pervasive influence, and are hard pressed to keep the commercial culture and its degraded values out of their children's lives;

WHEREAS, the aim of this corporate marketing is to turn children into agents of corporations in the home, so that they will nag their parents for the things they see advertised, thus sowing strife, stress and misery in the family;

WHEREAS, the products advertised generally are ones parents themselves would not choose for their children: violent and sexually suggestive entertainment, video games, alcohol, tobacco, gambling and junk food;

WHEREAS, this aggressive commercial influence has contributed to an epidemic of marketing-related diseases in children, such as obesity, type 2 diabetes, alcoholism, anorexia and bulimia, while millions will eventually die from the marketing of tobacco;

WHEREAS, corporations have latched onto the schools and compulsory school laws as a way to bypass parents and market their products and values to a captive audience of impressionable and trusting children;

WHEREAS, these corporations ultimately are creatures of state law, and it is intolerable that they should use the rights and powers so granted for the purpose of undermining the authority of parents in these ways;

THEREFORE, BE IT RESOLVED, that the U.S. Congress and the fifty state legislatures should right the balance between parents and corporations and restore to parents some measure of control over the commercial influences on their children, by enacting this Parents' Bill of Rights, including,

Leave Children Alone Act. This act bans television advertising aimed at children under 12 years of age. (federal)

Child Privacy Act. This act restores to parents the ability to safeguard the privacy of their own children. It gives parents the right to control any commercial use of personal information concerning their children, and the right to know precisely how such information is used. (federal, state)

Advertising to Children Accountability Act. This act helps parents affix individual responsibility for attempts to subject their children to commercial influence. It requires corporations to disclose who created each of their advertisements, and who did the market research for each ad directed at children under 12 years of age. (federal)

Commercial-Free Schools Act. Corporations have turned the public schools into advertising-free fire zones. This act prohibits corporations from using the schools and compulsory school laws to bypass parents and pitch their products to impressionable schoolchildren. (federal, state)

Fairness Doctrine for Parents. This act provides parents with the opportunity to talk back to the media and the advertisers. It makes the Fairness Doctrine apply to all advertising to children under 12 years of age, providing parents and community with response time on broadcast TV and radio for advertising to children. (federal)

Product Placement Disclosure Act. This law gives parents more information with which to monitor the influences that prey upon their children through the media. Specifically, it requires corporations to disclose, on packaging and at the outset, any and all product placements on television and videos, and in movies, video games and books.

16 On early-twentieth-century advertising to mothers, see Seiter (1993), chs. 2–3, and Marchand (1985), pp. 228–232. See Marchand, p. 231, for Wheatena and milk ads. For evidence of direct marketing to children in the 1930s, see Cook (2000b).

17 For an account of direct advertising to kids and its impact on requests to parents, see Stoneman and Brody (1981).

17 For a fascinating account of these issues, see Rappaport (2001). Shoplifting was an analogous situation: Merchants tolerated shoplifting by middle-class women because it was complementary with actual purchasing. For the United States, see Leach (1993). See also Abelson (1989) and Ohmann (1996).

17 Parental sentiments that television is not harmful were expressed in focus groups on kids and television conducted in Philadelphia by the Annenburg Public Policy Center. See Schmitt (2000), p. 24.

Chapter 2: The Changing World of Children's Consumption

19 Nickelodeon SUV ad from *Adbusters Magazine* (2000), p. 22.

19 On *Teletubbies'* promotional partners, see Commercial Alert, March 2000, available at http://www.commercialalert.org/index.php?category_id=1&subcategory_id=25&article_id=59. On the very young eating fast food, see Comiteau (2003), who reports that the youngest McDonald's age target is two to seven. For a critical view of *Teletubbies,* see Linn and Poussaint (1999).

19 On when brand loyalty and awareness develop, see Comiteau (2003). Comiteau reports on a 2000 Griffin Bacal study, which found that nearly two-thirds of mothers thought their children were brand aware by age three and one-third said age two.

19 On experts say three- to three-and-a-half-year-olds believe brands communicate personal qualities, see McNeal's statement in Comiteau (2003). See also McNeal (1999), pp. 202–206.

19 One in four chance of having a television in their room for preschoolers is from Woodward (2000), p. 4. Daily viewing time of just over two hours per day from Kaiser Family Foundation (1999), Table 10-A.

19 Upon arrival at schoolhouse steps, children evoke 200 brands from McNeal (1999), p. 206.

19 Seventy new toys figure from author's calculation. In 2000, 3.6 billion new toys were purchased in the United States. There are 52 million children in the twelve-and-under age group. This calculation assumes adults are not acquiring toys for themselves, but to counterbalance that, toy acquisition drops off by ages eleven and twelve. Number of toys from National Labor Committee (2002), p. 3.

9 Everyone brings their dELIA*s catalogue quote from Siegel, Coffey, and Livingston (2001), p. 117.

On Pokémon bans and adults' reactions, see Cook (2001).

Eight to thirteen year olds watching three and a half hours of television a day from Kaiser Family Foundation (1999), Table 8-A.

Children view an estimated 40,000 commercials per year reported in Strasburger and Wilson (2002), p. 37.

Three thousand requests per year from McNeal (1999), p. 80.

Fifteen billion dollars in advertising to children from McNeal, in private communication to author, March 25, 2004.

Fifty-two million figure in the zero-to-twelve demographic from U.S. Census of Population, available at http://factfinder.census.gov/servlet/BasicFactsServlet, Sex by Age for the Population Under 20 Years, p. 14. The exact figure is 52,190,294.

This prevents advertisers from sneaking ads into media that parents assume to be ad-free. (federal)

Child Harm Disclosure Act. Parents have a right to know of any significant health effects of products they might purchase for their children. This act creates a legal duty for corporations to publicly disclose all information suggesting that their product(s) could substantially harm the health of children. (federal)

Children's Food Labeling Act. Parents have a right to information about the food that corporations push upon their children. This act requires fast food restaurant chains to label contents of food, and provide basic nutritional information about it. (federal, state)

Children's Advertising Subsidy Revocation Act. It is intolerable that the federal government actually rewards corporations with a big tax write-off for the money they spend on psychologists, market researchers, ad agencies, media and the like in their campaigns to instill their values in our children. This act eliminates all federal subsidies, deductions and preferences for advertising aimed at children under 12 years of age. (federal)

Notes

Chapter 1: Introduction

9 For sources and more detail on these indicators of consumerism, see Schor (1998), especially ch. 1.
9 Data on shopping centers from 2002 NRB Shopping Center Census, from the National Research Bureau Shopping Center Database and Statistical Model, Table 1. Available at www.nrbonline.com.
9 On the growth of consumption, see Schor (1998), especially ch. 4.
9 Author's estimate of per capita apparel acquisitions using 2002 data. For details on data and methods, and a discussion of discard patterns, see Schor (2002).
9 On the decline of community and its connection to television viewing, see Putna (2000). Television ownership in the United States stood at 854 per 1,000 people 2002. Data from World Bank, Table 5.10, "The Information Age," available http://www.worldbank.org/data/databytopic/itc.html#ti.
9 Virtually every institution: The major exception is religious institutions.
12 80 percent of global consumer brands require tween strategy from Linds (2003), p. 14. Lindstrom also notes that "every marketing director has a sp budget allotment for tweens" (pp. 1–2).
13 The global tween study included only urban tweens who had the abilit online.
13 Global survey results and "bonded to brands" reference from Lindstrom (
13 For the rise in anxiety among children and the comparison to 1957 clin rates, see Twenge (2000).
14 On behavior modification: In 2003 the *New York Times* provided ongoir of conditions in these behavior modification programs in the light of p suits. See, for example, Weiner (2003).
14 Point on tweens' daily lives and media encouragement of anxiety is fro (2003), p. 197.
15 On toy accumulation in the 1870s, see Mergen (1992), p. 88.
15 On children and popular culture, see Tuttle (1992).
15 On moral panics, including Pokémon and Beanie Babies, see Coo
15 I note children's rich history as actors to avoid falling into the trap the past was a precommercial utopia free of the "profane" cultura market.
15 For Zelizer's analysis of the period 1870–1930, see Zelizer (198
15 Giroux quote on innocence from Giroux (1998), p. 265. See al from Jenkins and Walkerdine in the Jenkins volume.
15 For the argument that childhood is under attack, see Postman (has become common. See Stephens (1995b) and especially F
16 For evidence of the blurred boundaries, see Postman (1994)
16 For an argument against Postman and the disappearance th

21 *Nature of Kids* video and quotes from Rachel Geller, KidPower 2002 conference, May 6, 2002, Orlando, Florida.
21 KidPower workshop titles and "create an experience so engaging" from 2003 KidPower brochure. Conference brochures are usually available at www.kidpowerx. com.
22 The *Times* hired the Strottman Group to help plan its *Los Angeles Times* Kid City event, which took place in July 2003. Information from interview with Ron Coughlin, a principal of the Strottman Group.
22 Recent poll that children are aware of marketing efforts conducted by Widmeyer Communications for the Center for a New American Dream, February 2003, with 746 children aged nine to fourteen. Available at http://www.newdream.org/publications/bookrelease.html.
22 Barbie sales from Barbie Fun Facts, available at http://www.ideafinder.com/history/inventions/story081.htm. One hundred twenty million kids watching CTW from Del Vecchio (1997), p. 90. For a critique of *Sesame Street* and its impact on children's learning, see Healy (1999).
23 Eight percent of American population figure is author's calculation from reported 20 million customers a day served by McDonald's. Happy Meals comprise 20 percent of McDonald's sales, from presentation by Colleen Fahey, KidPower 2002 conference, May 7, 2002, Orlando, Florida.
23 Growth of children's purchasing power from 1989 to 1997 from McNeal (1999), p. 17. These figures are not adjusted for inflation. The 2002 figure ($30 billion) is from a private communication to the author from James McNeal, July 12, 2002.
23 Category breakdown for children's spending from McNeal (1999), p. 57.
23 Older kids spending of $170 billion from Teen Research Unlimited (2003), available at http://www.teenresearch.com/PRview.cfm?edit_id=152.
23 Two to three times per week and six items estimates from Rachel Geller, Gepetto Group, cited in White-Sax (1999).
23 Eighty percent of tweens shop with parents from *Kidscreen* Firstlook e-mail communication to author, October 3, 2002.
23 One in four going solo and median age of eight from McNeal (1999), p. 45.
23 On youthful shoppers buying for family needs, see Ahuja, Capella, and Taylor (1998).
23 On Alpharetta kids' village, see Lindstrom (2003), p. 215.
23 The $330 and $340 billion in direct influence and evoked, indirect influence from private communication to the author from James McNeal, March 25, 2004. See also McNeal (1999), p. 96, and Comiteau (2003).
23 Twenty percent growth per year from James McNeal, reported in Norris (2002).
23 Global tween influence spending over $1 trillion from Martin Lindstrom, BrandChild Web site, www.dualbook.com.
24 "Learning opportunities" phrase from presentation by Donna Sabino, KidPower 2002 conference, May 7, 2002, Orlando, Florida.
24 "When I was a kid I got to pick" quote from author's interview with Lisa Morgan (pseudonym).
24 Sixty-seven percent of car purchases figure from ad agency Millward Brown, available on the BrandChild Web site, www.dualbook.com. Millward Brown believes close to 80 percent of all brands purchased by parents are now subject to kid influence.
24 Griffin Bacal consumer panel data from *Kidscreen* (1999), p. 24.
24 Roper Youth Report data on six to seven year olds' consumer choices reported in White-Sax (1999).
25 Research done by one of my students refers to Greve (1995). Greve tested for the impact of parental time with and without children on parental discretionary expenditures using data from the Consumer Expenditure Survey, as well as an additional

data set she collected on upper-income families. Greve tested for guilt in her own data, but that variable is not available from the Consumer Expenditures Survey.

25 Eighty-nine percent of parents figure is from Penn, Schoen, and Berland (2001), a proprietary Nickelodeon study.

25 The phrase "bonded to brands" is from Lindstrom (2003).

25 Three hundred to 400 brands by ten year olds from McNeal (1999), p. 206. Brand-specific requests from McNeal (1999), p. 209.

25 The 89 percent figure is from Penn, Schoen, and Berland (2001).

25 Griffin Bacal study on children's brand awareness reported in Comiteau (2003). A 1999 Center for a New American Dream poll found that 22 percent of parents report their children began asking for brand-named items when they were ages two to three. Another 22 percent began their brand requests at ages four to five. Full discussion of this poll is in Chapter 9.

25 More closely bonded than kids anywhere and most brand-conscious generation claim from Lindstrom (2003), p. 13, and my interview with him.

26 On signs and sign wars, see Goldman and Papson (1996).

26 On sea-change in tastes and fashion houses driving the trend, see Kaufman (1999).

26 Upscaling in toys from Szymanski (1999), p. 62.

27 The number of toys sold increased by 20 percent from 1995 and North Americans consuming 45 percent of global production from units sold data available at http://www.toy-tma.org/industry/statistics/soi.html. See International Council of Toy Industries' World Toy Facts and Figures, March 2001.

27 MiniKin Kinder Salon example from presentation by Rachel Geller at KidPower 2002, May 6, 2002.

27 On cosmetic surgery between elementary and middle schools, see Quart (2003a), ch. 8.

27 FAO Schwarz birthday parties from Yazigi (1999).

27 "Crayons just won't do it" quote from Michael Sanson of *Restaurant Hospitality* magazine, cited in Sugarman (2000), p. F1.

27 Madame Alexander dolls from Leung (2002).

27 On corporate construction, see Steinberg and Kincheloe (1998). On media concentration, see Robert McChesney's excellent *Rich Media, Poor Democracy* (1999).

27 For a critique of Disney, including a discussion of racism and sexism in its characters, see Giroux (1999).

28 PBS and Nickelodeon have started a joint "educational" venture called Noggin. For a trenchant critique of the commercialism of PBS, see McChesney (1999).

28 Top-selling toy data from NPD Group, available at www.npd.com, TRSTS Top Ten Best Selling Toys ranked on units sold, Q1-2002.

28 On concentration among video game producers: In 2001, Nintendo had eight of the top twenty selling games, Sony had two, and Microsoft had one. See data at www.npd.com, Top twenty best-selling video game titles ranked on units sold in 2001.

29 Data on campaign contributions are from Common Cause, "Soft Money Donor Profiles," available at commoncause.org/laundromat/stat/top50.htm.

29 On the history of children's play, see Mergen (1992). See also Cross (1997), Sutton-Smith (1986), and Rotundo (1993).

30 On boys' outdoor play, see Rotundo (1993).

31 On only 25 percent of children's time as discretionary: These are my calculations from the data in Hofferth and Sandberg (2001b), Table 2. Their calculations of free time are slightly higher because they include shopping, studying, and household work as discretionary. Among children ages six to twelve, the corresponding figure for discretionary time is 24 percent. Time diaries were completed for 2,818 children in the sample.

This prevents advertisers from sneaking ads into media that parents assume to be ad-free. (federal)

Child Harm Disclosure Act. Parents have a right to know of any significant health effects of products they might purchase for their children. This act creates a legal duty for corporations to publicly disclose all information suggesting that their product(s) could substantially harm the health of children. (federal)

Children's Food Labeling Act. Parents have a right to information about the food that corporations push upon their children. This act requires fast food restaurant chains to label contents of food, and provide basic nutritional information about it. (federal, state)

Children's Advertising Subsidy Revocation Act. It is intolerable that the federal government actually rewards corporations with a big tax write-off for the money they spend on psychologists, market researchers, ad agencies, media and the like in their campaigns to instill their values in our children. This act eliminates all federal subsidies, deductions and preferences for advertising aimed at children under 12 years of age. (federal)

Notes

Chapter 1: Introduction

9 For sources and more detail on these indicators of consumerism, see Schor (1998), especially ch. 1.
9 Data on shopping centers from 2002 NRB Shopping Center Census, from the National Research Bureau Shopping Center Database and Statistical Model, Table 1. Available at www.nrbonline.com.
9 On the growth of consumption, see Schor (1998), especially ch. 4.
9 Author's estimate of per capita apparel acquisitions using 2002 data. For details on data and methods, and a discussion of discard patterns, see Schor (2002).
9 On the decline of community and its connection to television viewing, see Putnam (2000). Television ownership in the United States stood at 854 per 1,000 people in 2002. Data from World Bank, Table 5.10, "The Information Age," available at http://www.worldbank.org/data/databytopic/itc.html#ti.
9 Virtually every institution: The major exception is religious institutions.
12 80 percent of global consumer brands require tween strategy from Lindstrom (2003), p. 14. Lindstrom also notes that "every marketing director has a specific budget allotment for tweens" (pp. 1–2).
13 The global tween study included only urban tweens who had the ability to be online.
13 Global survey results and "bonded to brands" reference from Lindstrom (2003).
13 For the rise in anxiety among children and the comparison to 1957 clinic patient rates, see Twenge (2000).
14 On behavior modification: In 2003 the *New York Times* provided ongoing coverage of conditions in these behavior modification programs in the light of parental lawsuits. See, for example, Weiner (2003).
14 Point on tweens' daily lives and media encouragement of anxiety is from Lindstrom (2003), p. 197.
15 On toy accumulation in the 1870s, see Mergen (1992), p. 88.
15 On children and popular culture, see Tuttle (1992).
15 On moral panics, including Pokémon and Beanie Babies, see Cook (2001).
15 I note children's rich history as actors to avoid falling into the trap of assuming that the past was a precommercial utopia free of the "profane" cultural influences of the market.
15 For Zelizer's analysis of the period 1870–1930, see Zelizer (1985).
15 Giroux quote on innocence from Giroux (1998), p. 265. See also the contributions from Jenkins and Walkerdine in the Jenkins volume.
15 For the argument that childhood is under attack, see Postman (1994). This argument has become common. See Stephens (1995b) and especially Field (1995).
16 For evidence of the blurred boundaries, see Postman (1994), ch. 8.
16 For an argument against Postman and the disappearance thesis, see Allen (2001).

16 On early-twentieth-century advertising to mothers, see Seiter (1993), chs. 2–3, and Marchand (1985), pp. 228–232. See Marchand, p. 231, for Wheatena and milk ads. For evidence of direct marketing to children in the 1930s, see Cook (2000b).
17 For an account of direct advertising to kids and its impact on requests to parents, see Stoneman and Brody (1981).
17 For a fascinating account of these issues, see Rappaport (2001). Shoplifting was an analogous situation: Merchants tolerated shoplifting by middle-class women because it was complementary with actual purchasing. For the United States, see Leach (1993). See also Abelson (1989) and Ohmann (1996).
17 Parental sentiments that television is not harmful were expressed in focus groups on kids and television conducted in Philadelphia by the Annenburg Public Policy Center. See Schmitt (2000), p. 24.

Chapter 2: The Changing World of Children's Consumption

19 Nickelodeon SUV ad from *Adbusters Magazine* (2000), p. 22.
19 On *Teletubbies'* promotional partners, see Commercial Alert, March 2000, available at http://www.commercialalert.org/index.php?category_id=1&subcategory_id=25&article_id=59. On the very young eating fast food, see Comiteau (2003), who reports that the youngest McDonald's age target is two to seven. For a critical view of *Teletubbies,* see Linn and Poussaint (1999).
19 On when brand loyalty and awareness develop, see Comiteau (2003). Comiteau reports on a 2000 Griffin Bacal study, which found that nearly two-thirds of mothers thought their children were brand aware by age three and one-third said age two.
19 On experts say three- to three-and-a-half-year-olds believe brands communicate personal qualities, see McNeal's statement in Comiteau (2003). See also McNeal (1999), pp. 202–206.
19 One in four chance of having a television in their room for preschoolers is from Woodward (2000), p. 4. Daily viewing time of just over two hours per day from Kaiser Family Foundation (1999), Table 10-A.
19 Upon arrival at schoolhouse steps, children evoke 200 brands from McNeal (1999), p. 206.
19 Seventy new toys figure from author's calculation. In 2000, 3.6 billion new toys were purchased in the United States. There are 52 million children in the twelve-and-under age group. This calculation assumes adults are not acquiring toys for themselves, but to counterbalance that, toy acquisition drops off by ages eleven and twelve. Number of toys from National Labor Committee (2002), p. 3.
19 Everyone brings their dELIA*s catalogue quote from Siegel, Coffey, and Livingston (2001), p. 117.
20 On Pokémon bans and adults' reactions, see Cook (2001).
20 Eight to thirteen year olds watching three and a half hours of television a day from Kaiser Family Foundation (1999), Table 8-A.
20 Children view an estimated 40,000 commercials per year reported in Strasburger and Wilson (2002), p. 37.
20 Three thousand requests per year from McNeal (1999), p. 80.
21 Fifteen billion dollars in advertising to children from McNeal, in private communication to author, March 25, 2004.
21 Fifty-two million figure in the zero-to-twelve demographic from U.S. Census of Population, available at http://factfinder.census.gov/servlet/BasicFactsServlet, Sex by Age for the Population Under 20 Years, p. 14. The exact figure is 52,190,294.

21 *Nature of Kids* video and quotes from Rachel Geller, KidPower 2002 conference, May 6, 2002, Orlando, Florida.

21 KidPower workshop titles and "create an experience so engaging" from 2003 KidPower brochure. Conference brochures are usually available at www.kidpowerx. com.

22 The *Times* hired the Strottman Group to help plan its *Los Angeles Times* Kid City event, which took place in July 2003. Information from interview with Ron Coughlin, a principal of the Strottman Group.

22 Recent poll that children are aware of marketing efforts conducted by Widmeyer Communications for the Center for a New American Dream, February 2003, with 746 children aged nine to fourteen. Available at http://www.newdream.org/publications/bookrelease.html.

22 Barbie sales from Barbie Fun Facts, available at http://www.ideafinder.com/history/inventions/story081.htm. One hundred twenty million kids watching CTW from Del Vecchio (1997), p. 90. For a critique of *Sesame Street* and its impact on children's learning, see Healy (1999).

23 Eight percent of American population figure is author's calculation from reported 20 million customers a day served by McDonald's. Happy Meals comprise 20 percent of McDonald's sales, from presentation by Colleen Fahey, KidPower 2002 conference, May 7, 2002, Orlando, Florida.

23 Growth of children's purchasing power from 1989 to 1997 from McNeal (1999), p. 17. These figures are not adjusted for inflation. The 2002 figure ($30 billion) is from a private communication to the author from James McNeal, July 12, 2002.

23 Category breakdown for children's spending from McNeal (1999), p. 57.

23 Older kids spending of $170 billion from Teen Research Unlimited (2003), available at http://www.teenresearch.com/PRview.cfm?edit_id=152.

23 Two to three times per week and six items estimates from Rachel Geller, Gepetto Group, cited in White-Sax (1999).

23 Eighty percent of tweens shop with parents from *Kidscreen* Firstlook e-mail communication to author, October 3, 2002.

23 One in four going solo and median age of eight from McNeal (1999), p. 45.

23 On youthful shoppers buying for family needs, see Ahuja, Capella, and Taylor (1998).

23 On Alpharetta kids' village, see Lindstrom (2003), p. 215.

23 The $330 and $340 billion in direct influence and evoked, indirect influence from private communication to the author from James McNeal, March 25, 2004. See also McNeal (1999), p. 96, and Comiteau (2003).

23 Twenty percent growth per year from James McNeal, reported in Norris (2002).

23 Global tween influence spending over $1 trillion from Martin Lindstrom, BrandChild Web site, www.dualbook.com.

24 "Learning opportunities" phrase from presentation by Donna Sabino, KidPower 2002 conference, May 7, 2002, Orlando, Florida.

24 "When I was a kid I got to pick" quote from author's interview with Lisa Morgan (pseudonym).

24 Sixty-seven percent of car purchases figure from ad agency Millward Brown, available on the BrandChild Web site, www.dualbook.com. Millward Brown believes close to 80 percent of all brands purchased by parents are now subject to kid influence.

24 Griffin Bacal consumer panel data from *Kidscreen* (1999), p. 24.

24 Roper Youth Report data on six to seven year olds' consumer choices reported in White-Sax (1999).

25 Research done by one of my students refers to Greve (1995). Greve tested for the impact of parental time with and without children on parental discretionary expenditures using data from the Consumer Expenditure Survey, as well as an additional

data set she collected on upper-income families. Greve tested for guilt in her own data, but that variable is not available from the Consumer Expenditures Survey.

25 Eighty-nine percent of parents figure is from Penn, Schoen, and Berland (2001), a proprietary Nickelodeon study.

25 The phrase "bonded to brands" is from Lindstrom (2003).

25 Three hundred to 400 brands by ten year olds from McNeal (1999), p. 206. Brand-specific requests from McNeal (1999), p. 209.

25 The 89 percent figure is from Penn, Schoen, and Berland (2001).

25 Griffin Bacal study on children's brand awareness reported in Comiteau (2003). A 1999 Center for a New American Dream poll found that 22 percent of parents report their children began asking for brand-named items when they were ages two to three. Another 22 percent began their brand requests at ages four to five. Full discussion of this poll is in Chapter 9.

25 More closely bonded than kids anywhere and most brand-conscious generation claim from Lindstrom (2003), p. 13, and my interview with him.

26 On signs and sign wars, see Goldman and Papson (1996).

26 On sea-change in tastes and fashion houses driving the trend, see Kaufman (1999).

26 Upscaling in toys from Szymanski (1999), p. 62.

27 The number of toys sold increased by 20 percent from 1995 and North Americans consuming 45 percent of global production from units sold data available at http://www.toy-tma.org/industry/statistics/soi.html. See International Council of Toy Industries' World Toy Facts and Figures, March 2001.

27 MiniKin Kinder Salon example from presentation by Rachel Geller at KidPower 2002, May 6, 2002.

27 On cosmetic surgery between elementary and middle schools, see Quart (2003a), ch. 8.

27 FAO Schwarz birthday parties from Yazigi (1999).

27 "Crayons just won't do it" quote from Michael Sanson of *Restaurant Hospitality* magazine, cited in Sugarman (2000), p. F1.

27 Madame Alexander dolls from Leung (2002).

27 On corporate construction, see Steinberg and Kincheloe (1998). On media concentration, see Robert McChesney's excellent *Rich Media, Poor Democracy* (1999).

27 For a critique of Disney, including a discussion of racism and sexism in its characters, see Giroux (1999).

28 PBS and Nickelodeon have started a joint "educational" venture called Noggin. For a trenchant critique of the commercialism of PBS, see McChesney (1999).

28 Top-selling toy data from NPD Group, available at www.npd.com, TRSTS Top Ten Best Selling Toys ranked on units sold, Q1-2002.

28 On concentration among video game producers: In 2001, Nintendo had eight of the top twenty selling games, Sony had two, and Microsoft had one. See data at www.npd.com, Top twenty best-selling video game titles ranked on units sold in 2001.

29 Data on campaign contributions are from Common Cause, "Soft Money Donor Profiles," available at commoncause.org/laundromat/stat/top50.htm.

29 On the history of children's play, see Mergen (1992). See also Cross (1997), Sutton-Smith (1986), and Rotundo (1993).

30 On boys' outdoor play, see Rotundo (1993).

31 On only 25 percent of children's time as discretionary: These are my calculations from the data in Hofferth and Sandberg (2001b), Table 2. Their calculations of free time are slightly higher because they include shopping, studying, and household work as discretionary. Among children ages six to twelve, the corresponding figure for discretionary time is 24 percent. Time diaries were completed for 2,818 children in the sample.

31 On ten hours of weekly time for play among six to twelve year olds: Data are reported in Hofferth and Sandberg (2001a). The survey also included an additional category entitled "outdoors," which was twenty-nine minutes per week for six to eight year olds and forty-two minutes per week for the age-nine-to-twelve group. Some of that outdoor time is play.

31 On the comparison of children's time use between 1981 and 1997, see Hofferth and Sandberg (2001a, 2001b).

31 On stress and kindergartners, see Stolberg (2002).

31 Marketing studies reporting kids' feelings of time pressure are from a presentation by Wynne Tyree at KidPower 2002, reporting on KidID study.

32 Percentages of children who shop each week and do other activities are from Hofferth and Sandberg (2001b), Table 1. Average figures are my calculations for children ages six to twelve combined.

33 On the idea of postmodern childhood, see Buckingham (2000).

33 Media use data are from Kaiser Family Foundation Survey (1999) and available online at www.kff.org/content/1999/1535. For the youngest children, parents or caregivers gave responses. Daily television viewing by age from Table 8-A.

33 On 27.5 percent of kids spending more than five hours a day watching TV, see Kaiser Family Foundation (1999), Table 10-c. Author's calculations of eight to ten and eleven to thirteen year olds.

33 On television being on most of the time and during meals, see Kaiser Family Foundation (1999), chart 7, available at http://www.kff.org/content/1999/1535/. For the eight-to-eighteen age group, 47 percent reported TV was on most of the time.

33 Five hours and twenty-nine minutes average daily media use is from Kaiser Family Foundation (1999), Table 7, p. 19. Print media from Table 8-a. Forty-six percent of children with total media exposure of more than seven hours from Table 7, p. 19. On average, eliminating double-counting reduces the total by an hour per day.

34 Viewing times by race, income, and parental education from Kaiser Family Foundation (1999), Tables 8-C, 8-D, 8-E.

34 For conservatives' views on contemporary childhood, see Hymowitz (1999) and Mack (1997). On the demonization of youth, see Giroux (1997) and Jenkins's introduction to his 1998 collection on children's culture.

34 On 16.9 percent of children suffering food insecurity, see America's Children: Key National Indicators of Children's Well-Being (2001), Table ECON 4A. The 16.9 percent figure is sum of both food insecurity measures—with and without hunger. Available at www.childstats.gov.

34 A 1997 study found that 50 percent of children's calories are from added fat and sugar from Muñoz, Krebs-Smith, Ballard-Barbash, and Cleveland (1997).

34 On children's diets and the failure of 45 percent of children to meet any standards, see Indicators of Children's Well-Being, Appendix A, Detailed Tables, Table ECON 4.b Diet Quality, pp. 83–4, available at America's Children: Key National Indicators of Child Well-Being 1999, www.childstats.gov.

35 Data on prevalence of overweight children from Centers for Disease Control, Table 1, available at http://www.cdc.gov/nchs/products/pubs/pubd/hestats/overwght99.htm. Also see children's obesity rates from the Surgeon General's Call to Action 2001.

35 Statistics on eating disorders can be found at www.nimh.nih.gov/images/bluebox.gif. Among adolescent and young adult women in the United States, it is estimated that between 0.5 and 1.0 percent suffer from anorexia nervosa, 1 to 3 percent have bulimia nervosa, and 0.7 to 4 percent experience binge-eating disorder. There are limited data concerning the prevalence in males.

35 On regular smoking, five drinks in a row, and illegal drug use, see Indicators of Children's Well-Being, Appendix A, Detailed Tables, Tables BEH 1, 2, and 3. Available at

America's Children: Key National Indicators of Child Well-Being 1999, www.childstats.gov. Figures are rounded to the nearest integer.

35 More than 2,000 children and teens still start smoking every day from Smoking and Kids fact sheet, available at http://tobaccofreekids.org/research/factsheets/index.php?CategoryID=23.

35 Half of all high schoolers drinking from Christenson, Henriksen, and Roberts (2000).

35 *Pediatrics Journal* study on rising emotional and behavioral problems is from Kelleher (2000). A meta-analysis of anxiety studies from 1952 to 1993 also found significant increases in levels of anxiety; see Twenge (2000). Another study of trends over time found that children's problems worsened between 1974 and 1987, as measured by rising incidence for 45 out of 113 parent-reported problems. See Achenbach and Howell (1993).

35 Eight percent of adolescents with major depression and rising suicide rates are from http://www.nimh.nih.gov/publicat/childnotes.cfm.

35 On suicide rates by race, see *Mental Health: A Report of the Surgeon General* (1999), ch. 3, available at http://www.surgeongeneral.gov/library/mentalhealth/chapter3/sec5.html.

35 Worst level on self-reports in UCLA study from http://www.gseis.ucla.edu/-heri/norms_pr_ 01.html.

35 Findings from the MECA study are reported in *Mental Health: A Report of the Surgeon General* (1999), ch. 3, available at http://www.surgeongeneral.gov/library/mentalhealth/chapter3/sec5.html.

36 Data on children's problems from Child Development Supplement (one in five children were fearful) from Hofferth (1998). One in twenty-five were reported to have a behavior problem at school, pp. 8–9. Available at http://www.isr.umich.edu/src/child-development/timerep.html.

36 Fifty-nine percent of parents and warm behaviors data from Hofferth (1998), p. 9.

37 Children's top aspirations are from Roper Youth Report, reported by Dolliver (1998). In the 2000 report, among youth aged eight to seventeen, 56 percent dream about being rich, in comparison to 40 percent who dream about being a great athlete, being smarter (40 percent), or helping other people (37 percent).

37 Forty-four percent of kids daydreaming about being rich from KidID Study from JustKid Inc.; data provided to the author. The question wording is, "This is a list of things some kids daydream about and some kids do not. Please X the box that best describes if you daydream about these things a lot, some, not at all." December 2001. This was an in-school national survey of approximately 4,000 children.

37 Nearly two-thirds of parents report is from a poll conducted by the Center for a New American Dream, 1999. Sixty-three percent of parents agreed and strongly agreed with the statement (40 percent strongly agreed).

37 On the accumulating body of evidence on materialism, see Kasser (2002).

37 Data on youth materialism are from a data file for the Youth Materialism Survey provided by Marvin Goldberg. This was a nationwide, in-home survey of approximately 1,000 youths, aged nine to fourteen. For details, see Goldberg et al. (n.d.).

Chapter 3: From Tony the Tiger to *Slime Time Live*

39 On the Marshall Field's catalogue, see Cross (1997), pp. 11–12. On advertisers' primary appeal to adults, see pp. 30–31. On advertising to children from 1920 to 1940, see Marchand (1985), pp. 228–232.

39 On department stores, toy departments, and children's fashion shows, see Leach (1993), pp. 85, 103.

39 On children's radio shows and ads, see the discussion of Pecora (1998) in Strasburger and Wilson (2002), p. 39. Cook (2000b) also discusses some direct advertising to children.

39 On toys and television, see Committee on Communications (1992), p. 343, which argues that there is a "tight ring of commercialism around children's television from which young viewers cannot escape." Barbie would eventually become legendary, spawning a substantial literature. See McDonough (1999) and DuCille (1996).

40 On brand awareness and influence purchasing in the 1950s, see Munn (1958). Munn claims that 85 percent of children aged two to eight had high recognition of advertised products and wielded influence in 90 percent of homes. In the 1950s, there was also a wider range of products being advertised than the toys, cereals, and snack foods that came to dominate television ads by the 1960s. On the range of advertising products, see Kunkel and Roberts (1991). A Children's Advertising Review Unit study from 1991 finds that toys, cereals, and sugared snacks accounted for 75 percent of all commercials. But some new product types, such as videos and 900 numbers, were also being advertised.

40 On 1950s children's advertising as a low-creativity affair, not everyone agrees. In my interview with him, Paul Kurnit argued that the ads of the time were dynamic.

40 For an informative discussion of early television advertising to children, which covers Mickey Mouse, cereal characters, Barbie, the range of products, and types of selling techniques, see Alexander et al. (1998).

40 More than half of the most popular programs, see Schmitt (2000), p. 37, citing Nielsen data.

41 For James McNeal on his expertise falling on deaf ears, see the Preface to McNeal (1999).

41 Kurnit quotes and Kraft examples from my interview with Kurnit in Chappaqua, New York, November 15, 2002.

43 On advertisers' reliance on a common psychological model, there is one caveat, which is that their use of it is superficial, as I discuss in the concluding chapter.

43 For Daniel Cook's work, see his series of papers (2000a, 2000b, 2001) and his 2004 book. "Template of sorts" quote is from Cook (2000b), p. 494.

43 Lifebuoy and Shredded Wheat examples are from Cook (2000b), p. 494.

43 On the toddler stage as a marketing tool, see Cook (2000a, 2004).

44 For a discussion of teen and subteen age stages and clothing, see Cook (2004) and Cook and Kaiser (2003).

44 On children's timeless emotional needs, see Del Vecchio (1997), p. 28. For a related list of marketers' themes, see Nader (1996).

44 On sexual stereotyping and toys, see Seiter (1993).

45 On gender conventions in ads, Paul Kurnit articulated the conventional wisdom: "Capturing the boy is more difficult than capturing the girl, and that gets to some of the sexuality issues. . . . Girls in the marketing space tend to be a lot more relaxed in their skin than boys are."

45 On Kaiser findings on gender imbalance in programming and 63 percent, 78 percent, and 55 percent figures, see Signorielli (1997), Table 2, available at www.kkf.org.

45 Gender blending and examples trend from Rachel Geller of the Gepetto Group, presentation at KidPower 2002. For a perspective that begins with gender blurring but ends up stressing gender difference, see Gross (2002a).

46 An example of advocating the use of fear in children's entertainment as a way of satisfying the need to conquer fears is from Danny Kaye, a vice president of marketing at Universal Studios, who says that his goal is to give children entertainment that "challenges their senses by thrilling, exciting, unnerving, and even scaring them for

they understand that everything will be all right in the end." Cited in Del Vecchio (1997), p. 69.

46 Joanne Cantor on television and movies as a preventable cause of nightmares and anxieties is from Cantor (1998). See also Cantor and Mares (2001).

47 For a now-classic account of cool-hunting, see Gladwell (1997), reprinted in Schor and Holt (2000).

47 A recent survey in which 66 percent of kids say cool defines them is from the KidID survey of JustKid Inc. Data provided to the author and presented by Wynne Tyree at KidPower 2002.

48 On the shift from function to brand as the main attraction, see Lindstrom (2003), p. 82.

48 Gene Del Vecchio quote "part of cool" is from Del Vecchio (1997), p. 121.

48 On Traxtar marketing and its success, see Siegel et al. (2001), pp. 179–190.

48 On kids wanting to be older than they are, this is what Paul Kurnit had to say in our interview: "Emulation and aspiration work up, but only to a certain point. So if you want to capture six to eleven year olds, your bull's-eye is probably the eleven year old boy. . . . If you're looking for the eleven year old boy you're probably in a commercial casting a twelve or thirteen year old boy."

48 Douglas Holt quote on street as a potent commodity is from Holt and Schor (1998).

49 On sneaker marketing in the inner city, see Vanderbilt (1998), ch. 1.

49 On Hilfiger, see Smith (1997) and Spiegler (1997).

49 Paul Kurnit quote from his interview with O'Barr (2001).

50 On the cultural authority of marketers, see Holt (2002).

50 On these issues, see Kellner (1998), Holt (2002), and Frank (1997) on the backlash against advertisers and the subsequent marketing of cool.

50 The feedback loop is explored in the PBS special *Merchants of Cool,* available online at pbs.org/frontline/shows/cool/. Douglas Rushkoff quote from his essay "The Pursuit of Cool: Introduction to Anti-Hyper-Consumerism," available online at http://www.rushkoff.com/essay/sportswearinternational.html.

51 On cool-hunters' lists of what's hot and what's not, see Gladwell (1997), from which these items are drawn.

51 For an early recognition of the rise of antiadultism, see Nader (1996).

51 On the sale of youth rebellion to teens, see Nader (1996), ch. 4 and conclusion.

51 Nickelodeon's ratings are from *Kidscreen* magazine (2002), p. 33. On weekdays in 2002, Nickelodeon commanded a 2.7 audience share, a full point above the Cartoon Network; on Saturday mornings, its 4.2 share was 1.2 points higher than the number two.

52 The 1.1 million subscribers and 6.3 million readers from June 2003 data provided by Donna Sabino to the author.

52 On Nickelodeon's profitability, see Carter (2002). MTV Networks, to which Nickelodeon belongs, earned more than $3 billion in revenue in 2002. The statistic of 158 countries is also from this source.

52 "Whole premise of our company" quote by Lisa Judson, senior vice president of programming and executive creative director, cited in Hood (2000).

52 Sabino quote beginning "It's hard to be a kid" and thirteen criteria from interview with the author, July 2001.

53 Don Steinberg on Nickelodeon knowing what parents will accept is from Steinberg (2000).

53 On Sprite's success positioning itself as a youth brand, see *Merchants of Cool,* program 1911, *Frontline.* Available at www.pbs.org/wgbh/pages/frontline/shows/cool/etc/script.html.

53 The Sour Brite Crawlers example is from Siegel et al. (2001), p. 61.

54 "Nintendo ads" from Kline and de Peuter (2002), p. 265.
54 Nintendo marketer quote on targeting kids directly is from Kline and de Peuter (2002), p. 266.
54 Halpin quote from an interview with her at Reveries, available online at http://www.reveries.com/reverb/kids_marketing/halpin/index.html.
54 "Advertisers have kicked the parents out" quote from Mary Prescott (pseudonym), interview with the author, July 2001.
54 Crispin Miller quote from *Merchants of Cool* transcript, cited above.
54 Television dads quote from Kanner (2002), p. 45, and parents as nincompoops on p. 56. See also Hymowitz (1999), ch. 4, for a discussion of antifamilial attitudes in television.
54 Holly Gross quote from Gross (2002b).
55 On age compression, see Neil Postman's classic discussion (1994) from the point of view of the "disappearance of childhood." See also Hymowitz (1999), ch. 4, on what she calls the "teening of childhood." Other references on disappearance can be found in the notes to Chapter 10.
55 "By eight or nine they want 'N Sync" quote from Mary Prescott in 2001.
55 On the deliberate targeting of R-rated movies, see the prepared statement of the Federal Trade Commission, "Marketing Violent Entertainment to Children: Self-Regulation and Industry Practices in the Motion Picture, Music Recording, and Electronic Game Industries," available at www.ftc.gov/os/2001/07/violencetest.htm. For a discussion, see Grier (2001). On screening movies to nine and ten year olds, see Carvajal (2000).
55 On MTV watching, see Stanger and Gridina (1999), p. 11. My survey finds a third of ten to thirteen year olds watch MTV.
55 One of my favorite MTV anecdotes is from a seminar I gave to teachers in May 2002.
56 GI Joe age figures are from Paul Kurnit, who worked on the GI Joe account some years ago, from his KidPower 2002 presentation.
56 On *Seventeen* magazine's target audience, see Grier (2001), p. 12.
56 On the idea of the tween and its evolution from earlier categories of sub- and preteens, see Cook and Kaiser (2003).
57 On Abercrombie and Fitch thong underwear, an Associated Press (2002) story reports that the underwear has the words *eye candy* and *wink wink* printed on the front. These items prompted a protest e-mail campaign from two Christian groups, the American Family Association and the American Decency Association.
57 On WWE action figures, see Diane Levin (2003). See www.bicp.org for more information on WWE, as well as a campaign to oppose its marketing practices.
57 On four year olds targeted with toys tied to PG-13 movies, see Carvajal (2000).
58 Allison James quote from James (1998), p. 404.
58 Allison James quote beginning "It is thus of great significance" is from James (1998), p. 395.
58 Johann Wachs quote on grossing out Mom is from Chaplin (1999).
58 On adults and symbolic consumption, the story is more complicated with nonfood items. Parents care about symbolic issues such as what gender a product represents or its coding in terms of social class.
59 In addition to the Kool-Aid campaign, other beverage products have followed a similar strategy. For example, Siegel et al. (2001) recount their advice to the manufacturer of Sunny Delight: Tell her it's healthier, that it's great tasting and their friends like to drink it. "Appease the mom." Siegel et al. (2001), pp. 145–146, 188.
59 The origins of Happy Meals and "boring" quote from Colleen Fahey presentation at KidPower 2002.
60 Jerrie van Gelder quote on McDonald's from interview with the author, January 2002.

60 Teenie Beanie Baby Happy Meals described in Schlosser (2001), p. 47.
61 Wondergroup advice on preverbal babies from a presentation by Ivy Boehme and David Siegel at KidPower 2002.
61 On the Idell nag factor study, see Siegel et al. (2001), p. 75.
61 "Mom-centricity" quote is from Siegel et al. (2001), pp. 194–195.
61 Laurie Siegel quote is from her presentation at KidPower 2002.
61 On the idea that children should be the product's advocates, see Siegel et al. (2001), pp. 194–195.
62 Results from the 2002 poll on pester power by the Center for New American Dream Kids and Consumerism poll are available at http://www.newdream.org/campaign/kids/.
62 The finding that many parents believe kids know more about brands than they do is from the 1998 study by Penn, Schoen and Berland Associates, cited in Siegel et al. (2001), p. 117.
62 On kids reporting that they train their parents, see Siegel et al. (2001), p. 68.
62 Wynne Tyree quotes provided to me through written communications.
62 ACCUPoll backing off from previous advice is from 2003 KidPower Conference brochure.
63 Rachel Geller on toys and trans-toying from a PowerPoint presentation at KidPower 2002. "Almost" written as "(Almost!)" in original.
63 For views of child development experts, see Meltz (2002). See also Linn (forthcoming).
64 Susan Linn quote on "obscene value" from Meltz (2002).
64 For a collection of Gerbner's research, see Gerbner (2002). On television viewers overstating affluence, see O'Guinn and Shrum (1997). On television viewing and spending, see Schor (1998), ch. 4.
65 Nancy Shalek quote cited in Ruskin (1999).
65 On ads and children's emotional vulnerabilities, it's important to remember that it's hard to disentangle the effects of ads, programming, and the larger environment of consumer culture. Advertising is just one factor, and it interacts with other variables, such as a child's psychological makeup, social situation, family relationships, and daily life activities. On the other hand, the findings of my quantitative research, which include a rough measure of exposure to ads, suggest parents have good reason to be concerned about the cumulative impacts of marketing and advertising.
65 On the industry's stance, there's a bit of hypocrisy. Many in the industry believe in a Piagetian model of cognitive development, which implies that children's cognitive abilities develop in an age-based progression, which should be more or less constant over time. There's no reason to believe today's children are much more capable of understanding complex concepts such as the persuasive intent of advertising than those of the 1970s. This means the early research remains relevant. That, of course, is the view of the critics, who contend that the whole enterprise of advertising to children is inherently problematic.
66 On the accumulating body of evidence and expert opposition, see Federal Trade Commission (1978). For reviews of the evidence on children's ability to understand advertising, see Roedder John (1999), Gunter and Furnham (1998), Young (1990), Adler et al. (1980), Comstock (1991), Gunter and McAleer (1997), Valkenburg (2000), Strasburger and Wilson (2002), Martin (1997), and Kunkel (2001).
66 Academic sources on the impacts of advertising on children include Comstock (1991), Macklin and Carlson (1999), and Gunter and Furnham (1998).
66 The Palmer and McDowell study (1979) found that 53 percent of children could identify ads.
66 The Blosser and Roberts study (1985).

66 On the ineffectiveness of separators, see Strasburger and Wilson (2002) p. 46, and Comstock (1991), pp. 199–200.

66 On disclaimers, see Comstock (1991), p. 200.

66 There is debate within the literature about the theoretical underpinnings of these findings. In the Piagetian developmental framework, there are distinct stages for ages three to seven, seven to eleven, and eleven to sixteen. The inability to understand persuasive intent in the ages three to seven stage is attributed to the principle of "centration," or the inability to solve problems that require more than one component to a solution. Others, such as Young (1990) or Davies (1997), argue for a linguistic framework, which looks at when children can understand things like metaphor, ambiguity, irony, and so forth. The literature distinguishes commercial intent (the fact that commercials are there to sell products) with persuasive intent (the intention of the advertiser to persuade the viewer). Understanding of commercial intent develops before persuasive intent. In addition to the citations noted above, see also Buckingham (2000).

66 Fifty-three percent of first graders is from Robertson and Rossiter (1974). A more recent study is Wilson and Weiss (1992).

67 On the relation between television viewing time and understanding, see Faber, Perloff, and Hawkins (1982).

67 On children being less trusting of ads, see Roedder John (1999).

67 The 1994 study of middle school students is Boush, Friestad, and Rose (1994).

67 On children's defenses against ads, see Brucks, Armstrong, and Goldberg (1988) and Roedder John (1999).

67 On the impact of media literacy, see Roedder John (1999).

67 One study of nine and ten year olds and a media literacy film is Brucks, Armstrong, and Goldberg (1988).

67 Fooling kids about ads is discussed in the next chapter, in the context of Pepsi's Channel One ads.

67 On the influence of ads on purchases, see Roedder John (1999), Gunter and Furnham (1998), and Dietz and Strasburger (1991).

67 On food advertising and preferences, see Goldberg, Gorn, and Gibson (1978), Goldberg (1990), Borzekowski and Robinson (2001), and Reece, Rifon, and Rodriguez (1999).

67 Robinson's experiment on toy requests is Robinson et al. (2001).

Chapter 4: The Virus Unleashed

70 Information on POX from Alex Houston interview, plus PowerPoint presentation of the marketing plan provided to me by Houston.

72 Quote on "reinvigorating" the callers is from a presentation by two marketers involved in the POX launch that was given at the Advertising and Promoting to Kids Conference, September 10–11, 2001, and is contained in the APK conference booklet.

72 PowerPointed answer of "SCHOOLS!" is from APK conference booklet.

75 My conversation with Andrew Banks continued as follows: "No," I explained. "I am interested in issues of intrusion and privacy. With the 360-degree strategy, how could a person ever escape advertising?" Banks drew the line at paying people to sit in bars and praise particular brands without identifying themselves as marketers, a practice that had been exposed in the *New York Times* the week we spoke. But he defended other covert practices. Apparently, paying my best friend to get me to buy a product is absolutely fine with him.

75 Hollywood Product Placement is one such agency.
75 On B2K, 3LW, and the practice of seeding, see Holloway (2002).
76 On child sports endorsers, see Talbot (2003).
76 All information from an interview with Laura Groppe and company materials provided to me.
78 AOL estimate from Shinan Govani (1999), available at http://csmweb2.emcweb.com/durable/1999/02/10/p11s1.html.
78 Junior Mint product placement example is from United Placement Hall of Fame, available at www.upp.net/hall-of-fame.html. Other examples are from Creative Entertainment Services. Details at www.acreativegroup.com/ceshome/news_and_articles.html.
78 On M&M's and other branded food books, see Kirkpatrick (2000).
79 On virtual ads, see Elliott (1999). He quotes David Verklin of Carat: "You are seeing the first glimpse of the future of advertising, where the product and the program are integrated in a fashion that's more seamless than we ever could have imagined." The first example of a virtual ad was in March 1999, when Blockbuster, Coca-Cola, Evian, and Kenneth Cole ads were superimposed into an episode of *Seven Days*.
79 On Pepsi's documentary-style ads, see Fox (1996), pp. 50–52, 58.
80 See Center for Media Education (1996) for the original report on online abuses. For CME's one-year evaluation of COPPA's effectiveness, see CME (2001) and Aufderheide (2001). Available at www1.soc.american.edu/aufderheide/Research/kids.
80 Chen and Ringel "savvy marketers" quote on advergaming is from (2001).
80 Gap Branded Games is from a case study by Scott Randall, president of BrandGames, conference booklet, Fourth Annual APK Advertising and Promoting to Kids, September 10–11, 2001.
82 Anecdote on "This product cures cancer." Some details have been altered here to protect the identities of the companies involved.
83 Quote on "smart shopping tips and maximizing funds" is from the Santa Clara, California, Girl Scouts Web site, information on fashion adventure, available at http://www.girlscoutsofscc.org/girls/programs_35.html. Critical views of the Fashion Adventure program are available at commercialalert.org.

Chapter 5: Captive Audiences

85 On 80 percent of marketing dollars, see Wartella (1995).
85 On corporate sponsorship of public institutions, see Halpert (2001).
85 On commercial infiltration of public schools, there is now a large literature. See Molnar (1996), Consumers Union (1995), GAO (2000), Manning (1999a, 1999b, 1999c), Fox (1996), Jarvis (2001), and Golding (1999). There is also a large amount of online material available. See the Web sites of the Center for the Analysis of Commercialism and Education, and Commercial Alert. Consumers Union 1995, available at www.consunion.org/other/captivekids/evaluations.htm.
85 On the explosive rise of in-school commercialism after 1997, see Molnar (2002). The Commercialism in Education Research Unit of Arizona State University compiles an annual index of media reports of commercial activities in schools. The index began to rise in 1991 and nearly tripled between 1997 and 2000. See Molnar (2002), available at http://www.asu.edu/educ/epsl/CERU/CERU_Annual_Report.htm.
86 For statistics and an analysis of Channel One, see Hays (1999), Fox (1996), and Brand and Greenberg (1994). Ninety percent of all school days statistic is from the Center for a New American Dream and can be found at http://newdream.org/campaign/kids/facts.htm.

86 For an analysis of Channel One's content, see Fox (1996).
86 The annual price tag of $1.8 billion and $300 million is from Molnar and Sawicky (1998), pp. 6–8, available at http://www.asu.edu/educ/epsl/CERU/Documents/cace-98-02/CACE-98-02.htm.
86 Findings from the study of two Michigan schools are cited in Molnar (1996), p. 69.
87 The finding that students report feeling that advertised products are good for them is from Molnar (1996), p. 69.
87 The finding that children in poorer districts are more at risk is from Morgan (1993).
87 On Chris Whittle specifically targeting poor Latino districts, see Molnar (1996), p. 71.
87 On Channel One's foray into media literacy, see Manning (1999b). On kickbacks, see Trotter (2001).
88 Notable exceptions to Channel One's keeping its clients are the school districts of Seattle and Nashville, where Channel One has been banned as of 2004. For updates on Channel One, see commercialalert.org.
88 Information on Zapme! and its activities is available at www.commercialalert.org. See, especially, Commercial Alert press release, July 11, 2001.
88 Omaha gymnasium floor and Pennsylvania ads from Molnar (2002).
88 Oscar Mayer contest from Mayer (2003).
88 Centers for Disease Control figures of 94, 84, and 58 percent of schools offering soft drinks for sale are from fact sheet on Food Service, available at http://cdc.gov/nccdphp/dash/shpps/factsheets/fs01_food_service.html.
89 For a report on the Mike Cameron incident, see Molnar (1998), available at http://www.asu.edu/educ/epsl/CERU/Annual%20reports/cace-98-01.htm. A sampling of press coverage is available at http://www.adbusters.org/campaigns/commercialfree/toolbox/coke.html.
89 On the Texas school with soft drink exclusivity, see Quart (2003b).
89 On NetworkNext, see Lindeman (2001).
89 On free planners to New York City students, see Feuer (2002).
89 Sports as "fastest-growing areas" is from E. Fisher, writing in the *Washington Times,* March 9, 2001, cited by Molnar (2002), p. 9.
89 John Kellmayer quote from Russakoff (2001).
90 Tens of millions participating in Pizza Hut program and expansion to preschools from Schlosser (2001), p. 56.
90 For more information on these promotions, see past issues of *Not for Sale!,* the newsletter of the Center for Commercial-Free Public Education.
90 Contest examples are from Mayer (2003).
90 Weyerhauser summer program from Molnar (2002), p. 19.
90 On General Mills paying teachers, see Applebaum (2003), p. 24.
91 On the roots of current trends, see Molnar (1996).
91 On the content of corporate curricula, see Borowski (1999), who focuses on environmental curricula; Consumers Union (1995); Manning (1999c), p. 17; and materials from the Center for Commercial-Free Public Education.
92 Scholastic's in-school marketing is described in company promotional material. Data on total school enrollment are from the Department of Education Web site, http://nces.ed.gov//pubs2002/digest2001/tables/dt003.asp.
92 The Scholastic magazines example is from Consumers Union (1995), p. 11.
93 Examples of first-grade curricula are from "Information Packet on Commercialism in Schools," from the Center for Commercial-Free Public Education, March 20, 2000, provided to the author. Other examples include a Domino's pizza counting exercise and a Visa curriculum that promotes credit cards to kids by showing all the stuff kids can buy with a card.
93 On Care Bears and Clifford in preschools, see Hays (2003).

93 The Evan Shapiro quote on Court TV's curriculum is from the 2003 TeenPower Conference brochure.

94 Details on the Field Trip Factory are available from its Web site, www.fieldtripfactory.com.

94 Nearly 80 percent of materials biased from Consumers Union (1995). The report is available at www.consumersunion.org/other/captivekids/.

94 California administrator anecdote from Allen (1992).

94 Consumers Union quote on Exxon's energy cube, American Coal Foundation materials quote, and Chevron lesson plan are all from Consumers Union (1995), p. 5.

94 Incineration as "recycling" is from Jacobson (1995). Responsible clear-cutting is from Molnar (2002), p. 19.

94 Procter & Gamble's Decision Earth is from Consumers Union (1995), p. 5.

95 Plastics video incident and quotes are from Allen (1992).

95 Saudi Arabia and Israeli sponsorships are discussed in Molnar (1996).

95 The $521 figure is from Goodnough (2002).

96 Los Angeles and Oakland bans on soft drink sales are reported in Molnar (2002).

96 On the backlash to school commercialization, see Zernike (2001) and Manning (2001) on soft drinks, and www.commercialalert.org on Zapme! and Channel One. In 1999, the California legislature passed two bills limiting school commercialism.

96 On the Dodd-Shelby privacy provision, a coalition led by Commercial Alert, and including the right-wing groups Eagle Forum and Focus on the Family, was active in gaining this provision.

96 On industry opposition to the Maryland law, see LeDuc (2001).

97 The "most trusted name" quote is from Scholastic promotional materials.

Chapter 6: Dissecting the Child Consumer

99 This scene is my rendering from two interviews about her work with Mary Prescott.

101 On Levi Strauss going into kids' closets, see Gruber and Berry (1993).

102 Procter and Lucky Charms quotes are from Amanda Carlson (pseudonym).

103 "Rapport and friendship" quote is from a conversation with a marketer from the Martin Agency. Other information and Reynolds quote and clients are from Tabor (1999).

104 Drug study details were provided by Denny in a telephone interview and follow-up communication.

105 "Thoroughly and deeply implicated" and secrecy and danger quotes are from Sunderland and Denny (2003).

105 "Just say no [is] don't grow up" quote is from Sunderland and Denny (2003).

106 On Levi Strauss and Josh Koplewicz, including the "They were pretty blunt" quote, see Katz (1996). See also Isa (1996). Information on his current activities is from a personal communication, April 3, 2003.

107 The quote on aggressive marketing in schools is from Ron Coughlin's presentation at KidPower 2002.

108 "A little unfair" quote is contained in Katz (1996).

108 The "Money is what makes people go" quote is from Amanda Carlson.

110 The Adam Koval quote is from Margot Kelly, "The Science of Shopping," Canadian Broadcasting Company, December 3, 2002, available online at http://cbc.ca/consumers/market/files/money/science_shopping/.

111 Reiher is currently completing a book entitled *Innertainment: The Psychology of Entertainment and Its Impact on the Human Spirit,* which outlines what he calls age-appropriate entertainment enrichment experiences.

112 Another kid-marketed system is AcuPOLL, which claims to be the only large-scale quantitative methodology offering three distinct applications for kids in the five-to-seven, eight-to-ten, and thirteen-to-seventeen age ranges.

112 "Virtually every type of research" quote and data on Nickelodeon's research efforts are from interview with Sabino, July 2002.

112 Four stages of testing *Blue's Clues* are from Steinberg (2000), p. 698.

113 On focus groups in schools, see Tabor (1999).

113 Information on school-based studies is from e-mail communication with Pat Tobin, of Applied Research and Consulting, now the Michael Cohen Group.

115 "They kind of get over it" quote is from Amanda Carlson.

116 In the Strottman study, the marketers attempted to get permission in advance, but in cases where the store did not respond, they proceeded without approval.

Chapter 7: Habit Formation

119 On obesity reaching epidemic levels, see the Surgeon General's Call to Action, available at http://www.surgeongeneral.gov/topics/obesity/. On the doubling of obesity rates, see National Center for Health Statistics, "Prevalence of Overweight Among Children and Adolescents: United States, 1999," available at http://www.cdc.gov/nchs/products/pubs/pubd/hestats/over99fig1.html.

119 For new data from the Massachusetts Department of Public Health, see Smith (2002).

119 On media accounts, see, for example, *U.S. News and World Report,* August 19, 2003, which includes McDonald's Value Meal calories. See also Branch (2003). And for experts' views, Brownell and Horgen (2003).

120 The term *liquid candy* was used by the Center for Science in the Public Interest in its 1998 report, "Liquid Candy: How Soft Drinks Are Harming Americans' Health." The report found that one-fifth of one and two year olds and nearly half of all six to eleven year olds drink soda. The report is available at http://www.cspinet.org/sodapop/liquid_candy.html.

120 One study of Saturday morning children's television found 63 percent is from Gamble and Cotugna (1999). The quote on fruit and vegetable ads is on p. 264. Toy premiums in 20 percent of fast food restaurant advertising is from Reece, Rifon, and Rodriguez (1999), cited in Macklin and Carlson (2002), p. 241.

120 Forty percent fast food figure is from Byrd-Bredbrenner and Grasso (1999), p. 163.

120 The 1998 content study of prime-time viewing finding 23 percent and 40 percent is from Byrd-Bredbenner and Grasso (1999). They report that weekend daytime viewing hours were only 20 percent of prime-time viewing hours. Advertised diet as "antithesis of recommended diet" is on p. 163.

121 A read through *Nickelodeon* magazine is the author's calculation. The August 2001 issue of *Nickelodeon* had thirty-seven pages of ads. Five were for Nickelodeon's own magazines and products. Of the thirty-two other ads, nine were for candy and gum, eight were for other junk foods, and one milk ad promoted sugared milks. There were also two condiment ads (for syrup and mustard), four and a half pages of clothing and shoe ads, two and a half pages of ads for videos, one video game ad, one makeup ad, and one ad for tissues.

121 *Nickelodeon*'s target audience is from a private communication with Donna Sabino of Nickelodeon, December 2003.

121 Information on *Foodfight!* is from a news release by the movie's producer, Threshold Digital Research Labs, available in "Commercial Alert Criticizes Movie-Length Ad Targeted at Kids," news release, May 7, 2001, at www.commercialalert.org.

121 The $750 million figure for in-school food marketing is from Egan (2002).

121 The $33 billion figure and breakdown by types of food are from Nestlé (2002), p. 22.

122 McDonald's $500 million figure and 40 percent to kids are from Horgen et al. (2001), cited in Strasburger and Wilson (2002).

122 The Campbell Mithun Esty 1998 study is "National Study Reveals Kids' Favorite TV Ads," press release, Minneapolis, June 16, available at http://www.campbellmithun.com/news/archive.html, and is also reprinted in Strasburger and Wilson (2002), Table 7.2.

123 The licorice anecdote is from a presentation by Ron Coughlin, KidPower 2002.

123 On increasing sugar, another example is Saatchi and Saatchi's repositioning of Yoplait by adding more sugar and intensifying the flavor. See *Selling to Kids* (1998).

124 The eighteenth-century Irish discourse is from private communication with Professor Kevin O'Neal, Boston College, based on unpublished research.

124 On sugar's addictive properties, see Colantuoni et al. (2002).

125 On food companies' knowing of their products' addictive qualities, see Matthews (2003).

125 On decades of studies, see Goldberg (1990) on sugared cereals present in the home. See also Gorn and Goldberg (1982) for experimental evidence. Taras and colleagues is Taras et al. (1989), Borzekowski and Robinson is (2001), and the study of fourth and fifth graders is from Signorielli and Lears (1992), cited in Strasburger and Wilson (2002), p. 245.

125 The industry poll of parental attitudes toward food marketing is from Ebenkamp (2002). Television ads were the most frequently chosen influence (at 80 percent of parents). "Other kids" was second (61 percent), magazine ads and celebrity endorsements tied for third (21 percent), and newspaper ads (17 percent) and the Internet (11 percent) were also important.

126 On the prevalence of snacking and rise in fraction of calories, see Jahns, Siega-Riz, and Popkin (2001).

126 On Pepsi licensing its logo on infant bottles, see Jacobson (1998).

126 Fast food comprising 10 percent is from Cara Ebbeling of Harvard Medical School, reported in McLellan (2002).

126 The discussion of the companies' responses is in Barboza (2003). The quote by Kraft spokesman Michael Mudd from "Fat 'too tasty to remove' from consumers' diet" is in an article from *Food Ingredients First,* available at http://www.foodingredientsfirst.com/ newsmaker_article.asp?idNewsMaker=3898&fSite=AO545.

127 On Big Food's interest in AMP, see Day (2003b).

127 For Kraft's reassurances to investors, see "Investor Resources: Strategies for Growth," available at http://www.kraft.com/investors/strategies.html.

128 On the view that obesity depends on physical activity and individual physiology, see the comments of William S. Ohlmemeyer, an associate general counsel for Philip Morris, which owns Kraft, Oscar Mayer, and other brands, cited in Branch (2003).

128 The study on soft drinks and obesity is Ludwig (2001). The industry-funded Center for Consumer Freedom has attacked the Ludwig study.

128 That more than half of the average child's calories are from sodas, juices, and high-calorie drinks is from Cullen, Ash, Warneke, and Moor (2002), cited in Brownell and Horgen (2003), p. 102, n.22.

128 The arrangement between AAPD and Coca-Cola is discussed in Burros (2003).

128 For information on the relationship between Coke and the PTA, see commercialalert.org. On Coke's current school-based activities, see Day (2003a).

128 For a discussion of Tommy Thompson's address to the GMA, see Commercial Alert news release, "Go on the Offensive, Secretary Thompson Tells Junk Food Lobby," November 15, 2002.

129 On the obesity lobby and Henry Kravis, see Commercial Alert news release, "'Obesity Lobby' Will Carry Out CDC's New Program, Commercial Alert Charges," July 17, 2002.

129 VERB funding has been slashed from $125 million in 2001 to a projected $5 million in 2004. See Connolly (2003).

129 Other critics include Susan Linn, who reports that links on the VERB Web site connect to junk food ads. For a discussion of VERB and its Web site, see the interview with Susan Linn on Bill Moyers' *NOW,* a PBS program, available at http://www.pbs.org/now/printable/transcript_verb_print.html.

129 On the role of the food industry in challenging the WHO report, see Branch (2003). The Sugar Association's letter to the WHO, as well as the Bush administration letter (by William Steiger, special assistant to HHS Secretary Thompson) to the director-general of the WHO, J. W. Lee, are available at www.commercialalert.org. On the Sugar Association's efforts, see also Eilperin (2003).

129 McDonald's marketing goal of twenty visits per month is from Critser (2003), p. 28.

130 On kids just sitting around, Paul Kurnit articulated a similar sentiment: "You've got kids who are increasingly home alone, latchkey kids, you're got the after-school day part, which is the fourth meal and kids rule the kitchen. . . . So there's a level of kid independence today that is unprecedented."

130 On industry interference with the food pyramid, see Nestle (2002), ch. 2.

131 On Monsanto's lawsuits, see Mohl (2003). On rBGH, the FDA, and health impacts, see Green (2002). Green reports on the role of Michael Taylor, a Monsanto lawyer who went to the FDA during the period rBGH was being reviewed and approved. His ties to Monsanto were revealed, and he was then appointed at USDA. He subsequently returned to Monsanto. Critics have charged that the approval of rBGH, which occurred without human studies, and without original data being provided, was due to Monsanto's political influence.

132 Johann Wachs on parents' picking their battles is from Chaplin (1999), p. 65.

132 On cigarette advertising to kids, there is now a very large literature on its effectiveness. See Pierce et al. (1998) for a longitudinal study that finds that one-third of all smoking experimentation can be attributed to exposure to advertising and promotion.

133 A quarter of programming bought by alcohol companies is from Center on Alcohol Marketing and Youth (2002), p. 2, available online at http://camy.org/research/tv1202/.

133 Estimates of 15 percent, 1 percent, 89 percent, and overexposure on networks are from Center on Alcohol Marketing to Youth (2002), p. 2.

133 Alcohol ads common in popular youth magazines are from a fact sheet on magazines from the Center on Alcohol Marketing to Youth, available at http://camy.org/factsheets/index.php?FactsheetID=18#magazines002.

133 On Budweiser animal commercials as kids' favorite, see Hays (1998). Bud's "Whassup" campaign as kids' favorite is from a presentation by Abigail Hirschhorn at Kidscreen conference, September 11, 2001, citing the Zandl hot sheet.

133 More kids recognizing Bud frogs and Joe Camel than the vice president is from Stanger and Gridina (1999), Table 5.1.

133 On overexposure to beer ads, and MTV and Budweiser in particular, see Devaney (2001), p. 30.

133 The major content study of tobacco, alcohol, and drug advertising in movies is Roberts, Henriksen, and Christenson (1999). No G or PG films included illicit drug use. In the PG-13 category, 17 percent had illicit drug use. A higher prevalence claim is also from Roberts et al. (1992). A subsequent study of 250 top grossing movies is Sargent et al. (2001). See also Strasberger and Wilson (2002), ch. 6, for a review of the evidence on drugs and the media.

134 On cigarette product placement, see http://www.library.ucsf.edu/tobacco/2400.html. The Stallone contract is document 2401.02. *License to Kill* is document 2406.06.
134 On the increase in depictions of tobacco use in movies since the settlement, see the fact sheet produced by the Campaign for Tobacco-Free Kids, by Lindboom (2002), available at http://tobaccofreekids.org/research/factsheets/pdf/0216.pdf. See also: http://smokefreemovies.ucsf.edu/problem/moviessell.html.
134 Eighty percent of cigarette smoking in films is the top four advertised brands is from Sargent et al. (2001).
134 On television's depiction of addictive substances and statistics on 1998–99 shows and ads, see Christenson et al. (2000).
134 On Look-Look's campaign for Sky Vodka, see Goldstein (2000).
135 On record levels of advertising after the settlement, see Tobacco Industry Continues to Market to Kids, August 20, 2003, available at http://tobaccofreekids.org/research/factsheets/pdf/0156.pdf.
135 On recent advertising by tobacco companies, see the press release entitled "Groups Request Investigation of Philip Morris Schoolbook Covers," from Commercial Alert, January 3, 2001, available at commercialalert.org.
135 Knowledgeable advertisers is from author's interviews. On Philip Morris's record on antismoking messages, see "Philip Morris and Targeting Kids," fact sheet from Campaign for Tobacco-Free Kids, January 2, 2002, available at http://tobaccofreekids.org/research/factsheets/pdf/0011.pdf.
135 James Sargent study on movies and smoking is Sargent et al. (2001).
136 On tobacco as a gateway drug, see the references cited in Lowinson et al. (1997).
136 For the National Bureau for Economic Research study, see Saffer and Dave (2003).
136 For a California study, see Robinson, Chen, and Killen (1998).
136 The intimate knowledge claim is from a Denny interview.
136 On diet supplements, see Gugliotta (2000).
137 "Relently discussed" is from Sunderland and Denny (2003). This point also came up in my interview with Denny.
137 The study from *Pediatrics* showing that more than half of all concept music videos involve violence is called "Sexuality, Contraception and the Media," *Pediatrics* (2001), pp. 107–191, cited in Media and the Family fact sheet on MTV, available at http://www.mediafamily.org/facts/facts_mtv.shtml.
137 The study of MTV and violence is DuRant et al. (1997).
138 The $10.3 billion figure is from www.npdfunworld.com/fun.
138 "Inappropriate video games" as the number one item is from the Center for a New American Dream poll, May 2002, made available to the author. Also available at www.newdream.org. In Grand Theft Auto 3, the current best-seller from Rockstar Games, the player works for the mob stealing cars, killing, and maiming to avoid being caught.
138 The Robinson study is Robinson et al. (2001). The college student study is Anderson and Dill (2000). See also Dorman (1997), whose review of earlier literature is inconclusive. Funk and Buchman (1996) find that higher game playing is associated with lower self-esteem in seventh- and eighth-grade girls but not boys.
138 The Indiana University Medical School studies are described in "Violent Video Games Trigger Unusual Brain Activity in Aggressive Adolescents," press release from the Radiological Society of North America, November 30, 2002, available at http://jol.rsna.org/ pr/target.cfm?ID=94.
138 Grossman's views are set forth in Grossman and DeGaetano (1999).
138 The FTC report on marketing violent video games to underage youth is Federal Trade Commission (2000), available at http://www.ftc.gov/reports/violence/vioreport.pdf.
138 On the meta-analysis of video games, see Anderson (2003).

139 The joint statement on media and violence references 1,000 studies, but some sources put the number at 200 to 300. See Jones (2002), p. 29.
139 For the counterview, see Garbarino (1995), Levin (1998), and Carlsson-Paige and Levin (1990).
139 On the link between scientific findings and media reports about media violence, see Bushman and Anderson (2001).
140 The literature on the adverse effects of television is vast. On children, see MacBeth (1996), Stoneman and Brody (1981), Dietz and Strasburger (1991), Adler et al. (1980), Comstock (1991), Gunter and McAleer (1997), van Evra (1998), Singer and Singer (2001), Strasburger and Wilson (2002), and Healy (1990), in addition to previously cited references. See also Kubey and Csikszentmihalyi (2002). The AAP Web site, www.aap.org, has a wealth of information.
140 On addictions beginning in youth, see Lowinson et al. (1997).
140 On slot machines with children's themes, see Glionna (1999).

Chapter 8: How Consumer Culture Undermines Children's Well-Being

144 At one site, we included one small class of seventh graders because there were too few fifth and sixth graders.
144 See Kasser (2002) for a discussion of teen studies. One major exception to the lack of materialism studies is Goldberg et al. (n.d.), a national survey of materialism among nine to fifteen year olds. However, that study measures the extent of materialism and some of its correlates, but does not investigate the relationship between materialism and well-being, a central focus of the materialism literature. A second study of younger children, which was done after mine and uses my scale, is Engle and Kasser (2003).
144 Doxley has a school choice system that includes some more alternative school options. However, the survey was administered in the more traditional elementary schools. Therefore, I suspect the sample that was recruited was perhaps more representative of the population as a whole than a sample from the other three schools might have been.
145 Incomes in Doxley rose substantially in the 1990s, by more than 20 percent, compared to statewide growth of only 5 percent. Income data are from the U.S. Census and housing prices from real estate sites.
145 On the influx of professionals in Doxley: Part of it has been among East and South Asian families. Like many other places in the United States, Doxley has become more ethnically and racially diverse in recent years.
145 On schools' willingness to participate: In four of the five schools, both parents and children filled out consent forms before the children were permitted to participate in the study. In Doxley, a number of parents asked for copies of the survey in advance, and the teachers, principals, and I engaged in discussions with some parents. In one of the Boston schools, we used a passive consent form for parents because of prior experience indicating difficulty getting returned permission forms. All children filled out consent forms before taking the survey. Students who participated received an inexpensive pen or pencil as a gift.
147 On children's high level of uncertainty about their parents' degrees: Thirty-six and 42 percent reported postgraduate degrees, for mothers and fathers, respectively, with an additional 50 percent and 45 percent indicating that they didn't know whether their parents had them. One variable on which the children responded nearly identically may be worth noting: Forty-three percent of the children reported that their grades last year were "excellent" and 39 percent reported they were "good."

153 Twenty-five-hour figure from Kaiser Family Foundation (1999), Table 10-A. Figures for children aged eight to ten and eleven to thirteen are three hours and thirty-seven minutes per day. Author's calculation from daily to weekly hours.
160 The self-esteem scale is from DuBois et al. (1996); the Revised Children's Manifest Anxiety Scale is from Reynolds and Richmond (1979); the Children's Depression Inventory is from Saylor et al. (1984).
160 Anxiety levels are measured by sixteen yes or no items, for a total of 32 points. This scale is scored opposite to depression, so that higher scores indicate *less* anxiety. The average score was 27, indicating an overall low level of anxiety. Boston children were more anxious than those from Doxley by a difference of just over 1 point.
163 The question was asked about "the person who mostly takes care of you." Because that is a parent for virtually all of these children, I use that terminology.
163 The parental responsiveness measure is from the Authoritative Parenting Scale by Jackson, Jenriksen, and Foshee (1998). The four items taken from this scale are: "She (he) makes me feel better when I am upset," "She listens to what I have to say," "She is too busy to talk to me," and "She wants to hear about my problems."
166 On the limits of regression analysis: Another problem is the existence of a third factor, such as an emotionally deprived upbringing, which is responsible for both depression and consumer involvement. Focusing on reducing consumer involvement would have limited effectiveness as a strategy to combat depression, because it wouldn't be dealing with the root cause, namely upbringing.
166 On the structural equation estimates: We used AMOS for all estimates. In the structural equation models, the coefficients for the consumer involvement scale were very close in magnitude to the single equation models.
166 For similarities between the depression and anxiety measures, see Stark and Laurent (2001).
166 One variable that we looked at briefly but did not correlate with consumer involvement is happiness. This may be due to the fact that it is only a three-point scale with little variation in its distribution. Also, happiness was asked about in a single question rather than a well-validated psychological scale. Goldberg et al. (n.d.) also found no correlation between a single happiness question and their materialism scale.
172 On well documented by psychologists, see Kasser (2002) for a review of this literature. See also Kasser and Ryan (1993).
173 For a discussion of the impacts of television on reading, see MacBeth (1996).
173 For a review of the literature on play, see van der Voort and Valkenburg (1994).
173 The Kasser and Ryan study on materialism is (1993).
174 On materialist teens, see Kasser, Ryan, Zax, and Sameroff (1995) and, for a summary, Kasser (2002), ch. 2.

Chapter 9: Empowered or Seduced?

177 Richard Goldstein quote from "Roundtable on Values in Advertising," which appeared in *Advertising and Society Review* (2002).
177 Children "do not possess the cognitive ability" quote is from FTC (1978), pp. 2–4.
177 In 1991, the FCC reinstated the ban but interpreted it far more narrowly, in effect allowing all program-length commercials, except when additional, separate ads for the products appear within the program. On this point, see Strasburger and Wilson (2002), p. 67.
178 On Ralph Nader as a long-standing critic, see Nader (1996). This guide did an outstanding job of identifying many of the dominant marketing themes that I discussed in Chapter 3.

178 Activists' opposition to commercialization included a coalition among Commercial Alert, Obligation, and Junkbusters, which teamed up to protect the privacy of schoolchildren. Their efforts led to the demise of Zapme! and led N2H2 to stop market research in schools via Web browsers.
178 For George Gerbner's statement on corporations' becoming the dominant transmitters of culture, see Gerbner (1999) and Budd, Craig, and Steinman (1999).
178 The full text of "Watch Out for Children: A Mother's Statement to Advertisers," can be found at http://watchoutforchildren.org/.
178 The Hillary Clinton quote on "children as little cash cows" is in Nagourney (2000).
178 One industry publication quote is from Hood (2000), writing in *Kidscreen.*
178 "We are accused of manipulating" and other examples are from the KidPower 2003 brochure.
179 "We always try to put them" quote is from Lisa Morgan (pseudonym), interview with author.
179 "Kids have very little control" quote is from del Vecchio (1997), p. 71.
179 For some psychologists' view, see Kanner and Kasser (2000). See also Kanner and Gomes (1995) and Kasser and Kanner (2004).
179 Paul Kurnit quote on interview with Mack O'Barr (2001).
180 Bob Garfield quote and McNeal's "detestable" are from McNeal (1999), p. 148–149.
180 Judson "truth meter" quote is from Hood (2000).
180 Geoffrey Roche quote is cited in MacKinnon (2000).
180 "Kids have become a little more savvy" is from Jerrie van Gelder, interview with author.
181 Paul Kurnit quote that activists are overprotective is from O'Barr (2001).
181 Martin study is (1997). Later studies are more likely to use nonverbal measures, on which younger children do better.
181 For an exposition of these proadvertising arguments by Paul Kurnit, see O'Barr (2001).
181 For references on the impact of television, see Chapter 7.
181 On the argument that free television is a subsidy to low-income consumers, this is because low-income households watch relatively high levels of television but buy relatively low levels of consumer goods.
182 On the argument that the economy needs ads to avoid collapse, in 1995 the Ad Council, presumably worried about antiadvertising sentiment, ran a series of spots making these claims.
182 One example of the "ads are good" view is from Paul Kurnit: "Marketers need to stand up and proudly [say] that what we are doing is positive and has positive social implications in terms of kids and is helpful in terms of them growing up in this culture of ours. It teaches them to be aware and savvy consumers, gives them the opportunity to choose and select among products and ideas that they prefer" (O'Barr, 2001). Wynne Tyree made a similar point in a private communication to me: "Advertising empowers kids by giving them the information they need to make purchase decisions. Advertising tells them which products will taste great, what times shows they want to watch will air, and how to use things that might otherwise be confusing. They feel empowered by being 'in the know,' whether it's what new products to chat about at the lunch table or what new trick to do on a video game."
182 On the relationship between television viewing and critical facility, see Brand and Greenberg (1994). They found that students in Channel One schools, who see ads in school every day, view advertised products more favorably than do non–Channel One students. Van Evra (1998) reports that heavy television viewers have more favorable attitudes to commercials and products, pp. 95–100. For an opposing view, see Mangleburg and Bristol (1998). Both studies are of teens.

184 "David to the corporate Goliaths" is from Linn (2000).

185 The Center for a New American Dream poll was conducted in 2000. A full discussion is available in Schor (2001).

185 On how parents feel when pressured: the wording of this question was not ideal, on account of the word *pressure* in the statement and in the answer category.

185 A large majority of parents also agree that television "increases materialism" in children. See Woodward (2000), Figure 3.7.

186 The David Siegel quotes ("Give 'em a vitamin") are from his presentation at Kid-Power 2002.

186 The Peter Reynolds quote ("I want to save") is cited in Hood (2000). Learning Curve International, which markets Thomas the Tank Engine products, does not advertise directly to kids under the age of twelve.

187 Viselman quote on "ever since that study came out" is from Hood (2000).

187 Within the industry, concerns mainly getting lip service: I found relatively little public debate about the worthiness of the overall enterprise, and that discussion centers on certain "unethical" practices or "bad apples." Among published accounts, James McNeal is critical of overselling, deceptions, sexual innuendo, and violence, and Dan Acuff makes a similar plea for marketers to refuse products that are disempowering for kids, such as violent toys.

187 On the inability to be critical of the product, see the comments of Rich Goldstein, who expressed a similar view in "Roundtable on Values in Advertising," *Advertising and Society Review* (2002).

Chapter 10: Decommercializing Childhood

189 On "the way we never were," see Coontz (2000).

189 For discussions of postmodern childhood and its advocates, see Buckingham (2000) and Kincheloe (1998), among others.

190 The consumer sovereignty model is set out in most standard economics textbooks. For a critique of its relevance to existing consumer markets, see Schor (2000).

191 The hallmark of a collective action failure is that everyone would be better off if there was cooperation; when everyone acts in isolation, a worse outcome occurs. A classic example is standing at a concert to get a better view. Each person does it to enhance his or her own sight line. Once everyone is standing, no one's view is better, and everyone's legs get tired. It's impossible to sit down alone, because you can't see anything. Coordinated action could get everyone to sit down together, and improve everyone's situation. For a related perspective on issues of fashion, see Holloman et al. (1998).

193 On studio manipulation of ratings, see Kennedy (2002).

194 For networks' claims about educational programming, see the documentary history on the Center for Media Education Web site, www.cme.org. For current programs, see Schmitt (1999), available at http://www.appcpenn.org/05_media_developing_child/childrensprogramming/3hour-rule.pdf.

194 On industry guidelines on alcohol, the current system calls for no advertising on programs that have more than 50 percent underage viewers. But given that only 30 percent of the population is under age twenty-one and only 10 percent is in the age-eleven-to-seventeen category, the 50 percent threshold is quite lax. The FTC issued a report on this issue on September 9, 1999, but it affirmed the voluntary approach, despite companies' failure to abide by their guidelines. On the judicial side, the Supreme Court's 1980 ruling in the *Central Hudson* case, giving new protections to commercial speech, has led to two decades of decisions that make it difficult for

government to rein in advertising. (Central Hudson Gas and Electric Corp. v. Public Service Comm'n, 447 U.S. 557, 561 [1980].) In 2001, the Supreme Court unanimously sided with Lorillard Tobacco when it sued the State of Massachusetts for repeal of a law prohibiting tobacco billboards within 1,000 feet of schools, parks, or public playgrounds.

194 On forbidden fruit, see Grier (2001), p. 11.

194 On the invisibility of the TV ratings and the V-chip, see Schmitt (2000), available at http://www.appcpenn.org/05_media_developing_child/childrensprogramming/ppfr.pdf, and also other material on the Annenberg site.

196 For a discussion of taxation as an approach to consumption-related problems, see Frank (1999).

197 Information about Coke and the donation to the PTA is available at http://www.commercialalert.org/index.php/category_id/2/subcategory_id/34/article_id/187.

197 On schools and food sales: Schools should be required to reassess their compliance with the federal school lunch program. Activists have argued that the introduction of branded fast foods has put many schools in violation of the federal regulations.

198 Fifty-eight percent feeling pressure to fit in is from the Center for a New American Dream poll, available at www.newdream.org/publications/bookrelease.html.

199 For critiques of child development theory, see James, Jenks, and Prout (1998).

200 For a critique of Ariès, see Pollock (1984).

200 On social constructionism: There is a growing sociological and anthropological literature in child studies that tries to theorize and study children from nondevelopmentalist, social constructionist perspectives. Much of it is British. For example, James, Jenks, and Prout (1998) identify four sociological approaches. In addition to social constructionism, these include work that sees children as tribal, mainly existing within their own social worlds; as an oppressed minority group, analogous to racial minorities or women; and on a social structural basis, which looks at structural controls on children in schools, public spaces, and so forth. See also Stephen's Introduction to *Children and the Politics of Culture* (1995b). For gender differences in play, see Thorne (1993). On toys and culture, see Sutton-Smith (1986). For a collection of historical accounts, see Fass and Mason (2000). A related child-oriented literature can be found in cultural studies. This literature is particularly perceptive on the demonization of minority and poor youth in the United States. See, for example, Giroux (1997), Jenkins (1998), Kincheloe (1998), Kinder (1991), and Kellner (1998). On child abuse themes in popular culture, see Walkerdine (1997), Kincaid (1998) on the erotization of children, and Giroux on beauty pageants (1998) and Disney (Giroux, 1999). See also Steinberg and Kincheloe (1998). The cultural studies critique of adult ideologies of innocence is particularly enlightening.

200 For Postman on oral culture, see Postman (1994), p. 13–14. On literacy, see ch. 3. Postman's technological determinism has been criticized. See, for example, Luke (1989), who argues that childhood emerged earlier in Germany than France, on account of the Lutheran practice of giving all people access to Scripture.

201 On the idea of childhood as a right, see Postman (1994), p. 67.

201 On children not meriting special affection: This is not to say they did not merit affection at all. The historical evidence shows that they did. See Pollock (1984) for a discussion of the debates about adult affection for children.

201 On the evil child, see James et al. (1998), pp. 10–13.

202 For the argument that childhood is disappearing, see Postman (1994). This argument has become common. For example, see Stephens (1995b) and especially Field (1995).

202 On television and the disappearance of childhood, see Postman (1994), who also believed that television has contributed to the infantilization of adult culture in its

appeal to emotion rather than logic. Here Postman's own male, dualist, rationalist, and Enlightenment biases are particularly exposed.

202 "New realism": see Hymowitz (2003), p. 226; "far more than in other cultures": on p. 222.

202 On social conservatives' views: See Hymowitz (1999) and Mack (1997) for discussions of these debates.

203 "Merchants and marketers have always" quotation is from Kline (1993), pp. 18–19.

204 "Awakening their senses" quote is from the Edible Schoolyard Web site, http://www.edibleschoolyard.org.

205 On the reorganization of social space, see Zelizer (1985), ch. 1.

206 On the Swedish intiative: In the 1950s, a trio of Swedish pediatricians became concerned about high levels of injuries and pedestrian accidents among their nation's children. One response would have been to forbid children from crossing certain streets and limiting children's ability to go outside unescorted. The Swedish doctors pursued a different approach. Rather than take children out of a dangerous environment, they resolved to make that environment safe and embarked on a remarkable, indeed historic, campaign. New legislation incorporated principles of safety into frameworks for community planning and development, mandating attention when roads were built and buildings designed. As a result, schools were constructed with walkways and bicycle paths so children could walk or ride to them without having to encounter traffic. Residential streets were equipped with speed bumps. Speed limits were set to be consistent with what the traffic safety literature calls the weakest users, in this case, children. Traffic fatalities declined dramatically, to the lowest in the OCED, and less than half the U.S. rate, despite parity between the two countries before these initiatives began. For the history of the Swedish safety programs, see Bergman and Rivara (1991). On child injury rates, see Unicef (2001), Table 7, available at www.unicef-icdc.org. The campaign for child safety covered a variety of other injury factors such as drowning, poisoning, and traffic injuries from inside vehicles. One of its architects invented the child car seat. Sweden now leads the world in having the lowest rates for all forms of child injuries and deaths.

206 On Doxley Parents' critiques of consumer culture: Parents in Doxley revealed a wide range of objections to consumer culture, emanating from religion, sixties counterculture, and, for transplants to the East, a midwestern rural sensibility. Some displayed a standard middle-class desire to shield their children from certain low-brow aspects of popular culture. The mothers I interviewed objected to violent and sexist aspects of consumer culture, critiques that tend to be more prominent in the middle class. I raise this point not to pass judgment, but to remind us that attitudes about consumer culture are typically complex and infused with class and other sensibilities. There is an informative sociological literature on class differences in attitudes about consumer culture. Scholars have written about the ways in which parents with high-status aspirations for their children often screen out low-status, commercial products such as licensed characters from Hollywood or Tokyo, preferring products with upper-class and European origins, such as Paddington Bear, Madeleine, and Babar. The latter aren't considered commercial, even though they're licensed characters just as Ninja Turtles and PowerPuff Girls are. Middle-class parents have long articulated opposition to guns and other violent toys for boys. Feminist parents in the middle classes often try to limit certain stereotypical girl products, such as Barbie, or replicas of household appliances such as vacuum cleaners and cooking sets. These class differences are perhaps most clearly seen in the layout and inventories of toy stores. Mass marketers such as Toys 'R' Us divide toys by gender, sell mostly cheap toys from China, and are indiscriminate with respect to violent and rigidly gendered toys, or commercialization. Upscale toy stores are mostly unisex, special-

ize in European imports, skew to wood over plastic, and emphasize the educational value of their products. Williams (2003) has studied class differences in shopping behavior in mass-market and upscale toy stores. On these and related points, see also Bourdieu (1984) and Seiter (1993).

206 On TV restrictions: Some research findings suggest that restrictions on television are less effective than parents realize. In a study by the Annenberg Public Policy Center (Schmitt, 2000), when mothers and children from urban and suburban Philadelphia were asked separately about television rules, 71 percent of the mothers (of sixth and ninth graders) said they have television rules, but only half their children reported having rules. Only half of parent-child pairs agreed about whether they had rules (p. 26). According to Schmitt, "Children of all ages say they can easily get around their parents' rules about television. Out of twenty-eight children, only two third graders said that they never break their parents' rules about television" (p. 30). One reason the Doxley parents may have been more successful is that many of the mothers I interviewed are home with their children after school and directly monitor viewing. The fact that I interviewed only parents may have biased my findings, although the children's reported viewing times and restrictions are consistent with the parental reports.

207 On my own television experience: Part of what strengthened my resolve to exclude television from my children's lives was the suspicion that as they got older, restricting it would get difficult and eventually impossible. Allowing unrestricted access to television seemed out of the question, but I worried about endless negotiations. Removing the potential source of conflict seemed preferable.

208 For anecdotal evidence about the return to noncommercial activities, see Taylor (2003).

208 On eco-psychology, see Kanner and Gomes (1995).

208 My earlier books include *The Overworked American* and *The Overspent American.*

208 On time and other pressures on low-income families, see Heymann (2000).

208 Center for a New American Dream poll conducted in February 2003 and results are available at www.newdream.org/publications/bookrelease.html. About a fourth (23 percent) of those who don't spend a lot of time with their parents report that it is primarily because their parents are too busy because of work; 19 percent say it's because they're overscheduled with homework or school activities.

209 "We face a conflict of values" is from the text of "Watch Out for Children: A Mother's Statement to Advertisers," section II, available at http://watchoutforchildren.org/.

209 On children's productive practices, see Zelizer (2002) and Chin (2001).

209 On the correlation among materialism, parents, and children, see Goldberg et al. (n.d.).

210 The politics of the anticommercialism movement are interesting. Among its activists one finds both Ralph Nader and far-right senator Sam Brownback of Kansas. The right mainly opposes the sex, violence, and profanity of consumer culture. The left focuses more on commercialism, invasive marketing, corporate influence in schools, and public health. But there's also common ground, such as privacy. Some of the most determined critics of Channel One are religious conservatives. Not surprisingly, the two sides differ in their basic philosophies. The right mainly argues for cordoning off aspects of the adult world that it finds objectionable for children, and it tends not to extend criticism beyond the media to the corporations whose ads pay for entertainment. The left is critical of commercialism in both its child and adult variants and argues for more public and democratic control of space, media, and culture.

Afterword

213 For the likelihood of developing ADHD, see Christakis et al. (2004).
213 For the incidence of teasing and bullying, see Zimmerman et al. (2005).
213 Olshansky et al. (2005) look at longevity.
214 Data on sexual content of television shows is from Kaiser Family Foundation (2003).
214 The study of teens who watch more sexually explicit TV is Collins et al. (2004). On parents' views, see Kaiser Family Foundation (2004).
215 The Marciano letter is available at Concerned Women for America, cwfa.org.
216 The "so sexy so soon" phenomenon is explored in Levin (forthcoming).
216 The view that junk food could be "the next tobacco" is in Branch (2003).
216 Annual sugar consumption from Statistical Abstract (2005), Table 199, p. 131. Recommended allowance from USDA's pre-2005 guidelines. For a discussion of the politics of junk food, see Schor (forthcoming) and a series of press releases on the Bush administration's actions at commercialalert.org.
217 The actions of the Center for Consumer Freecom are chronicled in Sargent (2005).
217 Ellison (2005) looks at the Alliance for American Advertising.
217 Mayer (2005) reports on Kraft's announcement.

References

Abelson, Elaine. *When Ladies Go A'Thieving.* New York: Oxford University Press, 1989.

Achenbach, T., and C. Howell. "Are American Children's Problems Getting Worse?" *Journal of the American Academic of Child and Adolescent Psychiatry* 32(6):1145–1154, 1993.

Adler, Richard, et al. *The Effects of Television Advertising on Children.* Lexington, MA: Lexington Books, 1980.

Advertising and Society Review. "Roundtable on Values in Advertising." 3:1, 2002.

Ahuja, Roshan D., Louis M. Capella, and Ronald D. Taylor. "Child Influences, Attitudinal and Behavioral Comparisons Between Single Parents and Dual Parent Households in Grocery Shopping Decisions." *Journal of Marketing Theory and Practice* 6(1):48–62, 1998.

Alexander, Alison, et al. "A Content Analysis of Advertisements in Children's Television in the 1950s." *Journal of Advertising* 27(3):1–9, 1998.

Allen, David. "Is Childhood Disappearing?" Unpublished report, 2001.

Allen, Stewart. "Exxon's School Spill," *San Francisco Weekly,* December 9, 1992.

Anderson, Craig A. "Video Games and Aggressive Behavior." In Diane Ravitch and Joseph Vitieritti (eds.), *KidStuff.* Baltimore: Johns Hopkins University, 2003.

Anderson, Craig A., and Karen E. Dill. "Video Games and Aggressive Thoughts, Feelings, and Behavior in the Laboratory and in Life." *Journal of Personality and Social Psychology* 78(4):772–790, 2000.

Applebaum, Michael. "Don't Spare the Brand." *Brandweek,* March 10, 2003, pp. 21–26.

Ariès, Philippe. *Centuries of Childhood: A Social History of Family Life.* New York: Knopf, 1962.

Associated Press. "Abercrombie and Fitch Is Coming Under Fire—Again." May 22, 2002.

Aufderheide, Patricia. "Activities Available on Children's Websites: A Survey." April 17, 2001.

Barboza, David. "A Warning in Expanding Waistlines." *New York Times,* July 10, 2003.

Belk, Russell W. "Materialism: Trait Aspects of Living in the Material World." *Journal of Consumer Research* 12:265–280, 1985.

Bergman, Abraham B., and Frederick P. Rivara. "Sweden's Experience in Reducing Childhood Injuries." *Pediatrics* 88:69–74, 1991.

Blosser, B. J., and D. F. Roberts. "Age Differences in Children's Perceptions of Message Intent: Response to TV News, Commercials, Educational Spots, and Public Service Announcements." *Communications Research* 12:455–484, 1985.

Borowski, John F. "Schools with a Slant." *New York Times,* August 21, 1999.

Borzekowski, Dina L., and Thomas N. Robinson. "The 30-Second Effect: An Experiment Revealing the Impact of Television Commercials on Food Preferences of Preschoolers." *Journal of the American Dietary Association* 10(1):42–46, 2001.

Bourdieu, Pierre. *Distinction: A Social Critique of the Judgement of Taste.* Cambridge, MA: Harvard University Press, 1984.

Boush, D. M., M. Friestad, and G. M. Rose. "Adolescent Skepticism Toward TV Advertising and Knowledge of Advertiser Tactics." *Journal of Consumer Research* 21(1):165–175, 1994.

Branch, Shelly. "Is Food the Next Tobacco? As Obesity Concerns Mount, Companies Fret Their Snacks, Drinks May Take the Blame." *Wall Street Journal,* June 13, 2003.

Brand, Jeffrey E., and Bradley S. Greenberg. "Commercials in the Classroom: The Impact of Channel One Advertising." *Journal of Advertising Research* 34(1):18–21, 1994.

Brownell, Kelly, and Katherine Battle Horgen. *Food Fight: The Inside Story of the Food Industry, America's Obesity Crisis, and What We Can Do About It.* New York: McGraw-Hill, 2003.

Brucks, Merrie, Gary M. Armstrong, and Marvin E. Goldberg. "Children's Use of Cognitive Defenses Against Television Advertising: A Cognitive Response Approach." *Journal of Consumer Research* 14:471–482, 1988.

Buckingham, David. *After the Death of Childhood: Growing Up in the Age of Electronic Media.* Cambridge, MA: Polity Press, 2000.

Budd, Mike, Steve Craig, and Clay Steinman. *Consuming Environments: Television and Commercial Culture.* New Brunswick, NJ: Rutgers University Press, 1999.

Burros, Marian. "Dental Group Is Under Fire for Coke Deal." *New York Times,* March 24, 2003.

Bushman, Brad J., and Craig A. Anderson. "Media Violence and the American Public: Scientific Facts Versus Media Misinformation." *American Psychologist* 56(6–7):477–489, 2001.

Byrd-Bredbenner, Carol, and Darlene Grasso. "Prime-Time Health: An Analysis of Health Content in Television Commercials Broadcast During Programs Viewed Heavily by Children." *International Electronic Journal of Health Education* 2(4):159–169, 1999.

Cantor, Joanne. *Mommy I'm Scared: How TV and Movies Frighten Children and What We Can Do to Protect Them.* San Diego, CA: Harcourt Brace, 1998.

Cantor, Joanne, and Marie-Louise Mares. "Effects of Television on Child and Family Emotional Well-Being." In Jennings Bryant and J. Alison Bryant, eds., *Television and the American Family* (2nd ed.). Mahwah, NJ: Erlbaum, 2001.

Carlsson-Paige, Nancy, and Diane E. Levin. *Who's Calling the Shots? How to Respond Effectively to Children's Fascination with War Play and War Toys.* Philadelphia: New Society Publishers, 1990.

Carter, Bill. "He's Cool. He Keeps MTV Sizzling. And, Oh Yes, He's 56." *New York Times,* June 16, 2002.

Carvajal, Doreen. "How the Studios Used Children to Test-Market Violent Films." *New York Times,* September 27, 2000.

Center for Media Education. *Web of Deception: Threats to Children from Online Marketing.* Washington, D.C.: Center for Media Education, 1996.

———. *COPPA: The First Year, a Survey of Sites.* Washington, D.C.: Center for Media Education, 2001.

Center on Alcohol Marketing and Youth. *Television: Alcohol's Vast Adland.* Washington, D.C.: Center on Alcohol Marketing and Youth, December 2002.

Chaplin, Heather. "Food Fight." *American Demographics* 21(6):64–65, June 1999.

Chen, Jane, and Matthew Ringel. "Can Advergaming be the Future of Interactive Advertising?" New York: Fast Forward, 2001.

Chin, Elizabeth. *Purchasing Power: Black Kids and American Consumer Culture.* Minneapolis: University of Minnesota Press, 2001.

Christakis, Dimitri A., Frederick J. Zimmerman, David L. DiGiuseppe, and Carolyn A. McCarty. "Early Television Exposure and Subsequent Attentional Problems in Children," *Pediatrics* 113: 708–713, 2004.

Christenson, Peter G., Lisa Henriksen, and Donald F. Roberts. "Substance Use in Popular Prime-Time Television." Washington, D.C.: Office of National Drug Control Policy, 2000.

Colantuoni, Carlo, et al. "Evidence That Intermittent, Excessive Sugar Intake Causes Endogenous Opioid Dependence." *Obesity Research* 10(6), June 2002.

Collins, Rebecca L., Marc N. Elliott, Sandra H. Berry, David E. Kanouse, Dale Kunkel, Sarah B. Hunter, and Angela Miu. "Watching Sex on Television Predicts Adolescent Initiation of Sexual Behavior," *Pediatrics* 114:280–289, 2004.

Comiteau, Jennifer. "When Does Brand Loyalty Start?" *Adweek,* March 24, 2003.

Commercial Alert. "PBS Should Protect Children by Taking *Teletubbies* Off the Air, Coalition Says." News release, March 22, 2000. Available at: www.commercialalert.org.

———. "Commercial Alert Urges Parents to Fight Market Spies in Schools." News release, July 11, 2001. Available at: www.commercialalert.org.

Committee on Communications. "The Commercialization of Children's Television." *Pediatrics* 89(2):343–344, 1992.

Comstock, George. *Television and the American Child.* San Diego: Academic Press, 1991.

Connolly, Ceci. "Public Policy Targeting Obesity." *Washington Post,* August 10, 2003.

Consumers Union. *Captive Kids: Commercial Pressures on Kids at School.* Yonkers, NY: Consumers Union Education Services, 1995. Available at: www.consunion.org/other/captivekids/evaluations.htm.

Cook, Daniel Thomas. "The Rise of 'the Toddler' as Subject and as Merchandising Category in the 1930s." In Mark Gottdiener, ed., *New Forms of Consumption: Consumers, Culture, and Commodification.* Lanham, MD: Rowman and Littlefield, 2000a.

———. "The Other 'Child Study.' " *Sociological Quarterly* 41(3):487–507, 2000b.

———. "Exchange Value as Pedagogy in Children's Leisure: Moral Panics in Children's Culture at Century's End." *Leisure Sciences* 23:81–98, 2001.

———. *The Commodification of Childhood: Personhood, the Children's Wear Industry and the Rise of the Child-Consumer, 1917–1962.* Durham, NC: Duke University Press, 2004.

Cook, Daniel Thomas, and Susan B. Kaiser. "Betwixt and Be Tween: Age Ambiguity and the Sexualization of the Female Consuming Subject." Unpublished paper, 2003.

Coontz, Stephanie. *The Way We Never Were: American Families and the Nostalgia Trap.* New York: Basic Books, 2000.

Critser, George. *Fat Land.* Boston: Houghton Mifflin, 2003.

Cross, Gary. *Kids' Stuff: Toys and the Changing World of American Childhood.* Cambridge, MA: Harvard University Press, 1997.

Cullen, K. W., D. M. Ash, C. Warneke, and C. de Moor. "Intake of Soft Drinks, Fruit-Flavored Beverages, and Fruits and Vegetables by Children in Grades 4–6." *American Journal of Public Health* 92:1475–1478, 2002.

Davies, Marie. *Fake, Fact, and Fantasy: Children's Interpretations of Television Reality.* Mahwah, NJ: Erlbaum, 1997.

Day, Sherri. "Coke Moves with Caution to Remain in Schools." *New York Times,* September 3, 2003a.

———. "Keeping Food Tasty, Minus Salt and Sugar." *New York Times,* August 27, 2003b.

Del Vecchio, Gene. *Creating Ever-Cool: A Marketer's Guide to a Kid's Heart.* Gretna, LA: Pelican Publishing Company, 1997.

Devaney, Polly. "Pushing Products to the Poor and Impressionable." *Marketing Week,* March 21, 2001.

Dietz, William H., and Victor C. Strasburger. "Children, Adolescents and Television." *Current Problems in Pediatrics,* January 1991, 8–32.

Dolliver, Mark. "What Do I Want to Be When I Grow Up? Filthy Rich!" *Adweek,* October 5, 1998.

Dorman, Steve M. "Video and Computer Games: Effect on Children and Implications for Health Education." *Journal of School Health* 67(4):133–138, 1997.

DuBois, David L. "Early Adolescent Self-Esteem: A Developmental-Ecological Framework and Assessment Strategy." *Journal of Research on Adolescence* 6(4):543–579, 1996.

DuCille, Ann. "Toy Theory: Black Barbie and the Deep Play of Difference." In *Skin Trade.* Cambridge, MA: Harvard University Press, 1996.
DuRant, R. H., et al. "Tobacco and Alcohol Use Behaviors Portrayed in Music Videos: Content Analysis." *American Journal of Public Health* 87:1131–1135, 1997.
Ebenkamp, Becky. "The Color of Munchies." *Brandweek,* April 1, 2002.
Egan, Timothy. "In Bid to Improve Nutrition, Schools Expel Soda and Chips." *New York Times,* May 20, 2002.
Eilperin, Juliet. "U.S. Sugar Industry Targets New Study." *Washington Post,* April 23, 2003.
Elliott, Stuart. "Real or Virtual? You Call It." *New York Times,* October 1, 1999.
Ellison, Sarah. "Companies Fight for Right to Plug Kids' Food." *Wall Street Journal,* January 26, 2005.
Engle, Yuna, and Tim Kasser. "Why Do Adolescent Girls Idolize Male Celebrities?" Unpublished report, Knox College, 2003.
Faber, Ronald J., R. M. Perloff, and R. P. Hawkins. "Antecedents of Children's Comprehension of Television Advertising." *Journal of Broadcasting* 26:575–584, 1982.
Fass, Paula S., and Mary Ann Mason, eds. *Childhood in America.* New York: New York University Press, 2000.
Federal Trade Commission. Staff report on television advertising to children. Washington, D.C.: U.S. Government Printing Office, 1978.
———. *Marketing Violent Entertainment to Children.* Washington, D.C.: U.S. Government Printing Office, 2000.
Feuer, Jack. "Advertising Part of NYC Schools' Student Planners." *Adweek,* November 18, 2002.
Field, Norma. "The Child as Laborer and Consumer: The Disappearance of Childhood in Contemporary Japan." In Sharon Stephens, ed., *Children and the Politics of Culture.* Princeton, NJ: Princeton University Press, 1995.
Fox, Roy. *Harvesting Minds: How TV Commercials Control Kids.* New York: Praeger, 1996.
Frank, Robert. *Luxury Fever.* New York: Free Press, 1999.
Frank, Thomas. *The Conquest of Cool.* Chicago: Chicago University Press, 1997.
Funk, Jeanne, and Debra Buchman. "Playing Violent Video and Computer Games and Adolescent Self-Concept." *Journal of Communication* 46(2):19–32, 1996.
Gamble, Margaret, and Nancy Cotugna. "A Quarter Century of TV Food Advertising Targeted at Children." *American Journal of Health Behavior* 23(4):261–267, 1999.
Garbarino, James. *Raising Children in a Socially Toxic Environment.* San Francisco: Jossey-Bass, 1995.
Gerbner, George. "Foreword: Telling All the Stories." In Mike Budd, Steve Craig, and Clay Steinman, eds., *Consuming Enviroments.* New Brunswick, NJ: Rutgers University Press, 1999.
———. *Against the Mainstream: The Selected Works of George Gerbner.* New York: Peter Lang, 2002.
Giroux, Henry A. *Channel Surfing: Racism, the Media and the Destruction of Today's Youth.* New York: St. Martin's Press, 1997.
———. "Stealing Innocence: The Politics of Child Beauty Pageants." In Henry Jenkins, ed., *The Children's Culture Reader.* New York: New York University Press, 1998.
———. *The Mouse That Roared: Disney and the End of Innocence.* Lanham, MD: Rowman and Littlefield, 1999.
Gladwell, Malcolm. "The Coolhunt." *New Yorker,* March 17, 1997.
Glionna, John. "Slot Machine Designers Use Controversial Spin." *Los Angeles Times,* October 25, 1999.
Goldberg, Marvin E. "A Quasi-Experiment Assessing the Effectiveness of TV Advertising Directed to Children." *Journal of Marketing Research* 27:445–454, 1990.

Goldberg, Marvin E., Gerald J. Gorn, and Wendy Gibson. "TV Messages for Snack and Breakfast Foods: Do They Influence Children's Preferences?" *Journal of Consumer Research* 5:73–81, 1978.

Goldberg, Marvin E., Gerald J. Gorn, Laura A. Peracchio, and Gary Bamossy. "Understanding Materialism Among Youth." Unpublished report, Pennsylvania State University, n.d.

Golding, Daniel. "'Media Literacy' Sparks a New Debate over Commercialism in Schools." *Wall Street Journal,* December 17, 1999.

Goldman, Robert, and Stephen Papson. *Sign Wars: The Cluttered Landscape of Advertising.* New York: Guilford Press, 1996.

Goldstein, Patrick. "Untangling the Web of Teen Trends." *Los Angeles Times,* November 21, 2000.

Goodnough, Abby. "Teachers Dig Deeper to Fill Gap in Supplies." *New York Times,* September 21, 2002.

Gorn, Gerald, and Marvin E. Goldberg. "Behavioral Evidence of the Effects of Televised Food Messages on Children." *Journal of Consumer Research* 9:200–205, 1982.

Govani, Shinan. "Product Placement in Movies—Is It Really So Bad?" *Christian Science Monitor,* February 10, 1999.

Green, Ché. "Not Milk: The USDA, Monsanto and the U.S. Dairy Industry." *Lip Magazine,* July 8, 2002, available on alternet.org.

Greve, Karen. "The Impact of Parental Working Hours on Discretionary Expenditures on Children in Upper Income Families." Thesis submitted to the Department of Economics, Harvard University, 1995.

Grier, Sonya A. "The Federal Trade Commission's Report on the Marketing of Violent Entertainment to Youths." *Journal of Public Policy and Marketing* 20(1):123–141, 2001.

Gross, Holly. "Spotting the Marketing Opps in Blurring Gender Lines." *Kidscreen,* September 2002a, p. 53.

———. "Cracking the Tween Connection Code." *Kidscreen,* March 2002, p. 36–37.

Grossman, Dave, and Gloria DeGaetano. *Stop Teaching Our Kids to Kill.* New York: Crown, 1999.

Gruber, Selina, and Jon Berry. *Marketing to and Through Kids.* New York: McGraw-Hill, 1993.

Gugliotta, Guy. "Diet Supplement Marketers Target Kids." *Washington Post,* June 18, 2000.

Gunter, Barrie, and Adrian Furnham. *Children as Consumers.* London: Routledge, 1998.

Gunter, Barrie, and J. McAleer. *Children and Television* (2nd ed.). London: Routledge, 1997.

Halpert, Julie Edelson. "Dr Pepper Hospital? Perhaps, for a Price." *New York Times,* February 18, 2001.

Hays, Constance L. "The Media Business: Advertising Spots for Adults Appeal to Children." *New York Times,* March 26, 1998.

———. "Channel One's Mixed Grades in Schools." *New York Times,* December 5, 1999.

———. "Aided by Clifford and the Care Bears, Companies Go After the Toddler Market." *New York Times,* July 11, 2003.

Healy, Jane M. *Endangered Minds: Why Children Don't Think and What We Can Do About It.* New York: Touchstone, 1990.

Hewlett, Sylvia Ann, Nancy Rankin, and Cornel West. *Taking Parenting Public.* Lanham, MD: Rowman and Littlefield, 2002.

Heymann, Jody. *The Widening Gap.* New York: Basic Books, 2000.

Hofferth, Sandra L. "Healthy Environments, Healthy Children: Children in Families: A Report on the 1997 Panel Study of Income Dynamics." University of Michigan, November 1998.

Hofferth, Sandra, and John F. Sandberg. "How American Children Spend Their Time." *Journal of Marriage and Family* 63:295–308, 2001a.

———. "Changes in American Children's Use of Time, 1981–1997," in T. J. Owens and S. L. Hofferth, eds., *Advances in Life Course Research Series: Children at the Millennium: Where Have We Come From, Where Are We Going?* New York: Elsevier Science, pp. 193–229, 2001b.

Holloman, Lillian O., Velma LaPoint, Sylvan I. Alleyne, Ruth J. Palmer, and Kathy Sanders-Phillips. "Dress-Related Behaviorial Problems and Violence in the Public School Setting." *Journal of Negro Education* 65(3):267–281, 1996.

Holloway, Lynette. "Declining CD Sales Spur Labels to Use Street Marketing Teams." *New York Times,* September 30, 2002.

Holt, Douglas, and Juliet B. Schor. "Consumerism, the Commodification of Ghetto Violence, and Underclass Status." Unpublished report, Harvard University, 1998.

Holt, Douglas B. "Why Do Brands Cause Trouble? A Dialectical Theory of Consumer Culture and Branding." *Journal of Consumer Research* 29(1):70–90, 2002.

Hood, Duncan. "Is Advertising to Kids Wrong? Marketers Respond." *Kidscreen,* November 1, 2000.

Hymowitz, Kay S. *Ready or Not: Why Treating Children as Small Adults Endangers Their Future—and Ours.* New York: Free Press, 1999.

———. "The Contradictions of Parenting in a Media Age." In Diane Ravitch and Joseph P. Viteritti, eds., *Kid Stuff: Marketing Sex and Violence to America's Children.* Baltimore: Johns Hopkins University Press, 2003.

Isa, Margaret. "Consultants with Tender Faces: Big Companies Ask Children How to Sell to Children." *New York Times,* August 18,1996.

Jackson, C., L. Henriksen, and V. A. Foshee. "The Authoritative Parenting Scale: Predicting Health Risk Behaviors Among Adolescents." *Health Education and Behavior* 24:319–337, 1998.

Jacobson, Michael F. "Now There's a Fourth R: Retailing." *New York Times,* January 29, 1995.

———. *Liquid Candy: How Soft Drinks Are Harming Americans' Health.* Washington, D.C.: Center for Science in the Public Interest, 1998.

Jahns, Lisa, Anna Maria Siega-Riz, and Barry M. Popkin. "The Increasing Prevalence of Snacking Among U.S. Children from 1977 to 1997." *Journal of Pediatrics* 138:493–498, 2001.

James, Allison. "Confections, Concoctions and Conceptions." In Henry Jenkins, ed., *The Children's Culture Reader.* New York: New York University Press, 1998.

James, Allison, Chris Jenks, and Alan Prout. *Theorizing Childhood.* New York: Teachers College Press, 1998.

Jarvis, Steve. "Lesson Plans: Step Carefully When Strategy Includes Schools." *Marketing News,* June 18, 2001.

Jenkins, Henry, ed. *The Children's Culture Reader.* New York: New York University Press, 1998.

Jones, Gerard. *Killing Monsters: Why Children Need Fantasy, Super Heroes, and Make-Believe Violence.* New York: Basic Books, 2002.

Kaiser Family Foundation. *Kids and Media @ the Millennium.* Menlo Park, CA: Kaiser Family Foundation, 1999.

———. "Sex on TV3: A Biennial Report of the Kaiser Family Foundation." Menlo Park, CA: KFF, 2003.

———. "Parents, Media, and Public Policy: A Kaiser Family Foundation Survey." Menlo Park, CA: KFF, Fall 2004.

Kanner, Allen D. and M. E. Gomes. "The All-Consuming Self." In Theodore Roszak,

M. E. Gomes, and Allen D. Kanner, eds., *Ecopsychology: Restoring the Earth, Healing the Mind.* San Francisco: Sierra Club Books, 1995.

Kanner, Allen D., and Tim Kasser. "Stuffing Our Kids: Should Psychologists Help Advertisers Manipulate Children?" 2000. Available at: www.commercialalert/org.

Kanner, Bernice. "From *Father Knows Best* to *The Simpsons*—On TV, Parenting Has Lost Its Halo." In Sylvia Hewlett, Nancy Rankin, and Cornel West, eds., *Taking Parenting Public.* Lanham, MD: Rowman and Littlefield, 2002.

Kasser, Tim. *The High Price of Materialism.* Cambridge, MA: MIT Press, 2002.

Kasser, Tim, and Allen D. Kanner. *Psychology and Consumer Culture: The Struggle for a Good Life in a Materialistic World.* Washington, D.C.: American Psychological Association, 2004.

Kasser, Tim, and Richard M. Ryan. "A Dark Side of the American Dream: Correlates of Financial Success as a Central Life Aspiration." *Journal of Personality and Social Psychology* 65(2):410–422, 1993.

Kasser, Tim, Richard Ryan, M. Zax, and A. J. Sameroff. "The Relations of Maternal and Social Environments to Late Adolescents' Materialistic and Prosocial Values." *Developmental Psychology* 31:901–914, 1995.

Katz, Ian. "Josh Advises a Multinational Company on What's Cool . . . Josh Is 13." *Guardian,* August 17, 1996.

Kaufman, Leslie. "New Style Maven: 6 Years Old and Picky." *New York Times,* September 7, 1999.

Kelleher, Kelly J., et al. "Increasing Identification of Psychosocial Problems 1979–1996." *Pediatrics Journal,* June 1, 2000.

Kellner, Douglas. "Beavis and Butt-Head: No Future for Postmodern Youth." In Shirley Steinberg and Joe Kincheloe, eds., *Kinderculture.* Boulder, CO: Westview Press, 1998.

Kennedy, Louise. "The Rating Game." *Boston Globe,* June 30, 2002.

Kidscreen. "Preschoolers: An Emerging Consumer Set." July 1, 1999.

Kincaid, James R. "Producing Erotic Children." In Henry Jenkins, ed., *The Children's Culture Reader.* New York: New York University Press, 1998.

Kincheloe, Joe L. "*Home Alone* and 'Bad to the Bone': The Advent of a Postmodern Childhood." In Shirley Steinberg and Joe Kincheloe, eds., *Kinderculture.* Boulder, CO: Westview Press, 1998.

Kinder, Marsha. *Playing with Power in Movies, Television and Video Games.* Berkeley: University of California Press, 1991.

Kirkpatrick, David D. "Snack Foods Become Stars of Books for Children." *New York Times,* September 22, 2000.

Kline, Stephen. *Out of the Garden: Toys and Children's Culture in the Age of TV Marketing.* London: Verso, 1993.

Kline, Stephen, and Greig de Peuter. "Video Gaming and Postmodern Childhood." In Daniel Cook, ed., *Symbolic Childhood.* New York: Peter Lang Publishing, 2002.

Kubey, Robert, and Mihaly Csikszentmihalyi. "Television Addiction Is No Mere Metaphor." *Scientific American* 286(2):74–80, 2002.

Kunkel, Dale. "Children and Television Advertising." In Dorothy Singer and Jerome Singer, eds., *Handbook of Children and the Media.* Thousand Oaks, CA: Sage, 2001.

Kunkel, Dale, and Donald Roberts. "Young Minds and Marketplace Values: Issues in Children's Television Advertising." *Journal of Social Issues* 47(1), 1991.

Leach, William. *Land of Desire: Merchants, Power, and the Rise of a New American Culture.* New York: Pantheon, 1993.

Leduc, Daniel. "Legislators Urge Ban on Ads in Md. Schools." *Washington Post,* February 21, 2001.

Leung, Shirley. "Advertising: Happy Meals Angle for Little Girls' Loyalty with Well-dressed Dolls." *Wall Street Journal,* April 5, 2002.

Levin, Diane. *Remote Control Childhood? Combating the Hazards of a Media Culture.* Washington, D.C.: National Association for the Education of Young Children, 1998.
———. *Teaching Young Children in Violent Times: Building a Peaceable Classroom* (2nd ed.). Cambridge, MA, and Washington, D.C.: Educators for Social Responsibility and the National Association for the Education of Young Children, 2003.
———. "So Sexy, So Soon: The Sexualization of Childhood," in S. Olfman, ed., *Childhood Lost: How American Culture Is Failing Our Kids.* Westport, CT: Praeger, 2005.
Lindblom, Eric. "The Impact of Smoking in the Movies on Youth Smoking Levels." Campaign for Tobacco-Free Kids fact sheet, November 22, 2002.
Lindeman, Teresa F. "Ads in Schools: NetworkNext Signs Up 500 High Schools by Providing Mobile Computer." *Pittsburgh Post-Gazette,* July 11, 2001.
Lindstrom, Martin. *Brandchild.* London: Kogan-Page, 2003.
Linn, Susan. "Sellouts." *American Prospect* 11(22), 2000.
———. *Consuming Kids: The Hostile Takeover of Childhood.* New York: New Press, forthcoming.
Linn, Susan, and Diane E. Levin. "Stop Marketing 'Yummy Food' to Children." *Christian Science Monitor,* June 20, 2002.
Linn, Susan E., and Alvin F. Poussaint. "The Trouble with *Teletubbies.*" *American Prospect* 44:18–25, 1999.
Lowinson, Joyce H., et al. *Substance Abuse: A Comprehensive Textbook* (3rd ed.). Baltimore: Williams and Wilkins, 1997.
Ludwig, David. "Relation Between Consumption of Sugar-Sweetened Drinks and Childhood Obesity: A Prospective, Observational Analysis." *Lancet* 357:505–508, 2001.
Luke, Carmen. *Printing and Protestantism: The Discourse on Childhood.* Albany: State University of New York Press, 1989.
MacBeth, Tannis M., ed. *Tuning in to Young Viewers.* Thousand Oaks, CA: Sage, 1996.
Mack, Dana. *The Assault on Parenthood.* New York: Simon & Schuster, 1997.
MacKinnon, James. "Psychologists Act Against Ad Doctors." *Adbusters,* no. 28, Winter 2000.
Macklin, M. Carole, and Les Carlson. *Advertising to Children: Concepts and Controversies.* Thousand Oaks, CA: Sage, 1999.
Mangleburg, Tamara F., and Terry Bristol. "Socialization and Adolescents' Skepticism Toward Advertising." *Journal of Advertising* 27(3): 11–21, 1998.
Manning, Steve. "Students for Sale." *Nation,* September 27, 1999a.
———. "Channel One Enters the Media Literacy Movement." *Rethinking Schools* 14(2), 1999b.
———. "The Corporate Curriculum." *Nation,* September 27, 1999c.
———. "The Littlest Coke Addicts." *Nation,* June 25, 2001.
Marchand, Roland. *Advertising the American Dream.* Berkeley, CA: University of California Press, 1985.
Martin, Mary C. "Children's Understanding of the Intent of Advertising: A Meta-Analysis." *Journal of Public Policy and Marketing* 16(2):205–216, 1997.
Matthews, Robert. "Revealed—Food Companies Knew Products Were Addictive." *Telegraph* (UK), July 12, 2003.
Mayer, Caroline E. "Today's Lesson, Sponsored by . . . Corporate Cash Prizes Aid Schools, Court Customers." *Washington Post,* June 15, 2003.
———. "Kraft to Curb Snack-Food Advertising." *Washington Post,* January 12, 2005.
McChesney, Robert. *Rich Media, Poor Democracy.* Urbana: University of Illinois Press, 1999.
McDonough, Yona Zeldis, ed. *The Barbie Chronicles.* New York: Touchstone, 1999.
McLellan, Faith. "Marketing and Advertising: Harmful to Children's Health." *Lancet,* September 28, 2002.
McNeal, James. *The Kids Market: Myths and Realities.* Ithaca, NY: Paramount Publishing, 1999.

Meltz, Barbara. "Just Say 'Phooey' to the Food/Fun Link." *Boston Globe,* November 14, 2002.

Mergen, Bernard. "Made, Bought and Stolen: Toys and the Culture of Childhood." In Elliott West and Paula Petrik, eds., *Small Worlds.* Lawrence: University Press of Kansas, 1992.

Mohl, Bruce. "Got Growth Hormone?" *Boston Globe,* September 28, 2003.

Molnar, Alex. *Giving Kids the Business: The Commercialization of America's Schools.* Boulder, CO: Westview Press, 1996.

———. "Sponsored Schools and Commercialized Classrooms: Schoolhouse Commercializing Trends in the 1990s." August 1998. Available at: http://www.asu.edu/educ/epsl/CERU/Annual%20reports/cace-98–01.html.

———. "What's in a Name? The Corporate Branding of America's Schools. The Fifth Annual Report on Trends in Schoolhouse Commercialism." Tempe, AZ: Commercialism in Education Research Unit, 2002. Available at: http://www.asu.edu/educ/epsl/CERU/CERU_Annual_Report.htm.

Molnar, Alex, and Max B. Sawicky. *The Hidden Costs of Channel One: Estimates for the 50 States.* Tempe, AZ: Commercialism in Education Research Unit, April 1998. Available at: http://www.asu.edu/educ/epsl/CERU/Documents/cace-98–02/CACE-98–02.htm.

Morgan, Michael. *Channel One in the Public Schools: Widening the Gap.* Research report prepared for UNPLUG, 1993.

Munn, Mark. "The Effect of Parental Buying Habits on Children Exposed to Children's Television Programs." *Journal of Broadcasting* 2(2):253–258, 1958.

Muñoz, K.A., S. M. Krebs-Smith, R. Ballard-Barbash, and S. E. Cleveland. "Food Intakes of U.S. Children and Adolescents Compared with Recommendations." *Pediatrics* 100:323–329, 1997.

Nader, Ralph. *Children First! A Parents' Guide to Fighting Corporate Predators.* Washington, D.C.: Corporate Accountability Research Group, 1996.

Nagourney, Adam. "Mrs. Clinton Proposes Ban on Ads for Young Children." *New York Times,* September 27, 2000.

National Labor Committee. *Toys of Misery.* New York: National Labor Committee, 2002.

Nestle, Marion. *Food Politics: How the Food Industry Influences Nutrition and Health.* Berkeley: University of California Press, 2002.

Norris, Michelle. "Buy, Buy, Baby: Companies Taking the Fight for Consumer Loyalty to Kids." www.abcnews.com, May 10, 2002.

O'Barr, Mack. "Interview with Paul Kurnit." *Advertising and Society Review* 2:2, 2001.

O'Guinn, Thomas, and L. J. Shrum. "The Role of Television in the Construction of Consumer Reality." *Journal of Consumer Research* 24:278–294, 1997.

Ohmann, Richard. *Selling Culture: Magazines, Markets and Class at the Turn of the Century.* New York: Verso, 1996.

Olshansky, S. Jay, et al. "A Potential Decline in Life Expectancy in the United States in the 21st Century." *New England Journal of Medicine,* March 17, 2005.

Owens, T. J., and S. L. Hofferth, eds. *Children at the Millennium: Where Have We Come From, Where Are We Going?* New York: Elsevier Science, 2001.

Palmer, E. L., and C. N. McDowell. "Program/Commercial Separators in Children's Television Programming." *Journal of Communication* 29:197–201, 1979.

Pecora, Norma Odum. *The Business of Children's Entertainment.* New York: Guilford, 1998.

Penn, Schoen and Berland. Proprietary Nickelodeon study, 2001.

Pierce, John P., et al. "Tobacco Industry Promotion of Cigarettes and Adolescent Smoking." *Journal of the American Medical Association* 279:511–515, 1998.

Pollock, Linda A. *Forgotten Children: Parent-Child Relations from 1500–1900.* Cambridge: Cambridge University Press, 1984.

Postman, Neil. *The Disappearance of Childhood.* New York: Vintage, 1994.

Putnam, Robert D. *Bowling Alone: The Collapse and Revival of American Community.* New York: Simon & Schuster, 2000.

Quart, Alissa. *Branded: The Buying and Selling of Teenagers.* New York: Basic Books, 2003a.

———. "Welcome to (Company Name Here) High™." *New York Times,* July 16, 2003b.

Rappaport, Erika Diane. *Shopping for Pleasure: Women in the Making of London's West End.* Princeton, NJ: Princeton University Press, 2001.

Ravitch, Diane, and Joseph P. Viteritti, eds. *Kid Stuff: Marketing Sex and Violence to America's Children.* Baltimore: Johns Hopkins University Press, 2003.

Reece, Bonnie B., Nora J. Rifon, and Kimberly Rodriguez. "Selling Food to Children: Is Fun Part of a Balanced Breakfast?" In M. Carole Macklin and Les Carlson, eds., *Advertising to Children.* Thousand Oaks, CA: Sage, 1999.

Reynolds, Cecil R., and Bert Richmond. "Actor Structure and Construct Validity of 'What I Think and Feel': The Revised Children's Manifest Anxiety Scale." *Journal of Personality Assessment* 43(3):281–283, 1979.

Richins, Marsha L., and Scott Dawson. "A Consumer Values Orientation for Materialism and Its Measurement: Scale Development and Validation." *Journal of Consumer Research* 19:303–316, 1993.

Roberts, Donald, Lisa Henriksen, and Peter G. Christenson. *Substance Use in Popular Movies and Music.* Washington, D.C.: Office of National Drug Control Policy, April 1999.

Robertson, T. S., and J. Rossiter. "Children and Commercial Persuasion: An Attributional Theory Analysis." *Journal of Consumer Research* 1:13–20, 1974.

Robinson, Thomas N., et al. "Effects of Reducing Television Viewing on Children's Requests for Toys: A Randomized Controlled Trial." *Developmental and Behavioral Pediatrics* 22(3):179–183, 2001.

Robinson, Thomas N., Helen L. Chen, and Joel D. Killen. "Television and Music Video Exposure and Risk of Adolescent Alcohol Use." *Pediatrics* 102(5):e54, 1998.

Robinson, T. N., M. L. Wilde, L. C. Navracruz, K. F. Haydel, and A. Varady. "Effects of Reducing Children's Television and Video Game Use on Aggressive Behavior: A Randomized Controlled Trial." *Archives of Pediatric and Adolescent Medicine* 155(1):17–23, 2001.

Roedder John, Deborah. "Consumer Socialization of Children: A Retrospective Look at Twenty-Five Years of Research." *Journal of Consumer Research,* December 1, 1999.

Rotundo, E. Anthony. *American Manhood: Transformations in Masculinity from the Revolution to the Modern Era.* New York: Basic Books, 1993.

Rusakoff, Dale. "Finding the Wrongs in Naming Rights: School Gym Sponsorship Sparks Furor." *Washington Post,* December 16, 2001.

Ruskin, Gary. "Why They Whine: How Corporations Prey on Our Children." *Mothering,* November–December, 1999.

Saffer, Henry, and Dhaval Dave. *Alcohol Advertising and Alcohol Consumption by Adolescents.* National Bureau of Economic Research Working Paper # 9676. Cambridge, MA: National Bureau of Economic Research, 2003.

Sargent, Greg. "Berman's Battle." *American Prospect,* January 5, 2005.

Sargent, James D., et al. "Effect of Seeing Tobacco Use in Film on Trying Smoking Among Adolescents: Cross Sectional Study." *British Medical Journal* 323:1–16, 2001.

Saylor, Conway F., et al. "Children's Depression Inventory: Investigation of Procedures and Correlates." *Journal of the American Academy of Child Psychiatry* 23(5):626–628, 1984.

Schlosser, Eric. *Fast Food Nation: The Dark Side of the All-American Meal.* New York: Harper Perennial, 2001.

Schmitt, Kelly. *The Three Hour Rule: Is It Living Up to Expectations?* Philadelphia: Annenburg Public Policy Center of the University of Pennsylvania, 1999.

———. *Public Policy, Family Rules and Children's Media Use in the Home.* Philadelphia: Annenburg Public Policy Center of the University of Pennsylvania, 2000.

Schor, Juliet B. *The Overworked American: The Unexpected Decline of Leisure.* New York: Basic Books, 1992.

———. *The Overspent American: Upscaling, Downshifting and the New Consumer.* New York: Basic Books, 1998.

———. *Do Americans Shop Too Much?* Boston: Beacon Press, 2000.

———. "Do Children Need Protection from Marketers? The Commercialization of Childhood." Unpublished report, 2001.

———. "Cleaning the Closet: Toward a New Ethic of Fashion." In Juliet B. Schor and Betsy Taylor, eds., *Sustainable Planet: Solutions for the 21st Century.* Boston: Beacon Press, 2002.

———. "When Childhood Gets Commercialized, Can Children Be Protected?" *Mediactive,* forthcoming in 2006.

Schor, Juliet B., and Douglas Holt. *The Consumer Society Reader: An Anthology.* New York: New Press, 2000.

Schor, Juliet, John Shandra, and Robert Kunovich. "Does Consumer Culture Undermine Children's Well-Being? Results from a School Survey." Unpublished report, Boston College, 2004.

Seiter, Ellen. *Sold Separately: Parents and Children in Consumer Culture.* New Brunswick, NJ: Rutgers University Press, 1993.

Selling to Kids. "Food Company Repositions Yogurt for Kids." September 16, 1998.

Siegel, David L., Timothy J. Coffey, and Gregory Livingston. *The Great Tween Buying Machine: Marketing to Today's Tweens.* Ithaca, NY: Paramount Market Publishing, 2001.

Signorielli, Nancy. *A Content Analysis: Reflections of Girls in the Media.* Menlo Park, CA: Kaiser Family Foundation, 1997. Available at www.kkf.org.

Signorielli, Nancy, and M. Lears. "Television and Children's Conceptions of Nutrition: Unhealthy Messages." *Health Communication* 4:245–257, 1992.

Singer, Dorothy G., and Jerome L. Singer. *Handbook of Children and the Media.* Thousand Oaks, CA: Sage, 2001.

Smith, Paul. "Tommy Hilfiger in the Age of Mass Customization." In Andrew Ross, ed., *No Sweat: Fashion, Free Trade, and the Rights of Garment Workers.* New York: Verso, 1997.

Smith, Stephen. "State's Overweight on the Rise." *Boston Globe,* July 24, 2002.

Spiegler, Marc. "Marketing Street Culture." *American Demographics* 18(11):28–32, 1997.

Stanger, Jeffrey D., and Natalia Gridina. *Media in the Home: The Fourth Annual Survey of Parents and Children.* Philadelphia: Annenberg Public Policy Center of the University of Pennsylvania, 1999.

Stark, Kevin D., and Jeff Laurent. "Joint Factor Analysis of the Children's Depression Inventory and the Revised Children's Manifest Anxiety Scale." *Journal of Clinical Child Psychology* 30(3):552–567, 2001.

Statistical Abstract. *Statistical Abstract of the United States,* 2004–2005. Washington: Government Printing Office, 2005.

Steinberg, Don. "What Makes Nick Tick: Nickelodeon Is a Sensibility, a World, an All-Empowering Club: It's CNN for Children." In Paula Fass and Mary Ann Mason, eds., *Childhood in America.* New York: New York University Press, 2000.

Steinberg, Shirley R., and Joe L. Kincheloe, eds. *Kinderculture: The Corporate Construction of Childhood.* Boulder, CO: Westview Press, 1998.

Stephens, Sharon, ed. *Children and the Politics of Culture.* Princeton, NJ: Princeton University Press, 1995a.

———. "Introduction: Children and the Politics of Culture in 'Late Capitalism.' " In

Sharon Stephens, ed., *Children and the Politics of Culture.* Princeton, NJ: Princeton University Press, 1995b.

Stolberg, Sheryl Gay. "Stress Management for Kindergartners." *New York Times,* June 18, 2002.

Stoneman, Zolinda, and G. H. Brody. "The Indirect Impact of Child-Oriented Advertisements on Mother-Child Interactions." *Journal of Applied Developmental Psychology* 2:369–376, 1981.

Strasburger, Victor C., and Barbara J. Wilson. *Children, Adolescents and the Media.* Thousand Oaks, CA: Sage, 2002.

Sugarman, Carole. "Take My Order." *Washington Post,* June 7, 2000.

Sunderland, Patricia L., and Rita M. Denny. "Psychology vs. Anthropology: Where Is Culture in Marketplace Ethnography?" In Timothy Dewaal Malefyt and Brian Moeran, eds., *Advertising Cultures.* London: Berg, 2003.

Sutton-Smith, Brian. *Toys as Culture.* New York: Gardner Press, 1986.

Szymanski, Marianne. "Decoding the Kids' Psyche: Tips from the Toyzone." *Kidscreen,* March 1, 1999.

Tabor, Mary B. W. "Schools Profit from Offering Pupils for Market Research." *New York Times,* April 5, 1999.

Talbot, Margaret. "Why, Isn't He Just the Cutest Brand-Image Enhancer You've Ever Seen?" *New York Times Magazine,* September 21, 2003.

Taras, T. H., et al. "Television's Influence on Children's Diet and Physical Activity." *Developmental and Behavioral Pediatrics* 10:176–180, 1989.

Taylor, Betsy. *What Kids Really Want That Money Can't Buy.* New York: Warner Books, 2003.

Thorne, Barrie. *Gender Play: Girls and Boys in School.* New Brunswick, NJ: Rutgers University Press, 1993.

Trotter, Andrew. "Channel One Drops Cash Incentive Plan Aimed at Teachers." *Education Week,* September 21, 2001.

Tuttle, William M. Jr. "The Homefront Children's Popular Culture: Radio, Movies, Comics—Adventure, Patriotism and Sex-Typing." In Elliott West and Paula Petrik, eds., *Small Worlds.* Lawrence: University Press of Kansas, 1992.

Twenge, Jean M. "The Age of Anxiety? Birth Cohort Change in Anxiety and Neuroticism, 1952–1993." *Journal of Personality and Social Psychology* 79(6):1007–1021, 2000.

UNICEF. *A League Table of Child Deaths by Injury in Rich Nations.* Florence, Italy: UNICEF Innocenti Research Center, 2001.

U.S. General Accounting Office. *Public Education: Commercial Activities in Schools.* Washington, D.C.: U.S. Government Printing Office, September 2000.

U.S. News and World Report. "A Fat Nation?" August 19, 2003.

U.S. Office of the Surgeon General. *The Surgeon General's Call to Action to Prevent Obesity and Disease.* Washington, D.C.: U.S. Government Printing Office, 2001.

Valkenburg, Patti. "Media and Youth Consumerism." *Journal of Adolescent Health* 27(2):52–56, 2000.

Vanderbilt, Thomas. *The Sneaker Book.* New York: New Press, 1998.

Van der Voort, H. A. Tom, and Patti M. Valkenburg. "Television's Impact on Fantasy Play: A Review of Research." *Developmental Review* 14(2):27–51, 1994.

Van Evra, Judith. *Television and Child Development* (2nd ed.). Mahwah, NJ: Lawrence Erlbaum, 1998.

Walkerdine, Valerie. *Daddy's Girl: Young Girls and Popular Culture.* Cambridge, MA: Harvard University Press, 1997.

Wartella, Ellen. "The Commercialization of Youth: Channel One in Context." *Phi Delta Kappan* 76(6):448–455, 1995.

Weiner, Tim. "Parents Divided over Jamaica Disciplinary Academy." *New York Times,* June 17, 2003.

West, Elliott, and Paula Petrik, eds. *Small Worlds.* Lawrence: University Press of Kansas, 1992.

White-Sax, Barbara. "Wealthy, Savvy Kids Have Their Say." *Drug Store News,* June 7, 1999.

Williams, Christine L. "Kids in Toyland." Unpublished report, University of Texas at Austin, 2003.

Wilson, Barbara, and A. J. Weiss. "Developmental Differences in Children's Reactions to a Toy-Based Cartoon." *Journal of Broadcasting and Electronic Media* 36:371–394, 1992.

Woodward, Emory H. IV. *Media in the Home.* Philadelphia: Annenberg Public Policy Center at the University of Pennsylvania, 2000.

Yazigi, Monique P. "You Mean All Night at FAO Schwarz?" *New York Times,* November 14, 1999.

Young, Michael. *Television Advertising and Children.* Oxford: Oxford University Press, 1990.

Zelizer, Viviana A. *Pricing the Priceless Child: The Changing Social Value of Children.* New York: Basic Books, 1985.

———. "Kids and Commerce." *Childhood* 4:375–396, 2002.

Zernike, Kate. "Coke to Dilute Push in Schools for Its Products." *New York Times,* March 14, 2001.

Zimmerman, Frederick J., Gwen M. Glew, Dimitri A. Christakis, and Wayne Katon. "Early Cognitive Stimulation, Emotional Support, and Television Watching as Predictors of Subsequent Bullying Among Grade-School Children." *Archives of Pediatric and Adolescent Medicine* 159:384–388, 2005.

Index

Page numbers in *italics* refer to figures and tables.

Born to Buy

Discussion Points

1. Schor describes a marketing juggernaut of unprecedented size, scope, and sophistication. Why has marketing to children become so much more pervasive and extensive than in the past? What are the major strategies marketers are using in their communications with children?
2. How do you think children are affected by "tweening" (p. 56)? Do you think that children today are maturing at an earlier age? If so, why do you think that is?
3. Schor points out that advertisers have incredible influence over children's views. They are able to promote ideas, like "antiadultism," and manipulate points of view, such as what kids consider "cool." How did forces outside the family become so influential? How can parents regain their central role in educating and advising their children?
4. What do you think about the use of children in developing and marketing potential products? The author discusses some of the unaddressed ethical aspects of using children in this way, but marketers defend their actions, saying they are just trying to make products that kids will like. What about schools' participating in marketing plans? Do you think schools should be marketing-free zones?
5. On page 21, the author describes one marketing company's pitch in which children were represented as wild animals and the advertising companies as the British colonial hunter. Discuss this analogy.
6. Discuss the consumer involvement of children today. Juliet Schor states that children have taken on an increasingly active role in consumer decisions (p. 23). Why do you think that is? Do you think that this consumer involvement is detrimental or beneficial?
7. Discuss the relationship between children with behavioral problems and their participation in the consumer culture. What do Schor's survey results mean?
8. Discuss the similarities and differences in consumer habits among different demographics (economic, ethnic, urban/suburban, and others)? Do you believe any particular race or class is more vulnerable to certain marketing tactics? Why or why not?
9. Schor argues that cultural ideas about childhood have changed in the past 200 years. How do you understand that change? What does childhood mean to you? Do you think our society should go back to more traditional ideas of childhood?

10. Who do you believe should be held responsible for monitoring the impact of marketing to children? Do you agree with the advertisers that parents can just shut off the TV or simply say no in order to prevent advertisers from reaching their kids? Why or why not? What kinds of challenges do parents face?
11. In the late 1970s, the Federal Trade Commission was on the verge of enacting strict regulations on marketing to children, but the intervention of Congress prevented it from acting. Do you think it's time for the federal government to regulate ads to children? If so, what should it do?
12. Discuss different ways parents and teachers can help protect children from the growing consumer culture. After reading *Born to Buy,* do you feel a need to get more active on these issues, or do you feel that the commercialization of childhood is inevitable?

Interview with Juliet B. Schor

1. How did you come to write this book?

   In my previous two books, *The Overworked American* and *The Overspent American,* I analyzed the "culture of work and spend" that I believe has pervaded our society. Both those titles and all my previous work focused on adults. But as I was researching *Overspent,* which was mainly about social pressures to consume, it became clear to me that many of the most far-reaching and insidious changes in consumer culture were happening in children's and youth marketing. Children were being turned into consumers almost from birth, and by adolescence, their social worlds were almost totally constructed around cool commodities, brand names, and the latest, trendiest commercial music, films, and lingo. In contrast to my own (baby boom) generation, the commercial experience of today's young people appeared seamless. Earlier generations were consumers, but we also had powerful countervailing ideologies that rejected consumerism as a value system and a way of life. I worried about what would happen to the generations of kids who are growing up without those.

   My interest in this topic was also stimulated by the fact that I was experiencing these issues personally as the mother of two young children. I wanted to pass on a different value system to my children and was hoping to raise them in a far less commercial environment than that of the average American kid. We created a home environment that was TV and junk food free, and for quite a while was also free of video games and the Internet. As they aged, I confronted a series of challenges, from video games, to designer labels, to powerful peer effects, to high-sugar foods. In the process I have developed a point of view on how to navigate the challenges of consumer culture that is at odds with most of the conventional wisdom.
2. You did a lot of research for *Born to Buy.* What was your process like? How did you gather so much inside information? How much opposition did you face?

   Partly I was lucky. The foundation that selected me to participate in its visiting professor program wasn't worried about the fact that my work might be critical of the advertising industry. I don't know whether that's because it didn't know much about me or is open to critical perspectives.

The agency I was placed with was gracious, welcoming, and open. I wasn't really interested in proprietary information, which is traditionally the thing that agencies most worry about, so that helped. Once I was inside one agency, it was easy to make more contacts. I think that's because my initial contacts functioned like a seal of approval. I also benefited from the fact that so many practitioners are feeling ambivalent and guilty about their work. That was especially true as time went on and junk food marketing came under more scrutiny. I did face obstacles at some of the key institutions of youth marketing: MTV, Saatchi, and Channel One. Those firms are more experienced with criticism and guard their information very closely. I suspect that to get into them, I'd have had to use another process, because they don't typically help researchers or journalists they aren't confident will write uncritically. As I think back to the process, I sometimes still find it amazing that I was able to find out as much as I did.

3. How has the marketing and advertising industry responded to *Born to Buy*?

   I've had mixed reactions. I've been in touch with a few of my informants. Some have felt a bit betrayed, because they had no idea I would write something critical. At the same time, some of those same people also agree with much of what I'm saying and are glad I'm raising these issues, so they're conflicted. And there are some people I spent quite a bit of time with who have ignored me. Others have been friendly, but I know they're not happy with me. I wrote in the Afterword about how I haven't been able to get food marketers or companies to debate. However, Susan Linn and I did do a debate with Paul Kurnit and a representative from the Gepetto Group at an industry conference that was friendly and productive. I'm on my way to the annual KidPower conference next week to speak, which should be interesting. Overall, I'd say the varied receptions I've gotten parallel the range of opinion in the industry itself.

4. Are there specific factors that make children particularly vulnerable to marketers? Are children under more pressure now than in the recent past? Does their increased stress affect their vulnerability?

   Most child development experts and brain scientists emphasize that children's brains are not as capable as adults' when it comes to critical reasoning and impulse control. This is the basis of their arguments for restricting advertising to children. It's an important perspective. In addition to these biological and cognitive differences, one of the special vulnerabilities children are now facing is the high levels of stress, fear, and pressure they are living with. Those emotional states make them more receptive to marketing and the messages of "gotta have it, gotta be cool" that characterize so much advertising. I believe that the most savvy marketers have figured out how to capitalize on and exploit kids' stress. Nickelodeon is probably the most adept at that strategy. Nick's message to kids is that the adults in their world—parents and teachers, mainly—are the ones who are stressing them out, while Nick and the products they sell stand for fun and escape from that pressure. The other area of vulnerability is time stress in the family. Marketers take advantage of households where parents don't have a lot of time. I think that's particularly true with food. Parents have less time for cooking, which has created a shift toward fast foods.

5. In *Born to Buy,* you discuss age compression. What are some of the results of this practice, and what do you suspect the results will be as marketers continue to target younger and younger children?

   Age compression comes from marketers' observation that kids are getting older at a younger age. That's undoubtedly true. Marketers are trying hard to accelerate that trend because it allows them to market new kinds of products to kids. A classic example of this is real makeup for five- and six-year-old girls. It used to be there wasn't that much makeup marketed to kids, and it was fake. The idea was that they would be playing grown-up with these fake things. Now they market real makeup to girls. Even preschool girls wear nail polish and lip gloss. The sexualization of girls' fashion, which many parents are aware of and find problematic, is another example of age compression. Yet another is violent action figures for four year olds, such as World Wrestling action figures, or products from movies that are rated PG-13. Another example of age compression is when Hollywood studios were deliberately targeting nine-, ten-, eleven-, and twelve-year-old kids with R movies. They would actually bring them in for focus groups; there was a lot of internal documentation of this. So there was a bit of an outcry (in 2000), and studios said, "Okay, we will require either an ID or a parent for the R movies." They actually responded pretty significantly and changed the practice very quickly. And you might think "end of story." But what happened was they then shifted that violent and sexual content—and also, very interestingly, tobacco smoking—into PG-13 movies. There has been a disproportionate rise in tobacco smoking in PG-13 movies since this clampdown. Now many PG-13 movies are very much like what R movies were before the change. They show virtually all of a sex act, except actual copulation. They show near nudity. One could hardly imagine higher levels of violence than in some of these movies. This is a typical way of operating for these companies that are selling to children. They are not about to give up that youth audience. They repeatedly subvert the intentions of parents and regulators.

6. Has there been a backlash against marketing to kids?

   Yes. In the past year, things have begun to change. Some schools have opted out of exclusive soft drink contracts. And there are groups like Dads and Daughters, in Minnesota, which attempts to combat the effects of consumer culture on girls. They got a girls' clothing label to stop distributing T-shirts that read "Property of Boys Locker Room." In the Afterword I discuss many of the gains and even victories that activists have won in recent months.

7. In *Born to Buy,* you mention the lack of government involvement in monitoring marketing to children. What do you propose the government should do to better legislate marketing to children?

   First, government needs to clamp down on junk food marketing in public schools. The federal government has enormous power to regulate foods in schools that participate in its nutrition programs. So that's an easy and obvious place to start. Second, the FCC and FTC should address product placement, requiring disclosure for all paid product placements, in both child and adult programming. I'd love to see a law requiring that child marketers be required to affix their names to the ads they create, to insert some personal responsibility into the process. I also think that we should eliminate food advertising altogether in children's and teen programming. Diets shouldn't be driven by advertising of any kind.

8. What are the five most important things parents can do to protect their kids from the consumer culture?

In my view, the most important step is to dramatically reduce or eliminate television. This removes a source of ongoing exposure to ads and the insidious messages of children's consumer culture. It frees the parent from incessant nagging and the perpetual cycle of longing, acquisition, and disillusionment.

Second is to restrict Internet and video game use and to encourage creative, rather than highly commercialized, computer uses. The average American child spends much too much time in front of screens. Try to keep that within moderate limits. My children do use the computer, but they are not doing IM. They play Scrabble online. I don't let them spend much time on sites with a lot of advertising. When Neopets started "paying" children with online rewards for watching McDonald's commercials, it was obvious the time had come to eliminate Neopets.

Third, eat home-cooked, tasty dinners as a family. And as a corollary, don't go to fast food outlets. In my family, we eat together and cook virtually every night. It means we're all eating well, enjoying meals, and we don't get addicted to high-fat, high-sugar foods. Dinner helps create an emotional anchor for our children, which makes their lives easier. If the kids have athletic practice or a music lesson, we almost always schedule around it rather than give up on family dinner.

Fourth, find some noncommercial activities that you enjoy as a family, and cultivate them. We like to hike and climb small mountains. We listen to baseball on the radio. We read a lot. We cook and bake, and spend time socializing as a family with other families. We consciously try not to get overscheduled. Lately we've been doing crossword puzzles.

Fifth, walk your talk. Many of us are concerned about our children's consumerist orientation but fail to see how our own lifestyles embody high levels of materialism. We can't be hypocrites and succeed at raising decommercialized children. So if we don't want our children to be slaves to designer labels, TV, or junk food, we've got to cut out those things from our own lives. Especially as children grow, we need to practice what we preach. It sounds obvious, but it's vitally important. And while we're at it, if we really care about the commercialization of our children, it's worth getting active in our own communities about these issues.

About the Author

Juliet Schor, an economist by training, is professor of sociology at Boston College. She is the author of *The Overworked American* and *The Overspent American.* Schor is a founding board member of the Center for a New American Dream and a founding member of South End Press. She is married and has two children, and lives in Newton, Massachusetts.

"Schor's sharply intelligent *Born to Buy* . . . sheds light on how parents are demonized by anti-adult ads, and how parents have shifted from being gatekeepers who monitor their children's purchases to having what one marketer calls an 'unmanned tollbooth' approach to their children's spending and their exposure to media."

—*The New York Times Book Review*

"We worry about so many dangers to our children—drugs, perverts, bullies—but seldom notice the biggest menace of all: the multibillion-dollar marketing effort aimed at turning the kids into oversexed, status-obsessed, attention-deficient little consumers. Like her earlier books, Juliet Schor's *Born to Buy* is a brilliant exposé and call to action."

—Barbara Ehrenreich, author of *Nickel and Dimed*

"Juliet Schor . . . exposes the multibillion-dollar advertising schemes aimed at America's kids."

—*Time*

"Schor presents a disturbing picture of how children's sense of self is diminished by this barrage of ads. They begin to believe they are what they own."

—*USA Today*

"Juliet Schor is a human laser beam. Her careful research and brilliant analysis are presented in lucid prose. Plato defined education as teaching our children to find pleasure in the right things. Most parents do their best, but they are fighting a culture that educates our children to value all the wrong things. Children are suffering mentally, physically, and spiritually. Schor's book can put on us a path toward once again protecting our children. This may be the most important book of 2004."

—Mary Pipher, author of *Reviving Ophelia* and *Letters to a Young Therapist*

"In her artfully argued, important exposé, *Born to Buy,* Schor draws on interviews with marketers, academic research, and her own survey of Massachusetts fifth and sixth graders. The book is a worthy capstone to the consumer trilogy that Schor began with her best-selling *The Overworked American* (1991) and continued in *The Overspent American* (1998)."

—*Businessweek*

"Schor's book sounds a dire warning to parents about the pervasiveness and sneakiness of marketing to children, turning them into little 'I want' machines. Her outrage is a needed voice amid the din of kiddie commercialism."

—*Pittsburgh Post-Gazette*

"There must be a special circle of hell designed for those who came up with the notion of marketing to young kids, and if so, Juliet Schor is its Dante. This is a tremendous book, in the tradition of *Fast Food Nation.*"

—Bill McKibben, author of *Enough: Staying Human in an Engineered Age*

"What a fascinating and mobilizing book! No mother or father *intends* to turn over child rearing to the consumer culture, but the stress and speed of life wear down their resolve, making television, toys, electronics, and branding a kind of 'shadow parent' that literally spoils our children. Juliet Schor gives us ample evidence of the cost—to our children and society—of this drift into corporation-raised kids. *Born to Buy* will inspire anyone concerned with the next generation."

—Vicki Robin, coauthor of *Your Money or Your Life: Transforming Your Relationship with Money and Achieving Financial Independence*

"This extraordinarily well-researched book provides abundant evidence for commercialization of childhood in our society and offers the first hard research data on the negative effects of turning children into consumers."

—*The Boston Globe*

"Juliet Schor has established herself as a sharp observer and critic of American commercialism. In *Born to Buy,* this social analyst and concerned mother turns her attention to marketing for children, combining observation in the advertising industry, interviews in a Boston suburb, and close study of merchandising methods. Readers need not agree with all her arguments to learn plenty about how relations between children and merchandising media are changing, and what threats to children's well-being those changes are producing."

—Viviana Zelizer, author of *Pricing the Priceless Child* and *The Social Meaning of Money*